Code-Switching Lessons

Grammar Strategies for Linguistically Diverse Writers

Grade 3–6

by Rebecca Wheeler & Rachel Swords

*first*hand
An imprint of Heinemann
361 Hanover Street
Portsmouth, NH 03801
firsthand.heinemann.com

Offices and agents throughout the world

Library of Congress Cataloging-in-Publication Data
CIP data is on file with the Library of Congress

ISBN-13: 978-0-325-02610-7
ISBN-10: 0-325-02610-6

Design and composition by Catherine Arakelian
Photography by David Stirling

Printed in the United States of America on acid-free paper
14 13 12 11 10 VP 1 2 3 4 5

CONTENTS

Acknowledgments

MY FIRST THANKS GO to my astute collaborator, Rachel Swords. Rachel has been with me from the beginning, when she first took my graduate education seminar, *Language Varieties in American Schools,* in 2001. This past year, Rachel has completed our Heinemann project with me while working full time and being a loving mom to four children under the age of four! Thank you, Rachel, for your enduring commitment to recognizing the linguistic smarts and strong abilities of our linguistically diverse students.

Next, I thank all the teachers and students – my teacher education students at Christopher Newport University, teachers in diverse school systems with whom I've explored literacy in diverse classrooms, and teachers and students around the country who have written me with their code-switching experiences and inspirations. Your questions and concerns, your enthusiasm and insights have helped me deepen our work, to ever more translate theoretical linguistic insights into on-the-ground, practical materials for real teachers in real classrooms.

To Christopher Newport University in Newport News, Virginia, my home Department of English, and the Program of Teacher Preparation, I am profoundly grateful. My colleagues consistently encourage and affirm my work. The Office of the Dean has supported my research and writing with course releases. Indeed, this book was supported by a sabbatical grant from Christopher Newport University. I am so lucky to be a part of a smart, engaged faculty at this young liberal arts university. I *like, enjoy,* and *enduringly respect* my colleagues, both academic and administrative. Thank you for a fine academic home.

Heinemann. WOW! My editors, Tina Miller and David Stirling, are magicians of content and form. Tina's razor-sharp insight has honed our work in truly important ways, and David's sublime aesthetic sense has made *Code-Switching Lessons* not only a powerfully structured tool but a beautiful one also.

Finally, I come to my true heart home, my husband Lou. Thank you for always affirming the significance and trajectory of my work – reaching the often-forgotten children of America. Thank you for putting up with my middle-of-the-night and early-morning writing, and for hanging with me through the ups and downs. Thank you for us, for bringing gardens, whimsy, poetry, Rumi, Hafiz, and long soul explorations into my life. I promise to take more time for mischief and play! Here's to our life together!

—Rebecca Wheeler

THERE ARE MANY PEOPLE who helped make the writing of this book possible. I must begin by thanking Dr. Rebecca Wheeler. For the past ten years, Dr. Wheeler has championed the teaching of language through contrastive analysis. This book is the culmination of her constant support of both me and our work.

Newport News Public Schools has served as the forum in which all of my work has taken place. I thank Dr. Gale Lee (Supervisor, Elementary Title I Programs) for encouraging me to think outside the box, and for supporting innovative teaching methods.

I am also thankful for the support I have received as a teacher at Newsome Park Elementary. I thank Sherry Wolfson (former principal) for allowing me to work with teachers in an effort to implement code-switching in multiple classrooms. I thank my good friends and colleagues, Karis McDonald (reading specialist) and Analiese Smith (teacher), for always encouraging me to take the next step in introducing and implementing the concept of code-switching to a larger audience. I especially thank Analiese for embracing code-switching and for allowing me to work with her students over the past three years.

Of course this book would not have been possible without our editors, Tina Miller and David Stirling. They have believed in our work from the beginning. I am especially appreciative of their attention to detail, which has led to the creation of this beautiful book.

Finally, I must thank my family. They have been the greatest supporters of my work since the beginning. I thank my parents, Chet and Shari Sutphin, for always encouraging me to reach my full potential. I thank my husband, Thomas Swords, for his support during this project. He spent hours entertaining our four young children (Braedon, Savanna, Kylie, and Kelsie) so that I could write, and for that, I am so grateful. Finally, I thank my sister, Amy Howe, for listening to me vent about frustrations and for sharing in the excitement over this book. My family's support and encouragement was paramount in enabling me to complete this book.

—Rachel Swords

Introduction

In *Code-Switching Lessons*, we show you how to lay down the red pen and use successful strategies – contrastive analysis and code-switching – for teaching Standard English grammar in linguistically diverse classrooms. You'll discover that some of what look like errors in your kids' writing are actually the patterns of their vernacular language. In other words, students often write just as they speak – in the cadences, rhythms, and patterns they've used at home and in their neighborhoods from birth through the moment they step into your class. *Code-Switching Lessons* will demonstrate how to find these informal patterns in your kids' writing and use contrastive analysis to compare community English and formal academic English, helping your students build on their existing grammar knowledge to add new knowledge. Once you've equipped your students with explicit awareness of the differences between informal and formal English, we'll show you how to lead students to code-switch – to choose the language style to fit the setting, the time, place, audience, and purpose they have for communicating.

About Code-Switching

The resource you hold in your hand, *Code-Switching Lessons*, represents the fruits of an ongoing ten-year collaboration between me, a university teacher and educator, and Rachel Swords, an elementary school teacher and literacy specialist. I'm a linguist in the teacher education program at Christopher Newport University in Newport News, Virginia. Rachel teaches in a Title 1 school in Tidewater, Virginia.

How did *Code-Switching Lessons* come to be?

As a linguist, I began exploring the needs of language arts teachers in my local district, which serves a majority African American population (57 percent). I knew that many African American students speak a dialect distinct from that expected in school, and so I wondered:

- Does home speech crop up in school writing?
- If so, how do teachers respond to vernacular grammar in student writing?
- Are teachers successful in fostering Standard English mastery among vernacular speakers?
- What might basic linguistics offer to support teachers as they respond to vernacular grammar in student writing?

To answer these questions, I collected sample essays from one hundred students across five third-grade classrooms.

Then the real work began. In analyzing those essays, I was looking strictly at grammar, not spelling or punctuation or capitalization or sentence boundary issues (comma splices, run-ons, etc.). Instead, I was looking to see whether (and to what degree) home speech vernacular grammar transferred into student writing.

My Favorite Animal

My favorite animal is a giraffe. Every time I go to zoo I want to see the gi... frist. Giraffes is neat because is very tall. A giraffe nec... very long. It has long legs to... That is why they is so c...

Three days ago there was a Boysname max and alex they was at the moives watching a Scray Moive calla wear wolF.

When they was at there mom Said go to Sleep but they was scard they saw Sadows In the widow It was there dog they got So they told thery mom.

So they told they Sad we whena to go See a Scary moive in were scard.

My analysis revealed the following:

- Yes, community English does indeed transfer into students' school writing – considerably.
- Teachers handled the vernacular grammar in student writing by correcting it, of course.
- Students' mastery of Standard English patterns did not seem to be improving.

I knew from basic linguistics that in many cases the students weren't making mistakes but were simply following the patterns of their first dialect, and I knew from the research on developmental writing (Shaunessey, 1977; Taylor, 1991) that urban students continue to write in the vernacular cadences of home grammar even up into community college – all this after teachers' diligent and hard work correcting student grammar from the get-go, throughout elementary school, throughout middle and throughout high school. If correction didn't work, then what would?

In the fall of 2001, I brought my elementary-school data to my teacher education classes at Christopher Newport University. My students and I began working on the writing samples from over seventy student essays, complete with the full array of vernacular patterns. We explored dozens of vernacular grammar patterns that cropped up consistently in student writing. We then built "grammar translators," an early version of what has become our core graphic organizer, the code-switching chart. This type of chart enabled us to analyze, compare, and contrast the grammar of the home to the grammar of the school. We talked about home speech and school speech, about informal versus formal English, and about the research showing that correction does not work when teaching Standard English to vernacular-speaking students (Piestrup 1973; Taylor, 1991; Rickford, 1999).

That's when Rachel Swords stepped in. Rachel, one of the students in my class, was an in-service third-grade teacher at a Title 1 school. She decided to test out these ideas with her students. Rachel figured that she already had one approach to grammar that failed – the one where she corrected students over and over. Students had ended up feeling dumb, embarrassed, and reluctant to talk or write anymore. She figured that the worst that could happen with the new approach – code-switching and contrastive analysis – would be that she would have two approaches that failed to reach her African American students. She started talking with her students about using formal and informal English, about choosing language to fit the setting. She began developing and teaching code-switching lessons, choosing simple patterns first (possessives, plurals, and past time) before moving on to harder ones (subject–verb agreement, *was/were*, *am/is/are*).

"Her kids lit up, they became verbal again, and they became engaged in writing and reached for their voice."

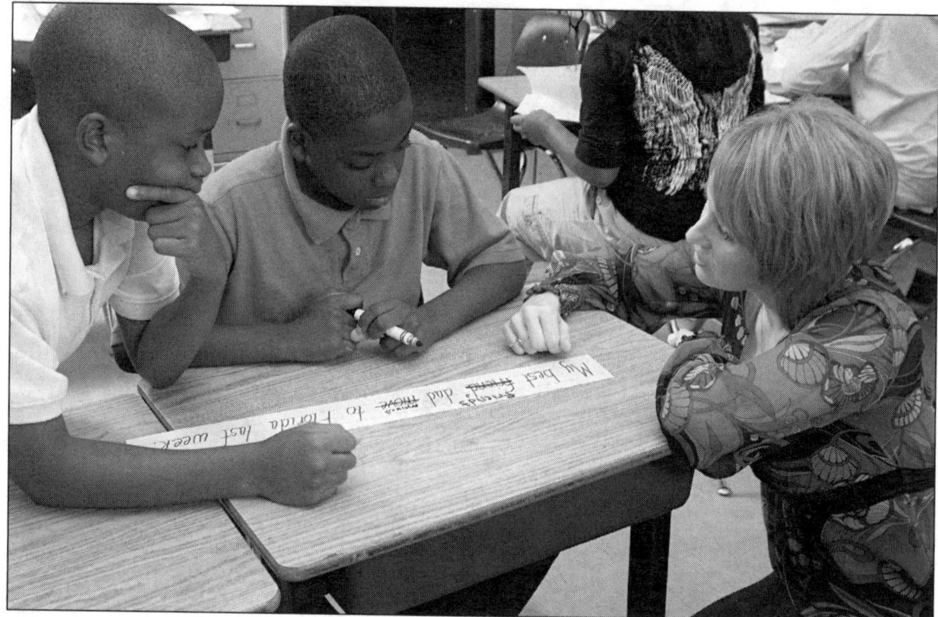

What Rachel found surprised her: Her kids lit up, they became verbal again, and they became engaged in writing and reached for their voice. By the end of her first year teaching code-switching, Rachel closed the achievement gap in her classroom. African American students either equaled (in math and writing) or outperformed (in science and social studies) their white peers on the year-end No Child Left Behind (NCLB) tests. These results have held constant ever since.

Thus began a collaboration that led to an article, a book, and now to these code-switching lessons. We're here to share the teaching moves and language that showcase how this linguistically informed approach actually looks and sounds in a classroom.

Why teach code-switching?

Code-Switching Lessons will speak to any teacher who finds that his or her classroom is becoming increasingly diverse. While fifty or sixty years ago the students filling our classes may have been overwhelmingly white native English speakers, that's clearly not the case now. Now multicultural, multilingual, multidialectical diversity is the norm. Our students come to us from down the block but also from Thailand and China, from South America and Latin America, and from Russia and the Ukraine. Our students are white but also Native American, African American, and Hispanic and come from the bayous of Louisiana as well as the boroughs of New York, with all the attendant differences in pronunciation, vocabulary, and grammar. With diversity of homeland comes diversity of languages, with English as a second language; with diversity of ethnic and U.S. regional groups comes diversity of dialects and diversity of culture. Our classrooms have become culturally and linguistically diverse, and we need teaching strategies that celebrate and use that diversity as a springboard to wider knowledge.

Code-switching develops kids' awareness of and attention to language differences and choices.

Building on the richness that children's oral language brings to the classroom, code-switching uses strategies of active discovery to help students recognize alternative language styles and own their language choices. We illustrate with two stories from Rachel's school.

Story #1: "The book uses formal"

Half of Rachel's students sat in the reading circle in the classroom of another teacher, Ms. Jones, as children read aloud. It was February, and Rachel's students had long since been familiar with the patterns of subject–verb agreement. Their whole class had worked through the code-switching lessons; they had discovered the informal patterns (*Mama walk to the store Saturdays*) and added the formal patterns (*Mama walks to the store Saturdays*) to their repertoires. The code-switching charts were up on the wall for their use during the writing process.

Ms. Jones had also been telling students about formal subject–verb agreement. She'd been marking their papers, writing in the missing -s on students' verbs, but it didn't seem to make much difference. And here, her students were reading out loud from a book written in Standard English, and they were leaving off the verb endings, just as they did in their writing, just as they did in their speaking.

The second-grade class was reading *The Paperboy* by Dav Pilkey. When Tarik's turn came, he read, "The paperboy know his route by heart."

The teacher interrupted him. "Read that again, more carefully."

Tarik reprised: "The paperboy know his route by heart."

"Again!" said the teacher. "Pay attention to the grammar!"

And Tarik read, "The paperboy know . . ."

By this time, the child was embarrassed, confused, and increasingly alienated from reading. Notice, he got the meaning – he would have had to understand the sentence in order to be able to speak through the grammar of his home language.

One of Rachel's students leaned over and whispered in his ear, "Look at the end of the word *know*. It's got an ending. You need to say that ending. I know you're using informal English, but the book uses formal and the teacher wants you to use formal. Just look at the endings on words and be sure to say them out loud" – powerful reading counsel from a second-grader.

Rachel's student had deeply understood the difference between the patterns of vernacular and Standard English and was able to explain the issue on the spot.

Story #2: "But Spy Mouse doesn't"

It was Rachel's very first semester teaching code-switching, back in 2001. She was just learning. That fall, she'd taught about formal and informal places and clothing and about formal and informal language, and she'd taught students about formal and informal grammar for showing possession and plurality and so on.

Students were working in writing workshop. In particular, David was writing another story in his series on Spy Mouse, the School Detective. This one was called "Spy Mouse and the Broken Globe." David was well into his writing when Rachel stopped by his desk.

"David," Rachel said, "I thought we'd talked about formal and informal English."

"Yes, Mrs. Swords," David replied.

"But did you understand? Did you understand when we talked about formal grammar and informal grammar?" Rachel pursued.

"Yes, I did, Mrs. Swords," David continued.

"Well, I'm disappointed. If you understood, why do you have informal English all through your writing?"

David was patient with his teacher. After all, she was venturing into new and different territory. "Mrs. Swords," David continued patiently, "*I* understand the difference between formal and informal English, but Spy Mouse doesn't."

Indeed, David had written his author's note entirely in Standard English, but he had used vernacular English to create character and voice for his mouse detective. Clearly, David was thinking about language and writing in writerly ways. Code-switching gave him the tools to make very savvy language choices.

"Code-switching gave him the tools to make very savvy language choices."

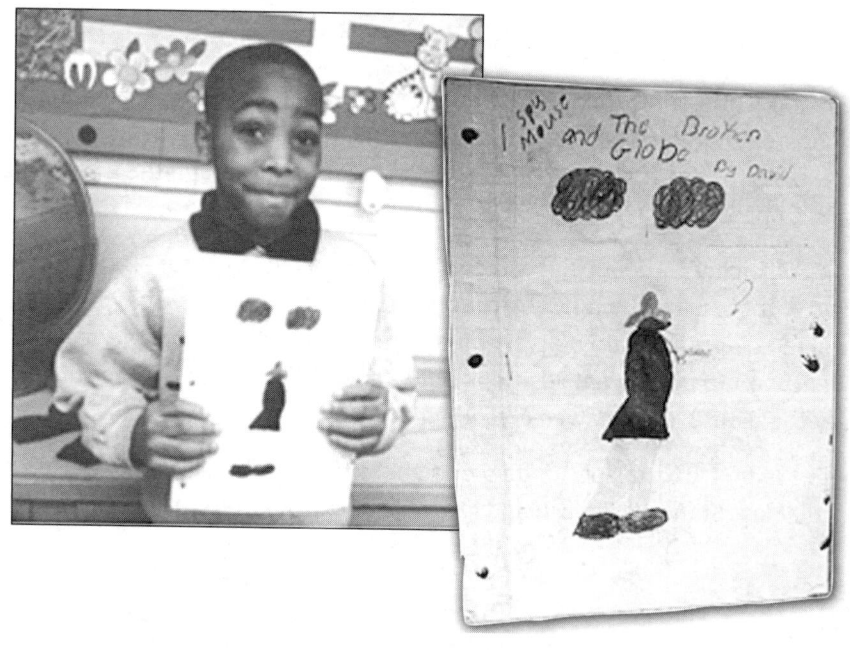

Code-switching works where correction doesn't.

Both experience and research tell us that correction just doesn't work very well to teach Standard English grammar; if correction worked, then by middle or high school, students wouldn't be making the same "errors." At our work sessions, teachers report that this sample of teacher response is pretty familiar:

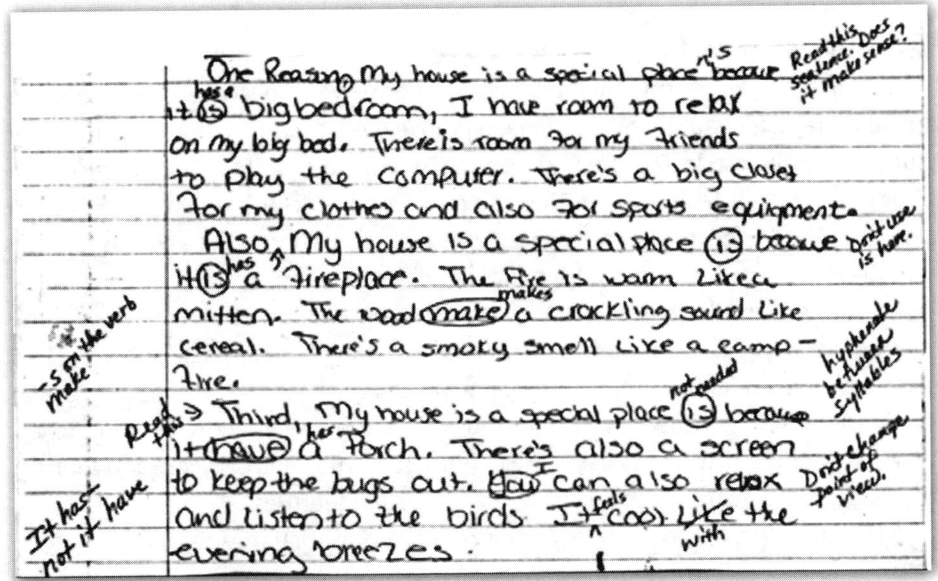

One Reason My house is a special place because it is big bedroom, I have room to relax on my big bed. There's room for my friends to play the computer. There's a big closet for my clothes and also for sports equipment.

Also, My house is a special place because It is a fireplace. The fire is warm like a mitten. The wood make a crackling sound like cereal. There's a smoky smell like a camp-fire.

Third, My house is a special place because it have a porch. There's also a screen to keep the bugs out. You can also relax and listen to the birds. It cool like the evening breezes.

Teachers correct vernacular grammar in student writing.

This eighth-grade teacher has put lots of effort into correcting student grammar, yet there's not a word about the student's strengths, like those enviable similes: "The fire is warm like a mitten" or "The wood make a crackling sound like cereal." Sure, there's a good deal of grammar work we'd do with this student, but more fundamentally, there's lots to celebrate in this student's writing. Could it be that the grammar blinded the teacher to the student's broader writing capacities?

You can bet, too, that the student who wrote this has received corrections on his or her papers all the way up through the years of elementary and secondary school, but here's an eighth-grade essay that uses the same vernacular patterns teachers have surely been correcting for eight years. Not surprisingly, teachers of developmental writing in community college report that these same grammar patterns populate their students' writing. The message isn't getting through. What gives?

Research corroborates what common sense tells us: "[W]hile various strategies can be useful for learning Standard English equivalents... [o]ne that does not work is correcting vernacular features" (Wolfram, Adger, & Christian, 1999, p. 122). Ironic, isn't it? The very strategy that seems so intuitive, so natural, and so necessary just doesn't work to teach Standard English. Piestrup, a language researcher over thirty-five years ago (1973) reported that with repeated correction, students "withdrew from participation in reading, speaking softly and as seldom as possible" (pp. 131–132). In other words, correction not only failed to teach Standard English but led students to opt out of the educational enterprise.

"Could it be that the grammar blinded the teacher to the student's broader writing capacities?"

By contrast, code-switching does work in teaching Standard English grammar to vernacular-speaking students. Experience has shown the success of code-switching, and so has research. Before Rachel began implementing code-switching, her African American students performed thirty points below their white peers on year-end tests. The very year she implemented code-switching, Rachel closed the achievement gap in her classroom, a result that has held constant ever since. Indeed, in 2006, the last year Rachel was a classroom teacher, 100 percent of her African American students passed 100 percent of the year-end tests.

Research studies affirm that linguistically informed approaches to the vernacular are far more successful than traditional ones. We have results from an experimental study set in third grade (Fogel & Ehri, 2000). Students taught "proper grammar" with traditional English techniques either improved 1 percent or actually got worse in using Standard English; by contrast, students who used contrastive analysis showed a nearly 100 percent increase in Standard English mastery (Fogel & Ehri, 2000).

Not limited to elementary contexts, these results hold true all the way up into community college. Hanni Taylor demonstrated (1991) that when she corrected students' vernacular grammar, they actually used more (not fewer) vernacular patterns but that the students who worked with contrastive analysis really improved. When Taylor taught students using the linguistically informed compare and contrast approach, students used 59 percent fewer vernacular features.

Not only in the United States (Adger, Wolfram, & Christian, 2007; Piestrup, 1973; Rickford, 1999; Rickford & Rickford, 2000) but also abroad in Norway, in Sweden, and in Canada (Rickford, 1999), scholar after scholar attest to the superiority of code-switching and contrastive analysis over the traditional methods for teaching the standard dialect to minority dialect speakers.

In summary, code-switching works, and it develops thoughtful language users. What better reasons are there to give it a try?

> **"Code-switching works, and it develops thoughtful language users."**

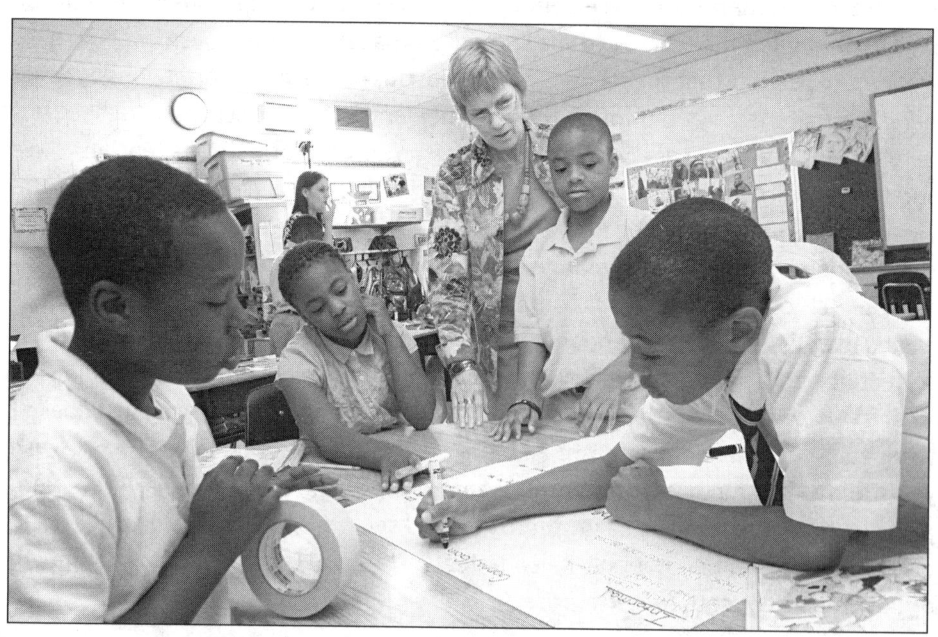

What are the essential features of a successful code-switching approach?

Refined over nearly ten years of classroom practice and grounded in research, *Code-Switching Lessons* has the following characteristics:

- It is grounded in student language, written and oral.
- It uses a graphic organizer as an analysis tool.
- It applies the scientific method to grammar discovery.
- It builds on the rules of vernacular and adds Standard English.

Code-Switching Lessons is grounded in student language.

Each year, we see the cadences of our kids' home speech grammar transfer into their school writing – our students often write just as they speak – so we make note of the common and most frequent vernacular patterns that we see in student writing. These become grist for our code-switching lessons. Then after we have worked on the "big-ticket" items in the writing process, we separate issues of mechanics (spelling, capitalization, and punctuation) from issues of grammar. At this point, we turn to our code-switching lessons to address Standard English usage.

Here's a sample from fourth-grade writing to get us started.

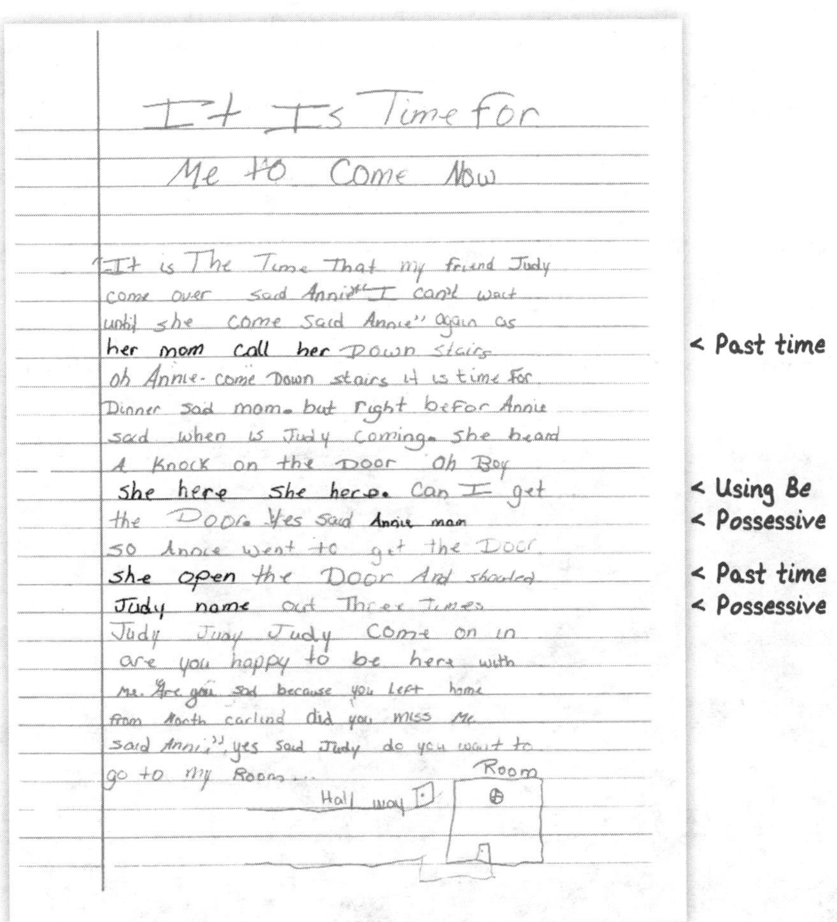

It Is Time For Me To Come Now

It is The Time That my friend Judy
come over said Annie" I can't wait
until she come said Annie" again as
her mom call her Down stairs
oh Annie- come Down stairs it is time for
Dinner said mom. but right befor Annie
said when is Judy coming. she heard
A knock on the Door Oh Boy
She here She here. Can I get
the Door Yes said Annie mom
so Annie went to get the Door
she open the Door And shouted
Judy name out Three Times
Judy Judy Judy Come on in
are you happy to be here with
me. Are you said because you left home
from North carlind did you miss me
said Annie", yes said Judy do you want to
go to my Room...

"It Is Time for Me to Come Now" by Darla

Code-Switching Lessons uses a graphic organizer as an analysis tool.

We do all our work using a core graphic organizer, a T-chart; we call it a **code-switching chart**. After we've found common vernacular patterns across student papers, we construct a code-switching chart that reflects the grammar contrasts at hand. Here's a sample code-switching chart for showing possession in vernacular (informal) and Standard (formal) English. We began with Darla's two possessive sentences and added several from her classmates' work.

SHOWING POSSESSION

INFORMAL	FORMAL
"Yes," said Annie mom.	"Yes," said Annie's mom.
She shouted Judy name.	She shouted Judy's name.
My goldfish name is Scaley.	My goldfish's name is Scaley.
Toni takes Joni ex-boyfriend.	Toni takes Joni's ex-boyfriend.
Christopher family moved to Spain.	Christopher's family moved to Spain.
I want to sing in the kid choir.	I want to sing in the kids' choir.
THE PATTERN	**THE PATTERN**
owner + owned	owner + 's + owned

Code-switching chart for Showing Possession

The left column contains student sentences illustrating the vernacular pattern we're addressing, possessive patterns, and the right column contains the Standard English equivalents.

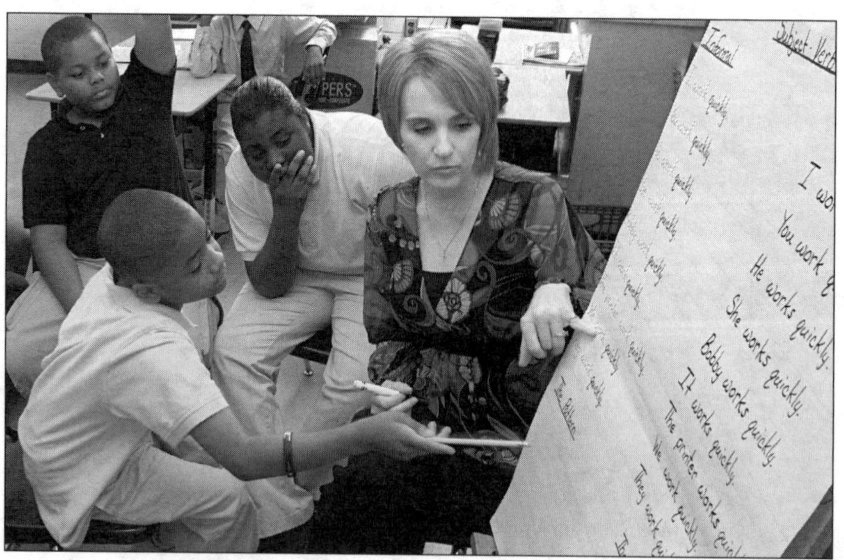

Code-Switching Lessons applies the scientific method to grammar discovery.

To address vernacular grammar in student writing, we draw on analysis and synthesis, critical thinking skills central to twenty-first-century literacy. Indeed, as you lead students in the discovery and learning of grammar patterns, you'll be following the steps of the scientific method.

SCIENTIFIC METHOD AS APPLIED TO GRAMMAR DISCOVERY

1. Collect data (student examples).
2. Examine data.
3. Seek grammar patterns.
4. Describe grammar patterns (a hypothesis).
5. Test the pattern.
6. Write the grammar pattern (the grammar rules).

Once we have built the code-switching chart, we lead students through these steps to discover the vernacular grammar pattern they're using in their school writing. Then, we build on that existing knowledge to add new knowledge, the corresponding pattern in Standard English.

Here's how the process goes: First, we lead students to discover the grammar pattern of informal English through the analytic and synthetic steps of the scientific method. To do so, we follow steps 2–6 once with the informal sentence in the left-hand column. Then, we apply the same process, following steps 2–6 again, for the Formal English sentences on the right. But this time we begin by exploring the formal sentences with an additional tool: comparison and contrast. We direct students' attention to the sentences in the Formal English column and ask, "What changed? How do the Formal English sentences here differ from the Informal English we just explored?" This lets us build on students' existing knowledge (the patterns of community English) to add new knowledge (academic English). We then lead students in analysis and synthesis, the steps of the scientific method, as they identify the grammar pattern for formal English.

Comparing and contrasting the grammar of the home to the grammar of the school is called **contrastive analysis,** a technique we've adapted from Second Language Acquisition (SLA) and English as a Second Language (ESL). In our lessons, we use contrastive analysis in service of Standard English as a Second Dialect (SESD). In this way, students develop explicit, conscious understanding of the differences between informal (vernacular) and formal (Standard) English.

Code-Switching Lessons builds on the rules of vernacular grammar to add the rules of Standard English.

While knowing the difference between vernacular and Standard English is a step, it's not our end result. We want students to be able to choose the language to fit the setting. That's code-switching – students making intentional choices in their language use! *Code-Switching Lessons* is all about empowering students to make conscious, effective choices in language and writing, to choose their language to fit the time, place, audience, and communicative purpose.

Central to *Code-Switching Lessons* is the understanding that informal or formal English is neither "right" nor "wrong" but rather appropriate or not to their situation. In our lessons, we never talk about "correcting" student grammar "errors" because, as we've shown, these linguistic patterns are not typically errors but are systematic vernacular rules. How, then, do we talk about grammar in a linguistically informed classroom?

NEW WAYS OF TALKING ABOUT LANGUAGE: FROM "ERROR" TO "PATTERN"

Instead of	Try this
Thinking in terms of • proper or improper • good or bad	**See language as** • appropriate or inappropriate • effective or ineffective in a specific setting
Talking about • right or wrong • correct or incorrect	**Talk about** • patterns • how language varies by setting
Thinking that students • make mistakes, errors • have problems with plurals, possessives, tenses, etc. • leave off an *-s*, *-'s*, *-ed*	**See your kids as** • following the grammar patterns of their home language
Saying to students • "should have," "are supposed to," "need to," "should correct"	**Invite students** • to code-switch (choose the language pattern to fit the setting)
Red notes in the margin • correcting students' grammar	**Lead students to** • compare and contrast language • build on existing knowledge to add new knowledge – Standard English • code-switch to fit the setting

Of course, this chart is just an illustrative guide. The real point is that we are always mindful of our language about language – and we urge our colleagues to be similarly mindful. As you talk about students' work, do you use terms that are neutral, or do you still talk in terms of error, mistake, and something missing? Can you catch yourself before you speak from a deficit perspective? It will take some time, but you'll get there. Teachers find that truly changing their language about language is a surprisingly challenging process. We believe that it's worth the effort – to see our kids as smart, linguistically robust, capable learners.

About Code-Switching Lessons

About *Code-Switching Lessons*

Code-Switching Lessons fits naturally into any writing block – most likely when students are revising or editing their work – when you notice the need for a grammar minilesson to highlight vernacular and standard alternatives. Rachel noticed that her students used the same home speech patterns year after year. She naturally and easily came to recognize a top-10 list of vernacular patterns common in her students' writing. In response, Rachel developed and sequenced the model lessons in this resource to help students add Standard English to their linguistic repertoires.

The Code-Switching Road Map

You will find that *Code-Switching Lessons* can be used in a number of ways. Regardless of how you use the book, we recommend that you wait at least four weeks into the school year before teaching any of these lessons. This will give you time to collect data and determine to what degree your students are in need of particular lessons. You may choose the book as a course of study in grammar. Since the lessons are roughly sequenced from simplest to most complex, you would simply begin with the first lesson in the first unit and work your way through the book. The units are designed to span from one to two weeks, depending on the needs of your students and the amount of time you dedicate to writing on a daily basis. After the final lesson is completed, you might discover additional grammar patterns that you'll want to teach using code-switching. If this occurs, you will have the foundation to create your own lessons for these additional grammar patterns. To support your work, we offer a good range of additional code-switching charts for other grammar patterns common in the writing of African American students.

Another way you can choose to use *Code-Switching Lessons* is to pick and choose the lessons that are most relevant to your students, based on your analysis of their work. In this case, we recommend teaching the first two or three units relatively early in the year to set students up for comparing and contrasting formal and informal language. Once you have introduced and explored the concept of code-switching, you can select additional lessons based on your students' needs. From this foundation, your students will be ready to tackle high frequency but harder patterns such as subject–verb agreement.

Code-Switching Lessons: The components

The core of *Code-Switching Lessons* is this lesson book, which contains all the direct instruction for establishing a foundation of language flexibility. The lessons develop writers' facility in choosing and using the language style most appropriate for a given audience and purpose. The Resources CD-ROM bound with this lesson book provides both resources to support the lessons and a variety of additional information – for example, Frequently Asked Questions and an extensive list of African American English patterns often found in school writing. In addition, check out the information in the *Code-Switching Lessons* section of www.heinemann.com.

Code-Switching Lessons: The units

This lesson book contains eleven units, each containing between two and four lessons. The units are organized into three main sections. The first section and the last section contain a single unit; they provide context for code-switching as a learning approach. Nine grammar units form the core of the program.

Unit 1: Diversity in Life and Language

We begin by anchoring in common daily experiences. We make use of students' intuitive understanding of how we all vary our self-presentation to fit the setting. We explore the idea of variation – for example, how places and clothing can vary from formal to informal. We brainstorm a list of places that are informal (McDonald's, picnics) and places that are formal (Olive Garden, holiday dinners). We brainstorm types of clothing that are more formal (suits, ties, dresses) or less formal (sneakers, jeans, T-shirts). Then we combine these, matching informal clothing to informal settings and so on. Finally, we extend the comparison to language, as we see formal and informal styles of greeting or vocabulary. From this point, we're ready to explore contrasts in vernacular and Standard English grammar, or what we call informal and formal English.

Units 2 through 10: Grammar patterns

Code-Switching Lessons offers lesson units addressing the top eight patterns we find in the writing of our own vernacular-speaking students from urban Tidewater, Virginia. These are the same patterns attested by teachers from all over the country and in the research literature on AAE (Charity et al., 2004; Craig and Washington, 2006; Green, 2002; Labov, 1972; Smitherman, 2000; Wolfram, 1969) . Most units focus on one grammatical contrast in Standard English and the vernacular variety of English spoken by many African American students. The first lesson in each unit leads students to discover a particular formal and informal English grammar pattern (possession, plurality, past time, and so on). Subsequent lessons in each unit develop students' mastery in identifying, defining, classifying, and practicing target grammar patterns. Each of the grammar units culminates with students editing their own writing to transition from vernacular to Standard English. The final code-switching unit explores the importance of vernacular in creating voice in literature and students' own narrative writing.

We organize the units by whether the grammar deals with nouns or verbs. We start with nouns, as those are the most straightforward. The last unit in the series of grammar patterns looks at how to respond when students write multiple vernacular patterns within one sentence.

NOUN PATTERNS	
Unit 2: Showing Possession	*I want to sing in the kid choir* vs. *I want to sing in the kid's choir*
Unit 3: Plural Patterns	*I have two brother* vs. *I have two brothers*
Unit 4: Reviewing Possessive and Plural Patterns	
VERB PATTERNS	
Unit 5: Showing Past Time	*Yesterday I turn on the TV* vs. *Yesterday I turned on the TV*
Unit 6: Subject–Verb Agreement	*She work hard* vs. *She works hard*
Unit 7: *Was/Were*	*We was working* vs. *We were working;* *They was working* vs. *They were working*
Unit 8: *Am/Is/Are*	*We is working* vs. *We are working;* *They is working* vs. *They are working*
Unit 9: Using *Be*	*She my best friend* vs. *She's my best friend*
MULTIPLE PATTERNS	
Unit 10: Multiple Patterns	

Why these patterns?

Simply put, these vernacular patterns

- Are the most frequently occurring ones in our African American students' vernacular English.
- Illustrate patterns in both noun phrases and verb phrases.
- Move from simple grammar to more complex grammar when taken together as a sequence.

In this way, students learn how to do contrastive analysis on the simpler patterns (noun patterns) before moving on to doing their work with the patterns that have the highest frequency but are the most difficult (verb patterns) and then on to handling multiple patterns in one sentence.

Unit 11: Character and Voice in Literature

The final unit comes full circle, affirming that diversity in life and language is natural and desirable. It demonstrates that through the choice of distinct language varieties, authors (including student authors) create character and voice. Without dialect diversity, literature wouldn't be literature.

Code-Switching Lessons: The lessons

As noted earlier, our code-switching instruction follows the scientific method in grammar inquiry. The direct instruction portion of every lesson, then, leads students to explore informal and formal grammar patterns in search of generalizations, comparisons, and contrasts. The broad outline of the approach you will find throughout direct instruction is represented in the following chart.

DIRECT INSTRUCTION IN *CODE-SWITCHING LESSONS*

	How We Teach	What Students Do
Examine data	• Unveil the code-switching chart. • Invite students to read sentences silently. • Read sentences aloud.	• Look at sentences to spotlight a grammar pattern.
Seek the grammar pattern	• Ask kids to look at underlined structures. • Ask kids what pattern they see in these structures.	• Talk about a common pattern they see in each sentence. • With your guidance revise or add to the rule if it doesn't match the data.
Describe the grammar pattern	• Ask students how we might state the pattern. • Restate the definition (grammar rule) in a simple form.	• Describe the pattern.
Test the grammar pattern	• Lead students to check each sentence.	• Read each sentence and restate the rule. • Determine if the rule describes all sentences. • Revise the rule if it does not fit all sentences.
Write the grammar pattern	• Write the pattern at the bottom of the list of sentences.	• Restate the grammar pattern.

LESSON WALKTHROUGH

Unit Introduction

Each unit is preceded by a brief introduction that does the following:

The Pattern explains the grammar patterns – informal and formal – that the unit explores

The Code-Switching Chart details the process we used to create the unit's code-switching chart

UNIT 3

Plural Patterns

The Pattern

In our students' papers, we noticed that vernacular-speaking students may show more than one by inserting a **number word** (*I have* two *dog*) or **another signal word** (*I have* many *friend*). At other times, no signal word appears in the sentence; instead, we know the student means more than one through **common knowledge** (*I should respect adult; In fall, people turn their clock back*). We will build on students' existing grammar knowledge to teach the formal pattern – *I have two dogs and two cats*. Thus, vernacular and Standard English both show plurality but follow different patterns.

Vernacular pattern:
number words
(*one, two, three*)
other signal words in the sentence
(*all, some, many, several*)
common knowledge
(we simply know that the sentence refers to more than one)

Standard English pattern:
noun + -*s*

The Code-Switching Chart

Identifying vernacular plural patterns in kids' work

Identifying vernacular instances of plurality in students' work is fairly straightforward. We just look for regular nouns that signal more than one and that would take -*s* to form the plural in Standard English.

These students have used the informal pattern for showing plurality:

In my family I have two dog and two cat. Duke is my favorite dog. He is a black lab. I just got him last week He is so cute and little but he

In my family I have two dog and two cat.

Christopher Newport was an inportant person in our history. He was a captain of a ship. Three ship sailed across the ocean when he came to Virginia. They

Three ship sailed across the ocean when he came to Virginia.

54 Code-Switching Lessons · Unit 3 · Plural Patterns

Choosing the examples

The first step in building a code-switching chart is to collect a range of student papers in which students follow the vernacular, or informal, pattern for plurality. We use these to pull example sentences for our chart. For our *Plural Patterns* chart, we're looking for examples of *regular* nouns. In the previous two samples, we readily find two examples – *I have two dog and two cat* and *Three ship sailed across the ocean.* In each case, the corresponding plural equivalent in Standard English would take an *-s*. We will not put nouns that would take an irregular plural form in Standard English on the chart (*ox, deer, fish*, and so on).

Creating the code-switching chart

Creating the Code-Switching Chart describes the example sentences that appear on the chart, followed by the informal and formal patterns.

As with all our compare and contrast charts, we set up a T-chart. We title our chart *Plural Patterns*. As always, we list informal sentences from student writing on the left, writing the formal translations next to them on the right. We use four to six sentences, remembering to correct any errors of spelling or punctuation or capitalization and to shorten the sentences so they fit on one line. We also remember to return any other vernacular grammar patterns to the Standard English equivalent to help students focus on the plural patterns only. Finally, we write *The Pattern* under each column of the chart, leaving space to write the pattern during the lesson.

We've chosen examples that illustrate each vernacular rule: number words, other signal words, and common knowledge. We order the examples to facilitate students' discovery of the vernacular patterns. Since number words are the most prototypic and straightforward, we put two examples with number words early in our list, and then we include an example or two with other signal words (*all, several, a bunch*, etc.), followed by one example illustrating common knowledge as the pattern for vernacular plural.

In order to direct students' attention to the vernacular pattern, we underline the number words or other signal words. For the sentences illustrating common knowledge, we don't underline anything.

Next, we translate each vernacular example into Standard English. For these, we underline the plural -*s*, the pattern for showing plurality in Standard English.

PLURAL PATTERNS

INFORMAL	FORMAL
I have <u>two</u> dog and <u>two</u> cat.	I have two dog<u>s</u> and two cat<u>s</u>.
<u>Three</u> ship sailed across the ocean.	Three ship<u>s</u> sailed across the ocean.
<u>All</u> of the boy are here today.	All of the boy<u>s</u> are here today.
Taylor loves cat.	Taylor loves cat<u>s</u>.
THE PATTERN	**THE PATTERN**
number words other signal words common knowledge	noun + -*s*

Now we're ready for the lesson!

LESSON WALKTHROUGH
Lessons

Following is a description of the lessons:

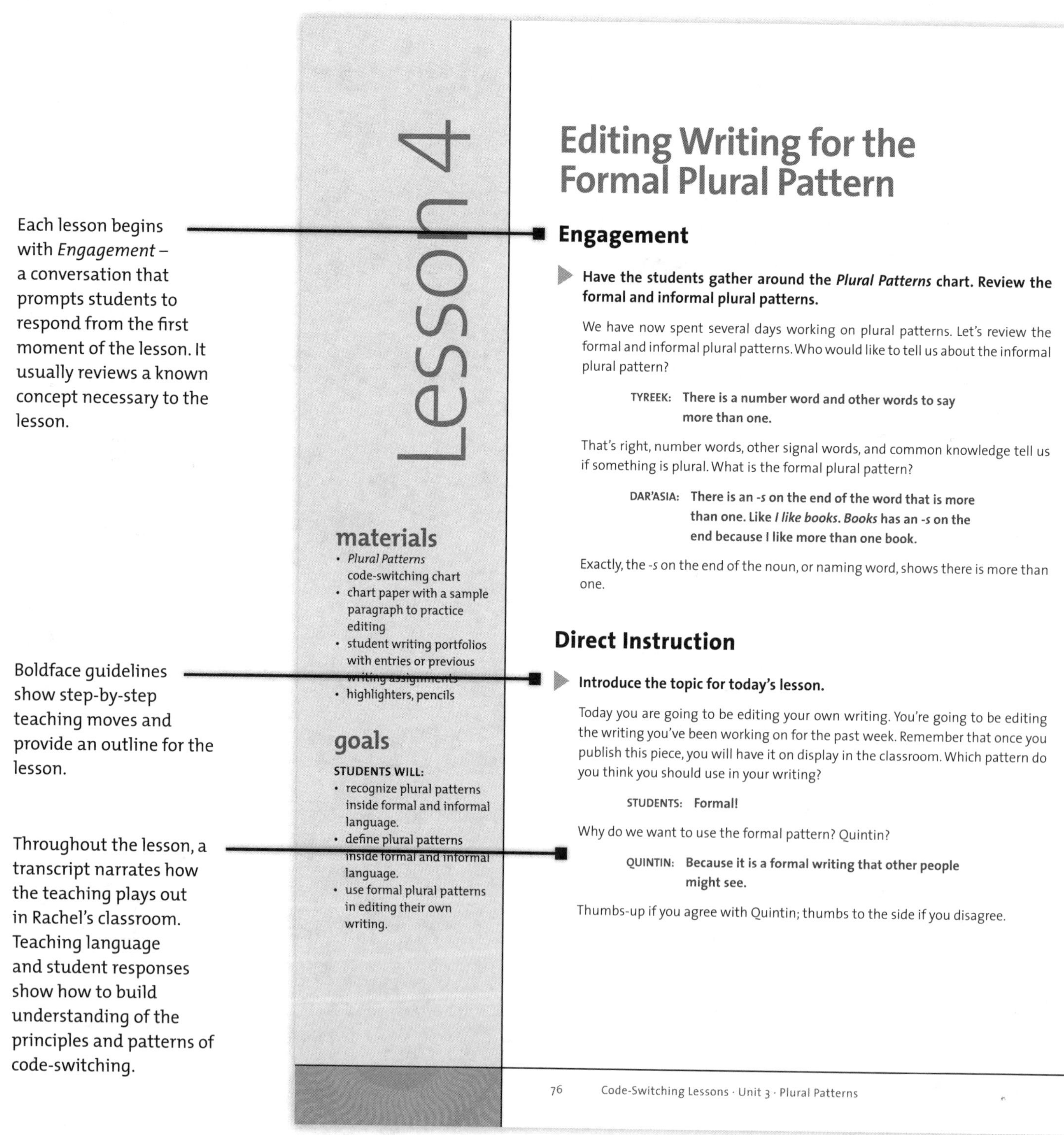

Lesson 4

materials

- *Plural Patterns* code-switching chart
- chart paper with a sample paragraph to practice editing
- student writing portfolios with entries or previous writing assignments
- highlighters, pencils

goals

STUDENTS WILL:

- recognize plural patterns inside formal and informal language.
- define plural patterns inside formal and informal language.
- use formal plural patterns in editing their own writing.

Editing Writing for the Formal Plural Pattern

Engagement

Have the students gather around the *Plural Patterns* chart. Review the formal and informal plural patterns.

We have now spent several days working on plural patterns. Let's review the formal and informal plural patterns. Who would like to tell us about the informal plural pattern?

TYREEK: **There is a number word and other words to say more than one.**

That's right, number words, other signal words, and common knowledge tell us if something is plural. What is the formal plural pattern?

DAR'ASIA: **There is an *-s* on the end of the word that is more than one. Like *I like books. Books* has an *-s* on the end because I like more than one book.**

Exactly, the *-s* on the end of the noun, or naming word, shows there is more than one.

Direct Instruction

Introduce the topic for today's lesson.

Today you are going to be editing your own writing. You're going to be editing the writing you've been working on for the past week. Remember that once you publish this piece, you will have it on display in the classroom. Which pattern do you think you should use in your writing?

STUDENTS: **Formal!**

Why do we want to use the formal pattern? Quintin?

QUINTIN: **Because it is a formal writing that other people might see.**

Thumbs-up if you agree with Quintin; thumbs to the side if you disagree.

76 Code-Switching Lessons · Unit 3 · Plural Patterns

Each lesson begins with *Engagement* – a conversation that prompts students to respond from the first moment of the lesson. It usually reviews a known concept necessary to the lesson.

Boldface guidelines show step-by-step teaching moves and provide an outline for the lesson.

Throughout the lesson, a transcript narrates how the teaching plays out in Rachel's classroom. Teaching language and student responses show how to build understanding of the principles and patterns of code-switching.

Model locating plural patterns in a piece of writing and editing for the formal plural pattern.

I have a paragraph written by a student a few years ago. The paragraph has both formal and informal plural patterns in it. However, since school writing usually needs to be formal, *all* of the plural patterns need to be formal, so I will need your help in making the entire paragraph formal by changing the informal plural patterns to formal. Let's start by reading the paragraph together. (I run my finger under the words as we read the paragraph together.) Let's look at each sentence, one at a time, and make sure the formal pattern was used. Every time we find a formal plural pattern, we are going to highlight it. If we find an informal plural pattern, we are going to make the pattern formal and then highlight it.

Jamestown

Last week all of the third-grade student took a trip to Jamestown. The student were divided into groups of two boys and two girl. All of the groups were given lists of thing to look for in Jamestown. There were twelve items on each list. My group only found some of the thing on the list. We saw two canoe and six longhouse that looked like the kind the Powhatan Indians used long ago. We were excited because both the canoes and the longhouses were on our list. However, we didn't see all three crop that the Powhatan Indians planted. Next time when we have a task on a field trip, I hope my group is able to finish.

Let's look at the first sentence. *Last week all of the third-grade student took a trip to Jamestown.* I see the word *all*, and I know that is a signal word, so there must be more than one student. Now I need to make the sentence formal by changing *student* to *students*. I'm going to add an *-s* to the end of it and highlight the word *students*. We'll do the rest of the paragraph together.

note

A customizable version of the paragraph "Jamestown" is available on the CD-ROM.

note

Our sample paragraph illustrates *only* vernacular examples of the grammar pattern we're exploring—here, plural patterns.

ways of talking

Note the positive language: we're not "correcting" *student;* we're "changing" it to formal English.

The Resources CD-ROM provides teaching tools for the lessons, including customizable versions of writing samples.

Ways of Talking suggests "language about language" that preserves a core code-switching principle: that language style is appropriate to a specific audience and setting.

LESSON WALKTHROUGH (CONT)

Guided Practice leads students through a writing activity that applies the lesson's patterns to appropriate situations

Instruction is driven by the scientific method—examine data, seek the pattern, describe the pattern, test the pattern, and write the pattern.

Guided Practice

Engage the students' help in locating and editing the remaining plural patterns.

Let's look at the next sentence. *The student were divided into groups of two boys and two girl.* Are there any plural patterns in this sentence?

JALANAY: **Two boys and two girl.**

That is actually two patterns. Let's look at the first one, *two boys.* Is that formal or informal?

STUDENTS: **Formal.**

JALANAY: **There is an *-s* on the end.**

Right, since *boys* ends with an *-s*, it is formal. Jalanay, would you highlight the formal pattern for us? (Jalanay highlights the word *boys.*)

What about *two girl*? Is that formal or informal?

STUDENTS: **Informal.**

How do you know?

DAWNNELLA: **It says *two* and that's it.**

The number word tells us that it is plural. What should we do to make it formal?

STUDENTS: **Add an *-s*!**

Andrew, would you please put the *-s* on the end of *girl.* (Andrew adds the *-s.*) Now you can highlight it because we made it formal. (Andrew highlights *girls.*) Let's read the sentence again and see if we found all of the patterns. *The student were divided into groups of two boys and two girls.* Did we find all of the patterns?

Jamestown

Last week all of the third-grade studentS took a trip to Jamestown. The studentS were divided into groups of two boys and two girlS All of the groups were given lists of thingS to look for in Jamestown. There were twelve items on each list. My

(I continue reading through the paragraph until all of the plural patterns are found. Students will highlight formal patterns and locate informal patterns, change them to formal, and then highlight them. Once students have located all of the patterns, I reread the entire paragraph.)

Good job, everyone. I'm going to hang this paragraph in the classroom as an example of editing for formal plural patterns.

Independent Practice

Independent Practice frees students up to work with the pattern with their own writing.

Have the students work independently to edit their own writing for the formal possessive pattern.

Now that we have edited a paragraph together, you are going to edit some of your own writing. You are going to read through your writing and do exactly what we just did with the Jamestown paragraph. Take your time. As you read through your work, look for examples of the plural pattern. If you find a formal plural pattern, highlight it. If you find an informal pattern, change it to formal and then highlight it. (I give students five to ten minutes to edit their own writing. I walk around the room as they complete the assignment and assist students who are having trouble with the assignment.)

what if...

it is taking too much time to complete the Guided Practice portion of the lesson?

Due to the length of the Jamestown paragraph, it may be necessary to complete only part of the paragraph during this lesson. You can then finish the paragraph during a subsequent lesson.

Sharing for Understanding

Sharing for Understanding lets students show off their own writing, synthesize their learning, and respond to the lesson.

Have the students gather in a circle to share examples of plural patterns they found in their own work. Make sure they bring their writing with them.

Now it's your turn to share some examples of the plural patterns that you found in your own writing. We're going to go around the circle, and each of you will share one sentence that contains a plural pattern. You'll need to pick one of your highlighted patterns. That means that all of the examples we share in the circle will be . . .

STUDENTS: **Formal.**

QUATASIA: **That's just like when we did possessives!**

It's exactly the same. Let's get started. If you would rather not share, just say "Pass," and we'll go on to the next person. Nije, would you like to get us started?

NIJE: **On Saturday my cousins spent the night at my house.**

Which word is plural?

NIJE: ***Cousins.* I put an *-s* on the end.**

Nice job. Quintin? (I continue around the circle in this fashion until everyone has a turn or until we run out of time.)

note

As the students share their sentences, periodically ask students how their sentence fits the plural pattern.

Assessment (on the following page, not shown here) provides guidance for monitoring your students' comprehension at the end of each lesson.

Lesson 4 · Editing Writing for the Formal Plural Pattern 79

Customizing *Code-Switching Lessons* to Your Own Classroom

Code-Switching Lessons demonstrates core principles and strategies that can extend far beyond the dialect we address in our lessons. The code-switching approach reaches concentrically out – to students who speak other U.S. dialects, to those who speak an international English (East Asian English, Caribbean English, British English, Australian English, etc.), and to students whose English is influenced by the grammar patterns of an entirely different native language (Thai, Russian, Greek, etc.). Code-switching can even help in your work with students who write in the casual cadences of spoken Standard English or text-messaging abbreviations!

Just as we have done while creating these lessons, you too can directly address the patterns your students need to expand their linguistic style repertoires:

- **Attune your ear and eye to your students' spoken language patterns.**
- **Collect examples of the patterns from your students' written work.**
- **Build your own code-switching charts.**
- **Follow the Code-Switching Lessons model to teach your patterns.**

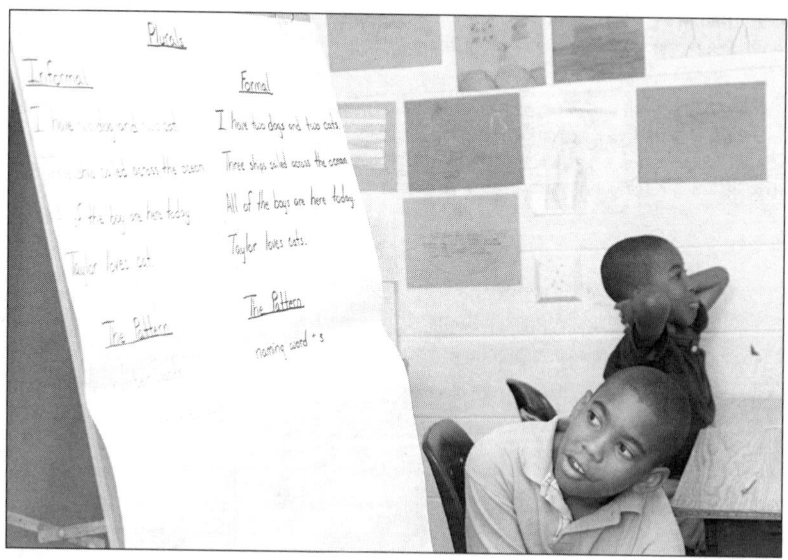
Plurals
Informal
Taylor loves cat.
The Pattern
Formal
I have two dogs and two cats.
Three ships sailed across the ocean.
All of the boys are here today.
Taylor loves cats.
The Pattern
naming word + s

Attuning your ear and eye to your students' spoken language patterns

Consider the following scenario. Let's say you're a first-year teacher in southwestern Virginia. As a teacher in Appalachia (the "territory encompass[ing] seven states . . . from West Virginia and Ohio to Georgia" (Montgomery, p. 244), you would surely find that students' home dialect transferred into school writing.

You have assigned your first essay in class and have received your students' first drafts. Of course, you will begin by focusing on the "big picture" items in the writing process – the students' focus, elaboration, concrete details, organization, sentence variety, and so on. After working on these macro issues, you'll turn to usage and mechanics. You come across examples like these: *There wasn't a church within twenty mile of us, The bear weighed four hundred pound, He cut it into four quarter, A few year after I moved here.* You immediately notice that students seem to be leaving off the plural *-s* right and left.

Now's the moment for a leap of faith. You know that languages are patterned and languages are made of dialects, which themselves are patterned. You know there could be a distinctive local language variety in your part of the country – indeed, you hear it! Further, it seems that many, many of your local students seem to leave off the *-s* while children who have moved to the area do not. You see lots of children in a local peer group using the same forms of language, which is a hallmark of a distinct grammar rule. Having taken that leap of faith, you understand that your students are not forgetting the *-s* but are following a different grammar pattern, one from their home community. Still, you know you want to extend their knowledge to the patterns of standardized American English.

Collecting examples of the patterns from your students' written work

Collect a range of student papers in which students follow the pattern you've noticed. You'll use these student papers to pull example sentences. For noun patterns, plan on ending up with four to six sentences for your code-switching chart. Students need that number to be able to identify grammar patterns. To get that many sentences, you'll probably collect eight to ten papers in which students used Appalachian plural patterns. Look for examples where the noun pattern happens in different parts of the sentence, maybe in subject position, in direct object position, in indirect object position, and so on. This broader range of papers will also let you filter out sentences that show the usage you're interested in but that may have inappropriate content. Finally, be sure to include examples that will let students fully test and refine the grammar rules they discover. For example, Appalachian English (AE) has more than one rule for showing plurality – AE shows plurality by context (words specifying amounts such as *twenty, four,* etc.) when the noun is a measure noun (*mile, pound, quarter*). But with non-measure nouns (*cat, table, bear cub*), the noun requires *-s*, so be sure to include an example or two of non-measure nouns so students can discover the full Appalachian English pattern for plurality. Now, with a good range of examples in hand, you'll build your code-switching chart.

Building your own code-switching charts

Your code-switching chart serves two functions. First, it helps you figure out the grammar pattern yourself. Second, once you've refined your own understanding of the grammatical pattern, you'll then use the chart to lead students to compare and contrast the grammar of the home and school in order to add academic English to their linguistic repertoire.

Here are the steps for building a code-switching chart:

1. Create the code-switching chart structure.

a. *Label the grammar pattern at the top of the page.*
You know that the pattern has something to do with different ways to express plurality, so we label the chart "Plurality." For more complex, difficult, or arcane grammar points, where a name is not so obvious, you can title the chart by just using examples (e.g., *Two Mile* vs. *Two Miles*), and that'll capture what the chart's about.

b. *Create two columns: Informal English and Formal English.*
In our lessons we use the terms informal and formal. However, how you title the two columns will reflect the subject matter you are exploring. Here, we could call the left-hand column "Appalachian English" and the right-hand column "Academic English," and that would be perfectly fine and correct.

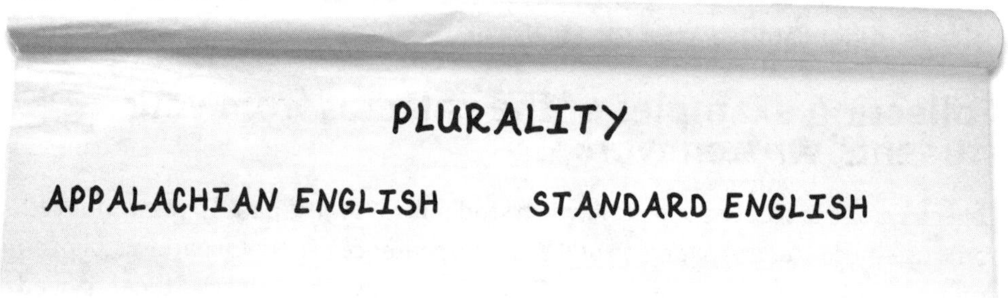

PLURALITY

APPALACHIAN ENGLISH STANDARD ENGLISH

Code-switching chart step 1: create the structure.

2. Adapt example sentences as necessary, and write them in the left-hand column.

In building charts, we may need to modify student sentences slightly. In order to help your students focus on the topic of the chart, you'll want to ensure that the only difference between your sentence and Standard English is the grammar point on which the chart focuses – here plurality patterns in Appalachian versus Standard English. That means you'll want to correct any errors in mechanics – correct spelling, capitalization and punctuation – and return any other vernacular or regional grammar patterns to Standard English equivalents.

Also, plan on editing student sentences to shorten them as necessary. It's important that examples fit on one line so that we preserve a visual parallel in the chart – one line of vernacular corresponds to one line of Standard English all the way down the chart. This helps students compare and contrast the informal and formal patterns and lock the grammar contrasts explicitly in their minds.

note

Of course, we teach punctuation, spelling, and capitalization, and integrate these into the editing time of our writing workshop. That's an activity distinct from our lessons on code-switching. *Code-Switching Lessons* focuses on grammar, the contrasts between vernacular and Standard English, or spoken and written English, so we make sure our charts focus students' attention uniquely on the grammar issue at hand.

3. **Translate each sentence in the left-hand column to Academic English.**

Once you build your left-hand column containing the adapted student sentences, write each sentence's Standard English equivalent next to it in the right-hand column. Again, make sure that each example occupies one line for the sake of visual clarity. And with this column, make sure the matching sentences are side by side to facilitate comparison and contrast.

4. **Underline the relevant grammar pattern.**

In the beginning of your code-switching work with students, plan on underlining the part of the sentence containing the relevant grammar pattern to help support student learning. Later, as students are more familiar with the process of analyzing sentences to find grammar patterns, they will increasingly take ownership and discover the patterns with much less teacher support.

5. **Write *The Pattern* under each column.**

Finally, write *The Pattern* under both columns, leaving enough space to describe the grammar pattern after students' discovery work. Labeling the pattern under both vernacular and Standard English columns reinforces the core linguistic insight underlying code-switching and contrastive analysis. Speakers who say or write "The bear weighed four hundred pound" are following a grammar rule; speakers who say or write "The bear weighed four hundred pounds" are also following a grammar rule – different rules, but rules nonetheless.

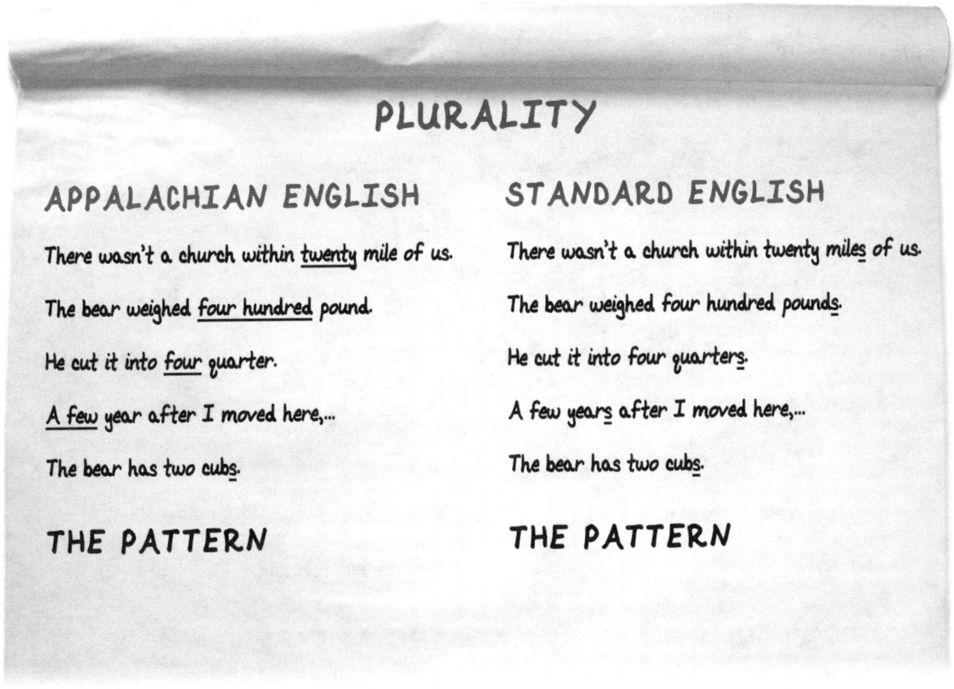

PLURALITY

APPALACHIAN ENGLISH	STANDARD ENGLISH
There wasn't a church within twenty mile of us.	There wasn't a church within twenty miles of us.
The bear weighed four hundred pound.	The bear weighed four hundred pounds.
He cut it into four quarter.	He cut it into four quarters.
A few year after I moved here,...	A few years after I moved here,...
The bear has two cubs.	The bear has two cubs.
THE PATTERN	THE PATTERN

The lesson-ready code-switching chart

note

When we unveil our code-switching chart, we make sure to tell students that we may have changed small parts of their sentences so that they can focus on the point we really want them to see . In this way, we can honor the students' voices while building an effective code-switching chart.

note

In working with students, be sure to stick to the sentences as written on the chart. Sometimes a student will say, "I say it different than that." Just thank the student, saying "For our work today, we are going to explore and analyze sentences from student writing. The sentences on the chart all come from students' papers. We want to see how these student sentences compare to formal English, so let's stick to the sentences on this chart, just exactly as they're written!"

In sum, here's the process you'll follow to build your code-switching chart, after you have collected examples of a pattern from your students' writing:

1. Create a chart structure, labeling the topic of the chart and creating two columns.
2. Adapt sentences as necessary, correcting spelling, capitalization, and punctuation, and shorten sentences to fit on one line. Return any other vernacular patterns to Standard English. Write four to six selected sentences under the left-hand column.
3. Translate each sentence in the left-hand column to Standard English.
4. Underline the relevant grammar pattern for both sets of sentences.
5. Write *The Pattern* under each column.

Following the *Code-Switching Lessons* model to teach your patterns

Once you have your code-switching chart, it's time to lead student discovery. The eleven code-switching units in this resource will provide ample examples and opportunity for practice. Take a look, too, at the lesson walk-through in the preceding section. Can you imagine substituting the Appalachian English code-switching chart for the one you see there? How would you describe the plural pattern you see in the Appalachian examples? How would you describe the pattern in the Standard English samples? Once you have a code-switching chart, the rest of the teaching approach falls right into place.

PLURALITY

APPALACHIAN ENGLISH	STANDARD ENGLISH
There wasn't a church within twenty mile of us.	There wasn't a church within twenty miles of us.
The bear weighed four hundred pound.	The bear weighed four hundred pounds.
He cut it into four quarter.	He cut it into four quarters.
A few year after I moved here,...	A few years after I moved here,...
The bear has two cubs.	The bear has two cubs.
THE PATTERN	**THE PATTERN**
Number words + measure noun	Noun + s
Other nouns + s	

Welcome to the Code-Switching Journey

Now, with a well-stocked rucksack for both you and your students, you're ready for your code-switching journey. When our students write as they speak, they're not making mistakes inside Standard English; instead, our kids are following the rules of a different language variety. Whether it's the dialect of the Appalachians or of the towns of Pennsylvania, whether it's the variety spoken in New York's boroughs, or on the streets of DC and Detroit, whether our students speak an International English or arrive in our classes as English Language Learners, patterns from their first dialect or language may transfer into their school-time writing. On the code-switching journey, we move beyond seeing students as a glass half full or half empty. Indeed, our kids are linguistically full to overflowing.

When you move from "error" to pattern, when you move from correction to contrast, your classroom transforms. As you lay down the red pen and learn linguistic insights and strategies to build on students' existing knowledge to add new knowledge – Standard English – your horizons will open. Students light up, returning to the educational enterprise. You join with students to choose the language to fit the setting. Through *Code-Switching Lessons*, you'll feel supported and freed to engage with the whole student as a thinker and collaborator in the writerly craft.

Welcome! Enjoy the code-switching journey!

1 Diversity in Life and Language

Lessons

THIS UNIT INCLUDES THE FOLLOWING LESSONS:

1. Identifying Informal and Formal Clothing
2. Identifying Informal and Formal Places and Situations
3. Identifying Informal and Formal Language
4. Recognizing Informal and Formal Language in Literature

This unit anchors all the code-switching work we do. Here we build the foundational understandings. Students should do the following:

- Learn to distinguish between the terms *informal* and *formal*.
  - Intuitively accessible, these terms help students focus on variation, a key component of our later work on grammar.
- Learn to use a T-chart to compare and contrast examples.
  - Students learn that the T-chart addresses a single topic.
  - Students learn to look for two columns (informal and formal).
  - Students learn that the entries in each column are similar.
- Come to understand that variation in life and language is necessary and desirable.
  - We all vary our style to fit the setting, time, place, audience, and communicative purpose. Children wouldn't wear school uniforms to the mall on Sunday; neither would they greet their friend "Good Morning, Tamisha. How might you be feeling today?" They'd choose a language style to fit the setting: "Hey girl, what's up?"

UNIT 1

Diversity in Life and Language

The Pattern

The goal of the first unit is to introduce students to the terms *formal* and *informal* by comparing and contrasting situations and settings they encounter in their everyday lives. In this unit, we are simply looking for examples of clothing, places, and language that are informal and formal. When we ask "What clothing is informal?" students intuitively and eagerly respond: T-shirts, sneakers, cutoffs. And they easily can volunteer formal examples: dresses, slacks, pants without holes.

The Code-Switching Chart

There are two ways in which our diversity charts differ from the code-switching charts in all later lessons:

- These charts are constructed *with* the children, whereas in later lessons, charts are constructed by the teacher on the basis of students' writing.
- The items populating the right- and left-hand columns are not usually informal and formal equivalents. For example, the *Places* chart may list *Chuck E. Cheese*, *ball park*, and *mall* in the informal column and *Olive Garden*, *Church*, and *School* in the formal column. While the first informal item names a restaurant (*Chuck E. Cheese*) and so does the first formal item (*Olive Garden*), the next item (*Ballpark*) doesn't have and doesn't need to have some formal equivalent on the chart. That's fine. Right now, we're focusing on students recognizing that contexts differ by levels of formality. Later, in the code-switching grammar units, each row in the charts will represent informal and formal equivalents, but not here in the foundational diversity unit.

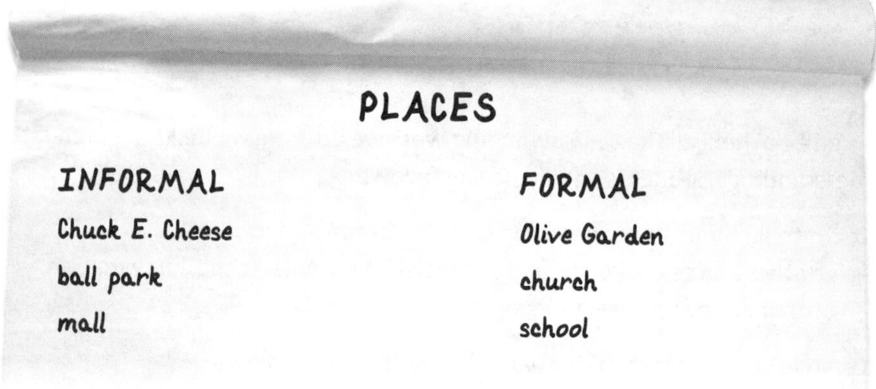

PLACES
INFORMAL
Chuck E. Cheese
ball park
mall
FORMAL
Olive Garden
church
school

Creating the code-switching charts

In this unit, we begin work with the T-chart, the graphic organizer that will underlie all our future work with students on code-switching. Just as we will in every lesson, we place the name of the category we're exploring (here, *Clothing* or *Places* or *Language*) at the top of the chart. Then we title the left-hand column *Informal* and the right-hand column *Formal*. This way, we will be able to lead the class in discovery of informal clothing or places or language and formal clothing or places or language.

In this unit we build three charts with the students, contrasting informal and formal clothing, places, and language. We'll demonstrate here with the clothing chart.

After exploring the meaning of the terms *informal* (casual, at home, among friends) and *formal* (fancy, dressed up), we invite the students to explore informal and formal clothing. We work on one column at a time, starting with either the informal or the formal side. Student discussion builds charts like this:

CLOTHING

INFORMAL	FORMAL
jeans	suit
T-shirt	tuxedo
sneakers	nice dress
basketball uniform	military dress uniform

Our diversity charts, of course, vary from year to year depending on the composition of our student body and the background of each class of students, but the goal is the same: to foster class discussion.

"What makes a suit formal?"

"What makes T-shirts informal?"

"Why are basketball uniforms informal but military uniforms formal?"

The important thing is to attune our students to observing diversity of style around them and to making choices to reflect different settings. This will underlie their later choices about which language fits a context.

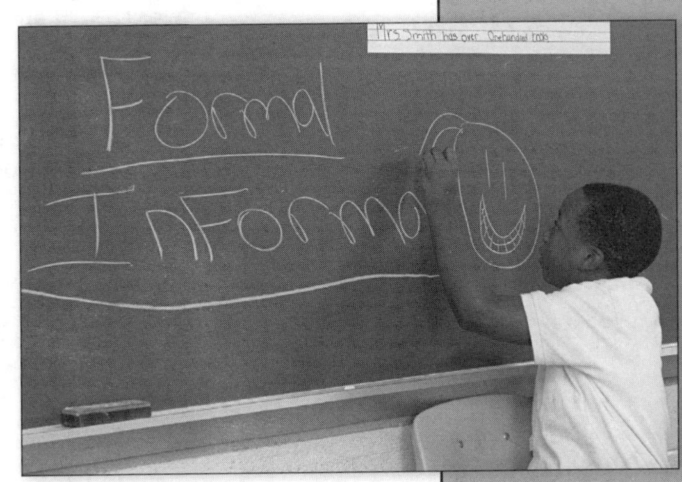

Lesson 1

Identifying Informal and Formal Clothing

Engagement

Gather the students in a central location around an easel with a T-chart that has been labeled *Clothing*, with *Informal* on the left and *Formal* on the right. Keep the chart covered for now. Prepare to introduce the ideas *formal* and *informal* by discussing different types of clothing the students wear.

For today's lesson, we're actually not going to do any writing. Isn't that weird? We're going to have a writing lesson without using writing! Today we're going to talk about clothing. Who likes clothing? (The students raise their hands.) I do, too. I love to go shopping for clothes. I want you to think about the kinds of clothes you wear to school.

NIJE: **Dress code.**

What does that mean?

NIJE: **Uniform.**

ONTIANA: **No jeans.**

Okay, a uniform, no jeans.

GARRETT: **Solid colors.**

SAMUEL: **Shirts with collars.**

Solid colors, shirts with collars. You really have to dress up to come to school, don't you? Now I want you to think of some other places that you might have to dress up to go to. What are some other places you dress up for before you go?

DAWNNELLA: **Church.**

ANDREW: **A nice restaurant.**

Now I want you to think of some places you don't have to dress up for. Where are some places you go that you don't need to get dressed up?

DESTINY: **The park.**

TYREEK: **When you're at home.**

The park, at home. Where else might you go that you don't need to dress up for? (I allow one or two more students to share.)

materials

- flip-chart paper with a T-chart labeled *Clothing*, with *Informal* on the left and *Formal* on the right
- a variety of magazines or catalogs
- two different colored sheets of construction paper for each student, one labeled *Informal*, the other labeled *Formal*
- markers, pencils, scissors

goals

STUDENTS WILL:

- recognize that variation is natural and desirable in life.
- recognize and use the terms *formal* and *informal* to describe clothing.

Direct Instruction

Introduce the purpose of today's lesson. Explain the meaning of the terms *formal* and *informal*.

Today we are going to be talking about how people dress differently at different times. As we talk about how people dress, we're going to use this chart. (I reveal the *Informal and Formal Clothing* chart.)

I want you to think about the clothes that you wear when you dress up. What kinds of clothes do you wear when you dress up or dress nicely?

ANDREW: **A suit.**

GARRETT: **A tuxedo.**

That would be pretty dressy! (I write the students' responses under the column marked *Formal.*)

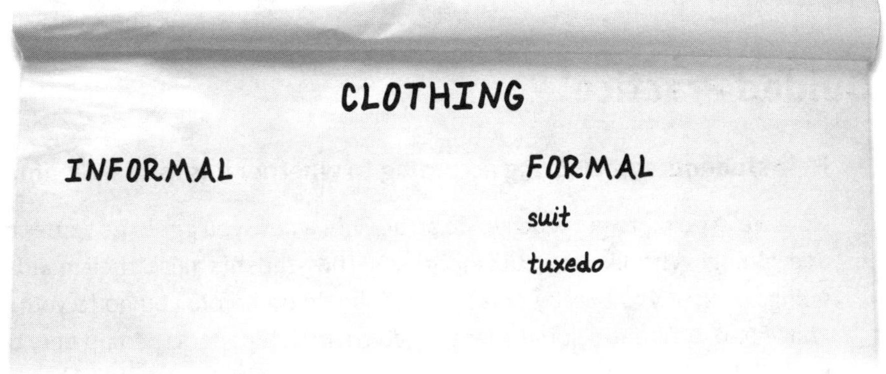

I'ANA: **A nice dress.**

BOBBY: **Pants without holes.**

Good. As you have given examples of clothing you would wear when you are dressing up, I've been writing them under this word. (I point to *Formal* on the chart.) It may be a word that you have not heard before. The word is *formal*. How many of you have heard that word before?

GARRETT: **I've heard it, but I don't know what it means.**

Well, *formal* means dressed up. So when I use the word *formal*, I want you to think dressed up. What do you look like when you dress up or wear formal clothes? (I allow three or four more students to share.) Now we're going to talk about this column. (I point to the word *Informal.*) The opposite of *formal* is *informal*. If formal means you have to dress up, what do you think *informal* means?

ONTIANA: **Not dressing up.**

Not dressed up! Exactly, *informal* means not dressed up, or casual. Let's think of some examples of informal clothing, or clothing that is not dressed up.

QUINTIN: **Jeans.**

DORIS: **T-shirt.**

ways of talking

Answers here aren't right or wrong. While we may not think that "pants without holes" are very formal, clearly the student does. What we do is ask students to articulate why a particular item is informal or formal. That's how we help cultivate students' sensitivity to contrasts across contexts.

Jeans, a T-shirt – those are informal. (I add them to the chart and allow four or five more students to share.) We have a good list up here. We have some examples of clothing that is formal and some examples of clothing that is informal.

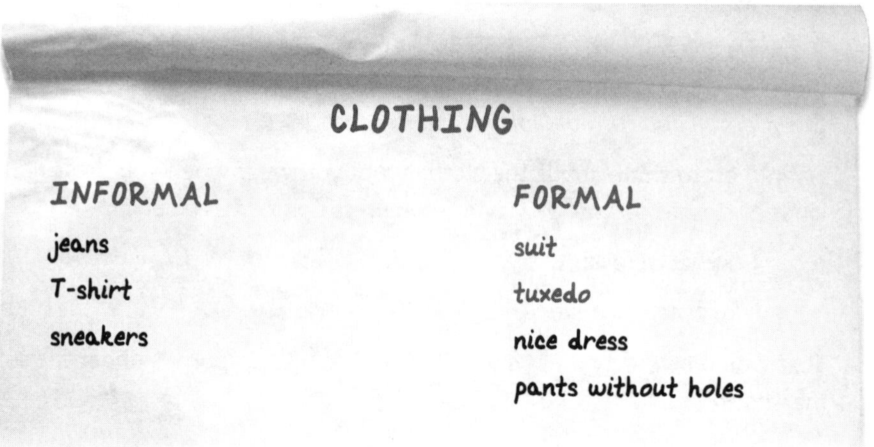

CLOTHING
INFORMAL
jeans
T-shirt
sneakers
FORMAL
suit
tuxedo
nice dress
pants without holes

Guided Practice

Help students sort clothing according to whether it is formal or informal.

Now we're going to get ready to do an activity where you get to do some cutting and gluing. Who likes to cut and glue? (The students raise their hands.) I'm going to show you exactly what you will be doing before you go to your seats. I have two different-colored sheets of construction paper taped up here on the wall. The yellow paper has the word *informal* written on it, and the blue paper has *formal* written on it. Your job will be to look through these magazines and catalogs to find examples of informal and formal clothing. I'm going to have you help me with a few pictures. (I hand out several catalogs and magazines.) Share with your neighbors. Raise your hand when you find a picture of something you would like to cut out.

I'ANA: **I found flip-flops.**

Do you think flip-flops are formal or informal?

GARRETT: **Informal. They look like the kind you wear to the beach.**

If you're wearing them to an informal place, they're probably informal. Go ahead and cut those out and glue them to our yellow informal list up here. Who else found a picture they'd like to cut out?

BOBBY: **I found pajamas.**

Do you think pajamas are formal or informal?

SEVERAL STUDENTS: **Informal.**

Why?

BOBBY: **They aren't fancy. You can't wear them to nice places.**

note

As students share what article of clothing they've found, ask why it's formal or informal. Students often answer by telling *where* they would wear the item, thus successfully anchoring their style to fit the setting.

Right. When you are getting dressed up, you don't put on a pair of pajamas! Cut the pajamas out, and glue them to our informal paper. Let's add a few more pictures.

> DORIS: **I found a suit.**

Would a suit be formal or informal?

> SEVERAL STUDENTS: **Formal!**
>
> ONTIANA: **It's really dressed up and fancy.**

Good. While you glue that to our blue formal paper, let's get a few more examples. (I allow two or three more students to share.)

Independent Practice

Have students create their own collages of *formal* and *informal* clothing. Explain the guidelines for the independent assignment.

Now that we've practiced finding formal and informal clothing together, it's time for you to showcase your brilliance by finding your own examples of formal and informal clothing. I've given each of you your own sheets of yellow and blue construction paper. Remember to look for examples of informal clothing and glue those examples to the yellow paper that has the word *informal* written on it. When you find examples of formal clothing, you're going to glue them to the blue paper that has *formal* written on it. I will be looking for at least five examples of each, so you should have at least five examples of formal clothing and at least five examples of informal clothing. You may get started. (As the students work, I walk around the room and discuss with them their reasoning behind designating certain clothing as formal or informal.)

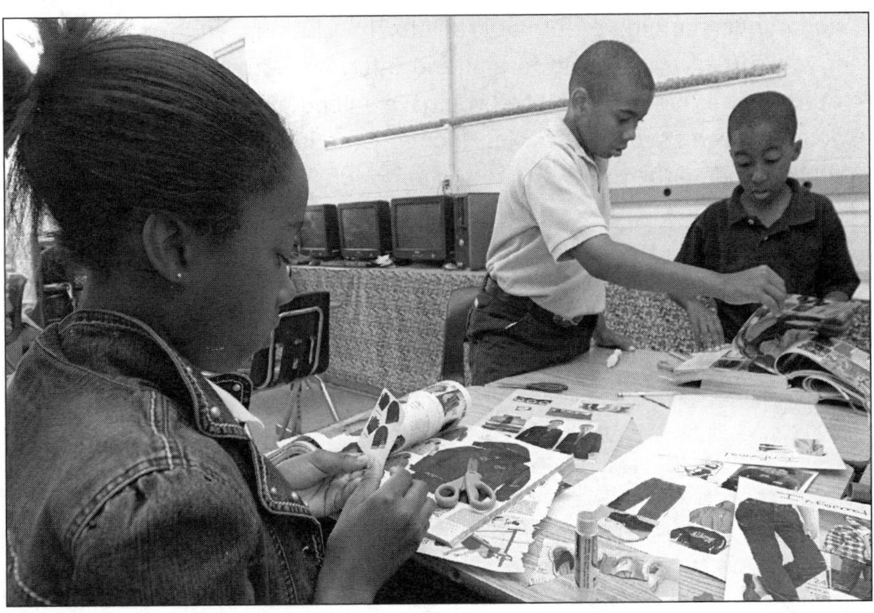

Sharing for Understanding

Have students share one example of clothing they used and explain how they determined whether it was formal or informal.

Let's form a circle so we can discuss some of your work. Make sure you bring your formal and informal papers with you. I want you to take a moment to choose your favorite picture; it can be formal or informal. Once you pick your favorite picture, I want you to think about how you decided if that particular piece of clothing was formal or informal. We're just going to go around the circle and share. I'll go first. (I hold up a piece of blue paper labeled *formal*.) I decided that this sweater (I point to the picture of a sweater I have glued to the paper) is formal because it looks dressy, like something I would wear to work. We'll go right around the circle. Quintin?

QUINTIN: **This tie is formal because you could wear it to school or church.**

TAJANTA: **This swimsuit is informal because it is not dressed up.**

Bobby? (We continue around the circle until everyone has had the opportunity to share.)

note

In their responses, students situate their choice of clothing relative to a context. We will use this foundation later on for talking about choosing style of language to fit the setting.

Conclude the lesson by allowing the students to assess their understanding of the lesson.

I want you to think about what we did today. We learned about the terms *formal* and *informal*, and we sorted clothing according to whether it was formal or informal. How well do you think you understand what the words *formal* and *informal* mean? Thumbs-up if you think you have a good understanding of formal and informal clothing, thumbs-down if you do not think you have a good understanding of formal and informal clothing, and thumbs to the side if you sort of understand formal and informal clothing. (The students show their thumbs.) Most of you feel you have a good understanding. Don't worry if you are having some difficulties, though, because we will continue to work on understanding the terms *formal* and *informal*.

Assessing the Lesson

To assess the students' understanding of formal and informal clothing, I evaluate their clothing collages. I expect them to have at least five examples of formal clothing and five examples of informal clothing because these are the criteria I gave them at the onset of the assignment. Next, I look at the selection of clothing the students used to represent formal and what they used to show informal. If I have any questions about their choices, I ask the students individually for an explanation. As long as they can validate their decisions, I accept the work as correct. The point of the assignment is to get students to think about clothing as formal or informal, as one step toward thinking more generally about choices we make in different contexts. As long as students understand the terms *formal* and *informal* and are able to explain them in relation to clothing, the lesson was successful.

Lesson 2

materials

- flip-chart paper with a T-chart labeled *Places,* with *Informal* on the left and *Formal* on the right
- a sheet of primary or lined paper that has been folded in half for each student
- markers, pencils

goals

STUDENTS WILL:

- recognize and use the terms *formal* and *informal* to describe clothing.
- recognize and use the terms *formal* and *informal* to describe a place or situation.
- draw a picture of themselves wearing both formal and informal clothing with a sentence describing where they are and what they are wearing.

Identifying Informal and Formal Places and Situations

Engagement

Gather the students around the easel with a T-chart that has been labeled *Places,* with *Informal* on the left and *Formal* on the right. Review the terms *formal* and *informal.* Lead the class in making a list of formal and informal places.

Yesterday we talked about the words *formal* and *informal.* What does the word *formal* mean?

DAWNNELLA: **It means to dress up.**

Formal means dressed up. Today we're going to start out by talking about some places that are formal. Where are some places you might go when you are dressed formally, or dressed up?

DORIS: **A wedding.**

That is really formal, isn't it! (I write *wedding* on the chart under the *Formal* column.) What else? (I allow several students to share. I record each response on the chart.) If *formal* means dressed up, what does *informal* mean?

QUINTIN: **Not dressed up.**

Where are some places you might go that are informal, or places you would not dress up for?

BOBBY: **At your house.**

When you're at home, you don't need to dress up. (I record his response.) Where else? (Several students respond, and I write their answers on the chart.)

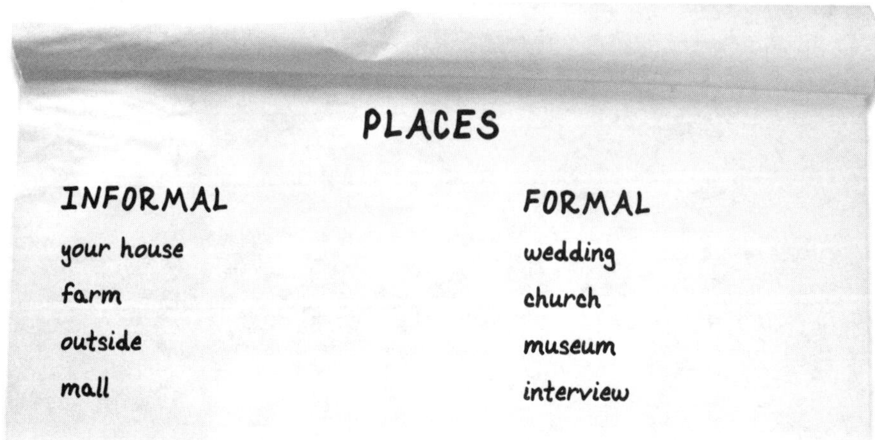

PLACES
INFORMAL
your house
farm
outside
mall
FORMAL
wedding
church
museum
interview

Direct Instruction

Introduce the topic for today's lesson. Demonstrate drawing and labeling an informal and a formal picture of yourself, with a sentence to describe each.

Now we have two charts. We have the chart we completed yesterday with the formal and informal clothing, and we have the chart we just did about formal and informal places. Today we're going to use both charts to help us draw pictures and write sentences. You will be drawing pictures of yourselves wearing formal clothing and informal clothing. Then you will be writing a sentence to go with each of these pictures. Let me show you what that will look like. You will each get a piece of paper that has already been folded in half. (I hold up a folded piece of paper.) On one half of the paper, you will draw a picture of yourself wearing informal clothing. Let me see. When I am being informal, I might wear flannel pajama pants and a T-shirt, so I'm going to draw a picture of myself wearing my flannel pajama pants. (I talk through the picture as I draw it.) Let me make sure I include little yellow stars and moons so that they look like the ones I own. Now I'm going to color my T-shirt blue, since that is the one I usually wear. I'm not going to wear any shoes with this, so I think I'm finished. Let me label my work by writing *Informal* above my picture.

Now I'm going to draw a picture of myself wearing formal clothing on the other half of the paper. I'm going to draw myself wearing my black skirt and white blouse. Let me add some earrings and some high-heeled shoes. Okay, looks good. I'll just label this picture by writing *Formal* over here. (I write *Formal* above the picture.)

ways of talking

Notice that the teacher models the assignment in its entirety, explaining her thinking as she goes. In this way, students see the teacher choosing his or her style to fit the context. We all vary our style to fit the context, a point that is central as we explore our language choices.

Now I need to write sentences explaining my clothing choices and where I wear these clothes. I'll start with the informal clothing. I usually wear this at home when I'm cleaning the house, so I'll write *I wear my flannel pajama pants and an old T-shirt to clean my house on Saturdays.* Now, I need to write a sentence about my formal clothes. These are clothes that I wear to school, so I'll write *I wear a skirt and a blouse when I go to school.* And there you have it. This is exactly what you will be doing!

Guided Practice

Guide the students through the process of creating formal and informal pictures with labels and writing sentences to go with them. Use the board or a large sheet of paper.

Let's practice doing this together on the board first. Let's start with informal clothing. What should we draw for informal clothing?

GARRETT: **Jeans and a football jersey.**

TEHJIA: **And a hat.**

Okay, Garrett, would you please draw that for us? While Garrett draws, who can tell me what else we need to do on the informal side before we start drawing our formal picture?

ONTIANA: **Write *Informal* on it.**

We need to label our picture. Ontiana, you can write *Informal* above our picture. What do we do next?

QUINTIN: **Draw a picture with formal clothes on.**

Exactly! What do we want to wear in our formal picture?

TAJANTA: **Dress code!**

What will that look like?

TAJANTA: **Brown pants and a shirt with a collar.**

While Tajanta draws our picture, who can tell me what we need to do next?

QUINTIN: **Write *Formal* next to the picture.**

Quintin's on fire today! Okay, Quintin, you can add our label. Now we need to write sentences to go with our pictures. We'll start with the informal picture. Where are we wearing our informal jeans and jersey?

NIJE: **At the park.**

Let's put that in a sentence that tells what the informal clothing is and where we are. You can use the example I did to help you.

NIJE: **I wear jeans and a football jersey to play at the park.**

Excellent! Would you like to write the sentence on our informal side? (Nije writes the sentence.) When you write your sentences, make sure you describe the clothes and name where you are. "I wear jeans and a football jersey to play at the park" is a great example. Let's look at the formal picture. How can we write a sentence that describes what we are wearing and where we would wear these clothes?

ANDREW: I wear my school uniform when I go to school.

You described the clothes and the place you are wearing the clothes. Nice job, Andrew. You can write our formal sentence on the board.

Independent Practice

▶ **Have the students create their own pictures and write their own sentences depicting themselves wearing formal and informal clothing in specific settings.**

Now that we've practiced the assignment, you get to a draw picture of yourself wearing informal clothing and a picture of yourself wearing formal clothing. Make sure you label your drawings. Then you are going to write a sentence for each outfit that includes a description of what you are wearing and the place you are wearing those clothes. Are there any questions? (The students shake their heads.) Okay, Bobby will hand out the papers, and you may get started. (I give the students ten to fifteen minutes to complete the assignment. As the students work, I assist students who are having difficulty.)

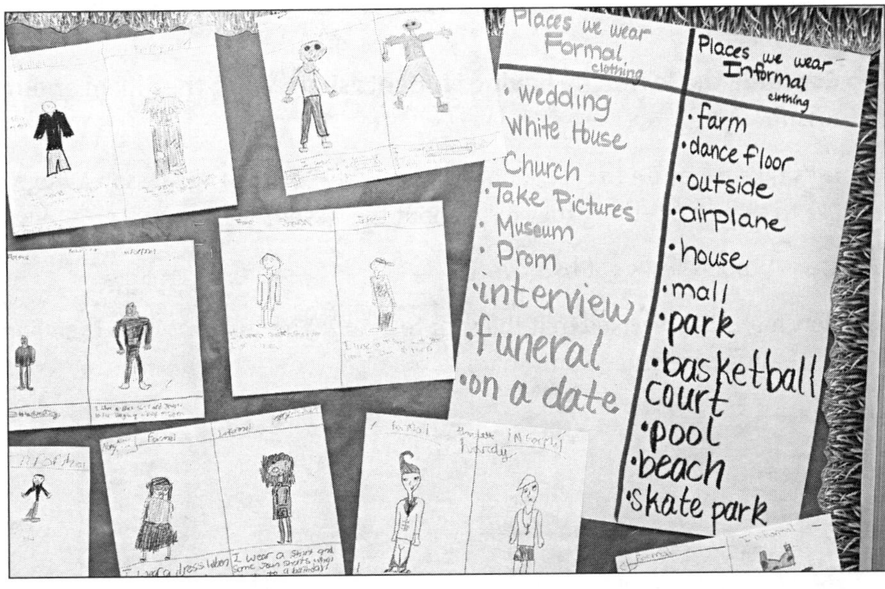

what if...

the sentence your student uses to explain the clothing and location is written informally?

It is important to stay focused on the goal of the lesson. Since I have not taught any formal grammar patterns, I cannot and do not expect my students to use them. If the other students questioned the grammar of the sentence, I might say, "What would you suggest Andrew write instead?" Once the student responded with a suggestion, I would leave it up to Andrew to decide whether to use his own sentence or the one offered by his classmate. I want to keep the focus of the lesson on formal and informal clothing and places.

Sharing for Understanding

Have students share their work with their group.

As I walked around the room, I saw some excellent drawings and some wonderful sentences. Let's take a few minutes to share your work with the class. Let's form a circle, and you can choose one of your sentences to share. Make up your mind now so when it is your turn, you'll be ready. If you don't want to share, just say "Pass," and we'll keep on moving. When it's not your turn, your job is to listen and decide if the sentence is describing informal clothing and an informal place or if the sentence is describing formal clothing and a formal place. If you think the sentence is describing formal clothing and a formal place, give a thumbs-up; if you think the sentence is describing informal clothing and an informal place, give a thumbs to the side. So that's a thumbs-up for formal and thumbs to the side for informal. Who would like to get us started? Dawnnella?

DAWNNELLA: **I wear my jeans with holes in them and my T-shirt when I play outside.**

Was that formal or informal? Show your thumbs. (The students show their thumbs.) Are they right, Dawnnella? Was it informal?

DAWNNELLA: **Yeah.**

Let's keep going. I'ana?

I'ANA: **I wear my swimsuit and flip-flops when I go to the beach.**

I see a bunch of thumbs to the side. Excellent. (I allow each student the opportunity to share a sentence in this manner.)

Conclude the lesson by having students share what they liked about the lesson.

Let's take a minute to think about what you liked about the lesson. Who would like to share something they liked about the lesson?

DORIS: **We got to draw.**

How many people liked that they got to draw? (The students raise their hands. I allow two more students to share.)

Assessing the Lesson

I collect the students' independent work to assess their understanding of formality as it relates to clothing and places. A student who understands the terms *formal* and *informal* and is able to apply them will have a picture that depicts acceptable formal and informal clothing. They will have labeled their work so that it is evident which side shows formal and which side shows informal. They will have written a sentence that describes the clothing and the place that correctly corresponds with each labeled picture. I do not grade for mechanics or grammar. Although these are both important, I did not use the writing process during this lesson, so students were not expected to edit their work. My evaluation is based solely on the purpose of the lesson.

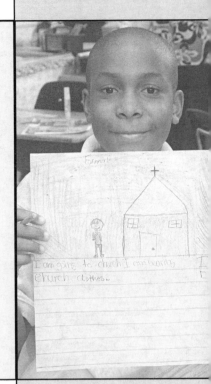

Lesson 3

Identifying Informal and Formal Language

Engagement

Gather the students around the easel with a T-chart that has been labeled *Language,* with *Informal* on the left and *Formal* on the right. Keep the chart covered for now. Review the terms *formal* and *informal.*

We have been learning about the terms *formal* and *informal*. What does *formal* mean?

HEZEKIAH: **It means to be dressed up.**

Formal means dressed up. Where are some places you might go when you're dressed up in your formal clothing?

ANDREW: **School.**

GARRETT: **A funeral.**

Yes, we dress up to go to school or a funeral. If *formal* means dressed up, what does *informal* mean?

DORIS: **It's like when you're not dressed up.**

Right, *informal* means not dressed up. *Informal* is the opposite of *formal*. Where are some places you might go when you are wearing informal clothing, when you're not dressed up?

SAMUEL: **The zoo.**

BOBBY: **The basketball court.**

Good examples. I think you're ready for today's challenge!

Direct Instruction

Introduce the topic for today's lesson.

We have talked about how clothing can be formal or informal. We've talked about how places can be formal or informal. Today we're going to talk about how language can be formal or informal. I want you to think about the ways you talk to different people. We're going to use this chart (I reveal the chart) to start our discussion.

LANGUAGE

INFORMAL	FORMAL

materials

- T-chart labeled *Language,* with *Informal* on the left and *Formal* on the right
- sheets of flip-chart paper for small groups
- markers, pencils

goals

STUDENTS WILL:

- recognize and use the terms *formal* and *informal* to describe a place or situation.
- recognize and use the terms *formal* and *informal* to describe language.
- write equivalent phrases using informal and formal language.

Discuss situations where students might use formal or informal language and what sort of greeting they would use in those situations.

I want you to think about the principal of our school. Which way do you think we should greet the principal of the school? Would you say "Yo man! Was' up?" or would you say "Good morning, Mr. B"?

STUDENTS (GIGGLING): **"Good morning, Mr. B."**

Yes, "Good morning, Mr. B" is a formal way to greet someone, and you would certainly want to greet the principal in a formal way. (I write *Good morning, Mr. B* under the *Formal* heading on the chart. I write *Yo man! Was' up?* under the *Informal* heading.) *Yo man! Was' up?* is an example of an informal greeting. Sometimes we have to dress up our language, like when we're talking to the principal. And sometimes we don't have to dress up our language, like when we talk to our friends.

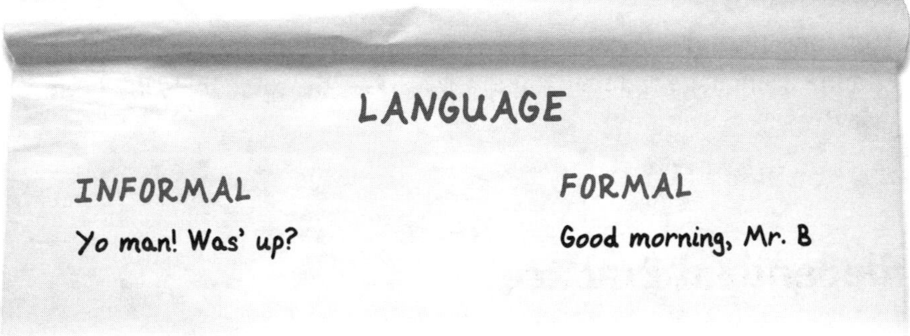

Can you think of any other people we would want to speak to using formal language?

ONTIANA: **The President of the United States.**

I would think we should use formal language if we get the chance to talk to the President of the United States. Who are some people we could speak with using informal language?

GARRETT: **Your best friend.**

You could certainly use informal language with your friends.

ways of talking

We move away from words like *right* and *wrong* or *correct* and *incorrect*. These are such absolute terms. Instead, we lead students to make more nuanced and contextualized judgments and choices – to choose their language and style based on time, place, audience, and purpose.

what if...

a student gives an informal example for the formal language column?

If Hezekiah had said "you crazy" was the formal translation for "you whack," I would have accepted his response and allowed him to record it on the chart. We haven't discussed any specific patterns yet. I am only looking for students to recognize that levels of formality exist in language. If another student was to challenge the formality of "you crazy," I would cultivate that discussion.

Guided Practice

Aid the students in adding informal and formal phrases to the *Language* chart.

I have already put an example of formal language and an example of informal language on our chart. Let's see if you can help me add some ways of speaking to the chart. Who thinks they have an example of informal language?

BOBBY: **You whack!**

That's pretty informal! How would you say that in a more formal way?

HEZEKIAH: **You're crazy!**

Okay, boys, you can write those on our chart.

Who else has an example of informal language?

QUATASIA: **Bling, bling.**

What would you say instead of "Bling, bling" if you were trying to be formal?

I'ANA: **Jewelry.**

Let's add that to our chart! Do you see how we came up with an example of informal language and then found a way to say the same thing in a more formal way?

STUDENTS: **Yes.**

Independent Practice

Have the students work in groups to create their own language charts that show examples of informal and formal language.

Now that we've had a chance to practice writing examples of informal and formal language as a class, you're going to work in groups of three to create your own charts. Your chart should look much like the one we worked on together. You will come up with an example of informal language and write it on the left side of the chart. Then change it to make it sound formal and write it on the right side of the chart. So for each informal example, you will have a formal example.

You must have at least five examples. You can have more than five examples, but no less. Take turns writing down the language examples so that everyone has a chance to write on the chart. Everyone in the group needs to agree before you write anything on the chart. Are there any questions? (I answer any questions and then give each group a piece of chart paper on which to record their examples. I give the students ten to fifteen minutes to work on their charts. I visit each group during this time to assist groups who are having trouble completing the assignment or working together.)

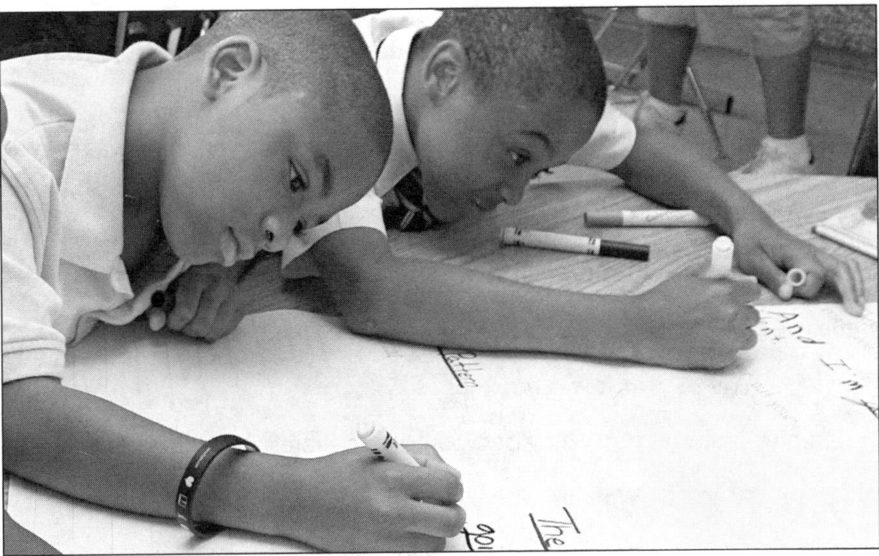

Sharing for Understanding

Allow each group to share some examples from their charts with the whole class. Add these examples to the class chart.

I heard some very lively discussions as you were working on your charts! I think we need to share some of the language examples you came up with in your groups. Let's come on back to the carpet so we can all see the charts. As a group, I need you to decide on one example that you would like to share with the class. You will read both the informal and formal forms of your example. As you listen to different groups share, your job is to decide if the informal and formal examples mean the same thing. So if the examples a group shares do mean the same thing, you're going to give a thumbs-up. If you don't think the examples mean the same thing, you're going to give a thumbs-down, and we will discuss the best way to make the informal example into a formal example. After each group shares their example, you can write it on the class chart we started earlier. Let's have Quintin, Ontiana, and Andrew get us started. Which informal example did you choose to share?

ANDREW: **Homies.**

How did you make that formal?

ONTIANA: **Friends.**

Thumbs-up or thumbs-down? I don't see any thumbs-down, so you can add *homies* and *friends* to the class chart. (Each group has an opportunity to share in this manner.)

Conclude the lesson by allowing students to share what they found easy and what they found difficult about the lesson.

I want you to think about what we did today. What did you think was easy about today's lesson, and what did you find to be difficult? Let's start with what was easy. Who would like to share?

TYREEK: **The informal stuff was easy.**

So you didn't have any trouble writing the informal examples?

TYREEK: **No, it was fun, too!**

Learning is always fun! Who else would like to share something they found easy?

GARRETT: **Working with my group was easy.**

You must have gotten along well! (I allow one or two more students to share.) Who would like to share something they found difficult?

NIJE: **Some of the formal ones were hard.**

You found it difficult to make some of your informal examples formal?

NIJE: **Yeah.**

That's something we'll be working on in the future. Any other difficulties? (I allow one or two more students to share.) Great job today!

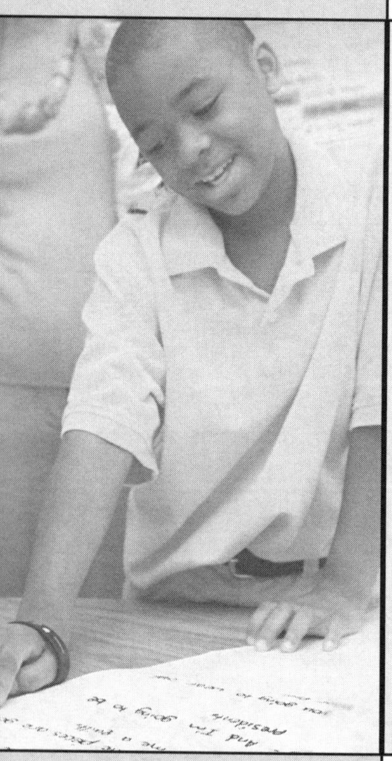

Assessing the Lesson

I base the success of this lesson on the discussions that take place regarding formal and informal language. The purpose of the lesson is to think about language in terms of understanding formality and in terms of choosing language to fit the setting. In order to determine if students have an understanding of this, I have to hear the conversations they have while they are creating their own charts; for this reason, I spend a few minutes with each group. I also evaluate the lesson based on what the students say when they share their favorite language examples. Before students can examine grammatical patterns, they must see language in terms of style that varies from setting to setting. Therefore, I want to make sure all of my students leave this lesson with that understanding.

Recognizing Informal and Formal Language in Literature

Lesson 4

Engagement

▶ **Have the students gather around the *Informal and Formal Language* chart they helped to create in Lesson 3. Review informal and formal greetings.**

Yesterday we talked about how language can be informal sometimes and how it can be formal sometimes. I want you to think about the different ways we greet people. What are some informal ways we can greet people?

ONTIANA: **What up?**

GARRETT: **Whatcha doin' dog?**

Those are good examples of informal ways we can greet people. Let's get a few formal examples of ways to greet people.

ANDREW: **How are you doing, sir?**

I'ANA: **Good afternoon.**

Nice job. I think you have a good understanding of how we can use informal language sometimes and of how we can use formal language at other times. Isn't it great that you have these language choices?

Direct Instruction

▶ **Introduce the topic for today's lesson. Read the first few pages of *Flossie and the Fox*, and then discuss the use of informal and formal language by the characters in the story.**

Today we are going to read a story called *Flossie and the Fox*. This story is about a fox and a little girl named Flossie. I want you to listen to the way Flossie and the fox speak. One of these characters speaks informal English, and one of them speaks formal English. I'm going to read a few pages, and then I'm going to ask you which one speaks informally and which one speaks formally, so listen very carefully. (I read the first several pages of the book aloud, through the page on which Flossie and the fox meet.) Who thinks they know which character speaks informally and which character speaks formally? Raise your hand if you think Flossie speaks informally. I see a lot of hands! What made you think Flossie was the informal speaker?

DORIS: **She said "I be Flossie."**

I can see you were listening very closely! Does anyone have an example of the fox saying something formal?

SAMUEL: **He said "top of the morning to you."**

That sounds pretty formal!

materials

- a copy of *Flossie and the Fox*, by Patricia McKissack
- flip-chart paper
- markers, pencils

goals

STUDENTS WILL:

- recognize that variation is natural and desirable in life.
- recognize and use the terms *formal* and *informal* to describe language.
- locate examples of *formal* and *informal* language in literature.

what if...

the students are unable to determine which speaker is formal and which is informal?

If the students cannot distinguish between the formal and informal speaker, I offer more support by writing some key sentences on chart paper. For Flossie, I might write *I be Flossie Finley and I reckon I don't know who you be either.* For the fox, I might write, *Top of the morning to you and at your service.* I would then read these sentences aloud. Between the visual and audio presentation of the sentences, most students will be able to recognize that Flossie speaks informally while the fox speaks formally.

Guided Practice

Guide the students in identifying sentences from the story as formal or informal.

As I continue to read the story, I want you to listen for examples of formal language and examples of informal language. If you think you hear an example of formal language, I want you to hold up one finger. If you think you hear an example of informal language, I want you to hold up two fingers. Let's practice a few sentences together. "I reckon I don't know who you be either." (The students hold up two fingers.) You're right. That is an informal sentence. Let's try another example. "How do a fox look?" (Most of the students hold up two fingers again.) Oh, I thought I'd be able to trick you with that one, but you are on your game today! Let's try one more before I finish reading the story. "And what is your name?" (Most of the students hold up one finger.) If you held up one finger to show that the sentence was formal, you were right! You all are excellent listeners!

Independent Practice

Read the remainder of the story while the students continue to hold up one finger when they hear formal language and two when they hear informal language.

As I continue to read the story, I want you to continue to hold up one finger every time you think you hear an example of formal language and two fingers every time you think you hear an example of informal language. When I finish reading, I'm going to ask you to share some specific examples of formal and informal words or sentences from the story, so you will need to be listening carefully. I expect everyone to participate! (I read the remainder of the story. The students hold up one or two fingers when they think they hear an example of formal or informal language.)

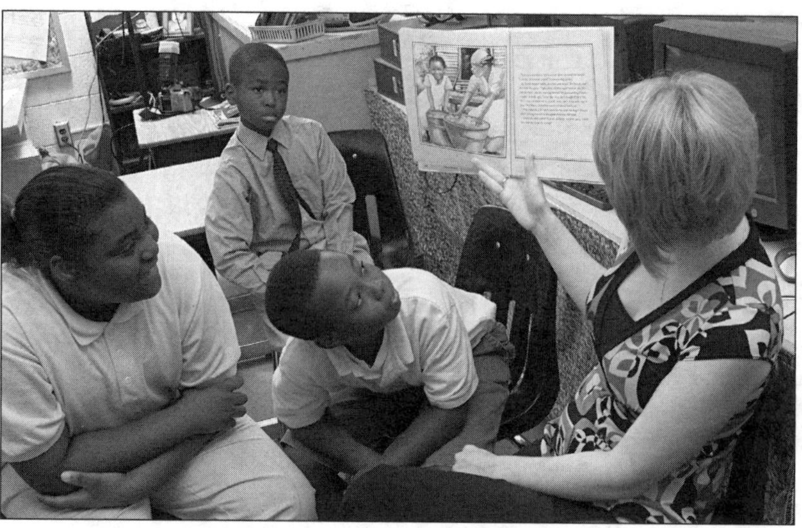

Sharing for Understanding

Allow students to share some examples of formal and informal language that they heard in the story. Create a chart to show these.

I told you that you would have the opportunity to share some examples of informal and formal language from the story. Who has an example of informal language from the story?

> ANDREW: **"A fox be just a fox."**

Good example. (I write it on the chart under the Informal heading.) Who has another example?

> DAJON: **"Shucks! You aine no fox."**

Good. (I add the sentence to the chart and allow two or three more students to share.) Now let's see if we can add some examples of formal language to the chart. Who has a formal sentence from the book?

> NIJE: **That part where fox calls the cat "a fine creature."**

"A fine feline creature."

> NIJE: **Yeah, that's it.**

That's a great example. (I add it under the Formal column on the chart and allow three or four more students to share.)

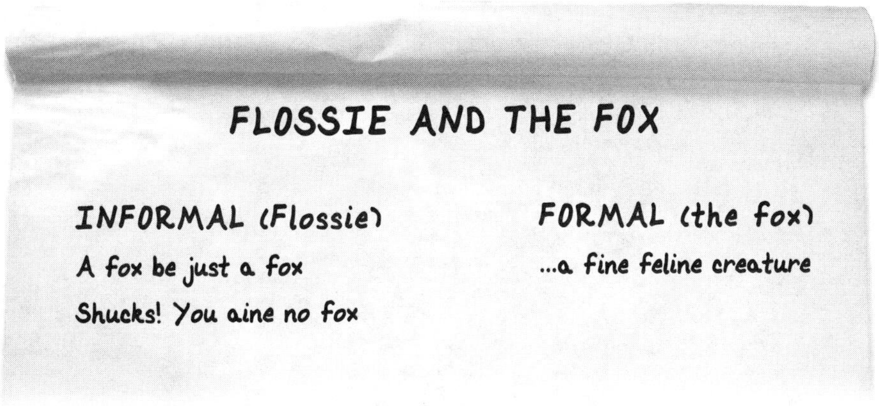

FLOSSIE AND THE FOX

INFORMAL (Flossie)
A fox be just a fox
Shucks! You aine no fox

FORMAL (the fox)
...a fine feline creature

Conclude the lesson by asking the students to share how the characters' language helped to make the story more interesting.

Why do you think Patricia McKissack, the author of *Flossie and the Fox*, chose to use different language styles for her characters? Why do you think she had Flossie speak informally and the fox speak formally?

> SAMUEL: **It made the story better.**

> DAJON: **Yeah, it was more fun to listen to.**

what if...

the students are unable to recall any sentences from the story?

I provide sentences if the students cannot remember any specific examples themselves. I might say, "one sentence that really stuck out to me was . . . " or "listen to this sentence and tell me whether you think it is formal or informal."

I agree. It wouldn't have been as entertaining if both Flossie and the fox spoke the same way. Plus, people do not all speak the same way in real life, do they? (The students shake their heads.) It would be pretty boring if everyone sounded exactly alike.

Assessing the Lesson

In this lesson, I am simply looking to see that the students notice differences in language styles. The goal of this lesson is for students to listen for differences in language and then to evaluate language as formal or informal. Since we have not studied any grammatical patterns at this point, I am not expecting accuracy. I am primarily concerned with student participation during this lesson. As we continue to learn about language and study particular grammar patterns, I will expect students to correctly identify language as formal or informal.

Showing Possession

2

Lessons

THIS UNIT INCLUDES THE FOLLOWING LESSONS:

1. Defining Formal and Informal Possessive Patterns
2. Classifying Formal and Informal Possessive Patterns
3. Practicing the Formal Possessive Pattern
4. Editing Writing for the Formal Possessive Pattern

Possessive patterns are an excellent choice for your first grammar lesson. Since the vernacular pattern for showing possession is so straightforward, it's a good one for introducing students to the concept and the process of discovery learning with the compare and contrast charts. For this reason, we always start with possession, even if only a few of our students use this informal pattern: "*I play on Derrick team.*"

Showing Possession

The Pattern

In our classroom, students often write sentences like *My goldfish name is Scaley* or *I play on Derrick team.* These students are showing possession following a different pattern than found in Standard English:

Vernacular pattern:
owner + thing owned

Standard English pattern:
owner + 's + thing owned

The Code-Switching Chart

The main tool for the lessons in this unit is a compare and contrast code-switching chart containing informal possessive patterns and their formal translations.

Identifying vernacular possessive patterns in kids' work

We readily find instances of vernacular possessive patterns in our students' work. Here are some writing samples in which students have used the informal pattern for showing ownership:

Then they came back to get me then we went to my Aunt house and I had to wait outside then I went in and they all sayed suprise.

We went to my aunt house.

My Favorite Animal

My favorite animal is a giraffe. Every time I go to the zoo I want to see the girffes frist. Giraffes is neat because it is very tall. A giraffe neck is very long. It has long legs too. That is why they is so cool.

A giraffe neck is very long.

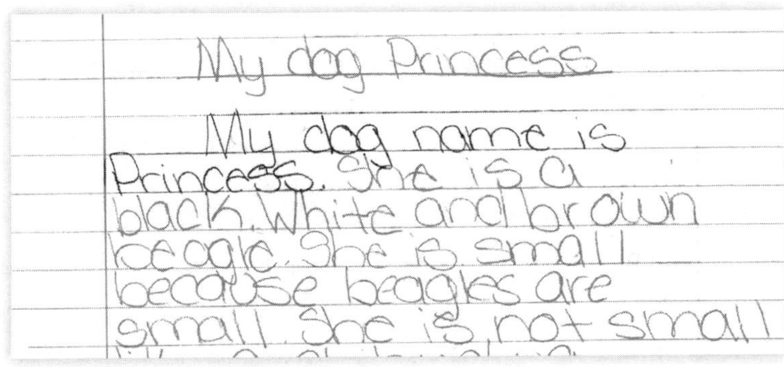

My dog Princess

My dog name is Princess. She is a black. White and brown beagle. She is small because beagles are small. She is not small

My dog name is Princess.

Choosing the examples

In choosing examples for our code-switching charts, we look for sentences with two nouns sitting side by side (*aunt house, giraffe neck, dog name*). The first noun, the owner, is a full-fledged noun, not a pronoun of any sort. The highlighted sentences above are three good examples for our compare and contrast chart. A nice feature of these examples is that they illustrate that the vernacular possessive pattern can occur in different parts of the sentence, in the subject position and as the object of a preposition.

Not just any examples of possessives go into the informal column. Inside *Moon Cycle*, the student writes *The earth spin on it axis.*

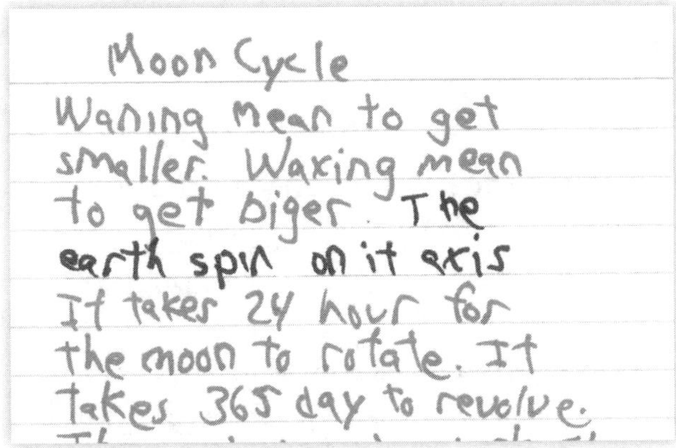

Moon Cycle

Waning mean to get smaller. Waxing mean to get biger. The earth spin on it axis It takes 24 hour for the moon to rotate. It takes 365 day to revolve.

While it is true the student hasn't followed the formal Standard English pattern (*The Earth spins on its axis*), this example does *not* go on the Showing Possession chart. Why? Because the owner, *it*, is not a common or proper noun; it's a pronoun. The grammar pattern we're working on right now deals only with the pattern **owner + thing owned**, where both the **owner** and the **thing owned** are full nouns, either common or proper.

Finally, we'll want four to six examples for the code-switching chart, and we'll want to be sure that the examples show possession occurring in different parts of the sentences, with a variety of kinds of subjects (pronoun subjects, full noun phrase subjects, and so on).

Creating the code-switching chart

As with all our compare and contrast charts, we set up a T-chart, or tree map. We title this one *Showing Possession* and list our informal sentences from the students' work on the left, writing their formal translations next to them on the right. In early lessons like this one, when students are just beginning to look at language, we underline the contrasting parts of each sentence to highlight the comparison. Finally, we write *The Pattern* under each column of the chart, leaving space to write the pattern during the lesson.

SHOWING POSSESSION

INFORMAL	**FORMAL**
We went to my aunt house.	We went to my aunt's house.
A giraffe neck is very long.	A giraffe's neck is very long.
My dog name is Princess.	My dog's name is Princess.
I made people beds.	I made people's beds.
Be good for Annie mom.	Be good for Annie's mom.
THE PATTERN	**THE PATTERN**
owner + what is owned	**owner + *'s* + what is owned**

Support student's comparison of the patterns on your charts by:

- writing between four and six sentences to fill out your Informal column.
  Fewer than four is just too few, and more than six is unnecessary to illustrate the grammar pattern.
- editing the informal sentences to focus on only one vernacular pattern.
  For example, if we were to add the sentence *I go over my dad house,* we would change it slightly, recasting it as *I go over to my dad house.*
- correcting any errors in spelling, capitalization, or punctuation.
- shortening the examples so that each sentence fits on one line.
- underlining the contrasting patterns.
  Later, when students become adept at comparison, you might have them identify the contrasting parts of the informal and formal sentences.

Defining Formal and Informal Possessive Patterns

Engagement

Gather the students in a central location around an easel with a T-chart that has been labeled *Showing Possession* with *Informal* on the left and *Formal* on the right. Keep the chart covered for now. Review the terms *formal* and *informal*.

We have been talking about the terms *formal* and *informal*. Remember that *formal* is dressed up or fancier and *informal* is not dressed up or casual. Someone used the word *casual* earlier this week. Who can tell me a time that you would wear something casual or speak informally?

ANDREW: **Outside**

When you're outside, you might speak informally.

ONTIANA: **With your family**

Yes, you might speak informally with your family. Now, who can give me an example of a time you would wear something formal or speak formally?

SAMUEL: **At school.**

Yes, you would want to use formal language at school – at least most of the time. Any other times you would want to use formal language?

DAR'ASIA: **If you're talking to the President.**

Wow! If you had the chance to talk to the President, you certainly would want to speak formally!

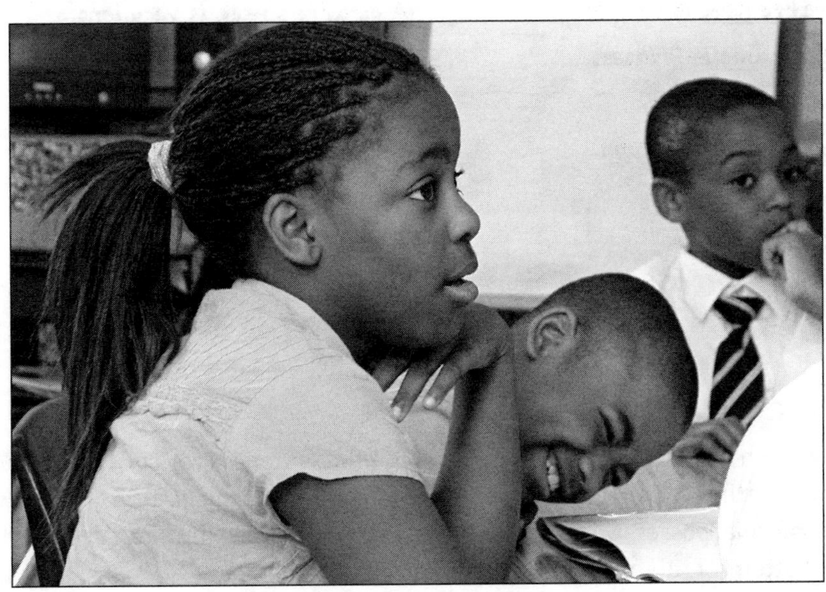

Lesson 1

materials

- *Showing Possession* code-switching chart
- flip-chart paper
- markers, pencils, paper

goals

STUDENTS WILL:

- recognize possessive patterns inside formal and informal language.
- define possessive patterns inside formal and informal language.
- distinguish between informal and formal possessive patterns.
- write sentences using informal and formal possessive patterns.

Direct Instruction

Introduce the topic for today's lesson. Define key concepts.

We are going to talk about some specific patterns for speaking formally and informally today. We are going to look at the patterns for using possessives. Does anyone know what that word *possession* means? (The students shake their heads.) I'll tell you what a possession is – a possession is something that you own, something that belongs to you. For example, I own a blue truck. The blue truck is one of my possessions. I want you to think of something that you possess – something you own.

> BOBBY: **A Nintendo.**

Bobby owns a Nintendo, so a Nintendo is one of his possessions. It is something that belongs to Bobby. Who else has an example of something they possess?

(I allow several students to give examples while reiterating the word *possession*.)

Show students the *Showing Possession* code-switching chart.

I have taken some sentences that I found in your writing and created a chart for us to use. Some of these sentences use formal English and some use informal language.

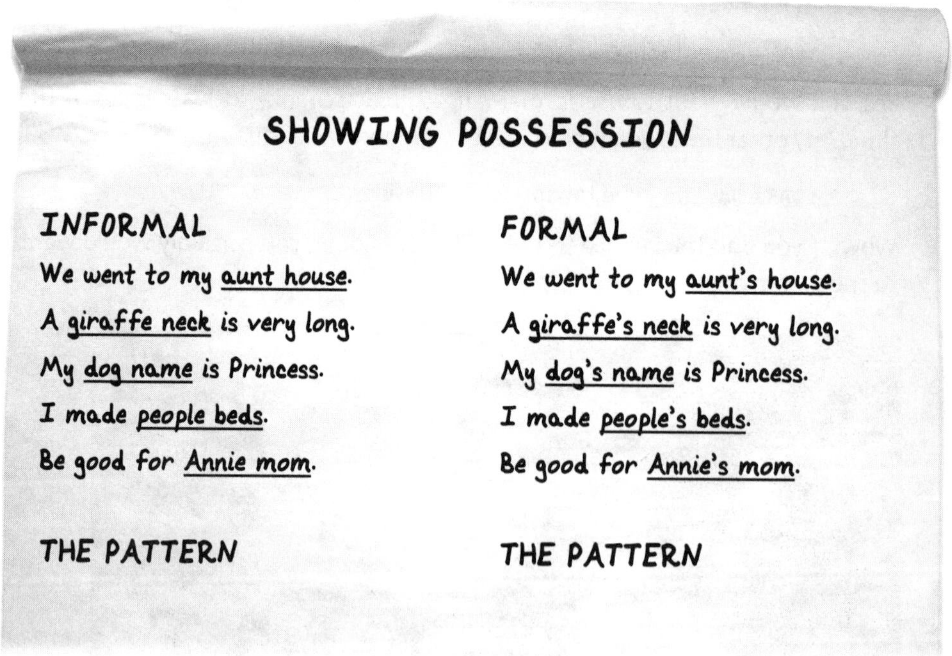

SHOWING POSSESSION

INFORMAL	FORMAL
We went to my aunt house.	We went to my aunt's house.
A giraffe neck is very long.	A giraffe's neck is very long.
My dog name is Princess.	My dog's name is Princess.
I made people beds.	I made people's beds.
Be good for Annie mom.	Be good for Annie's mom.
THE PATTERN	THE PATTERN

Initial code-switching chart, *Showing Possession*

Now, I don't want you to say anything about the sentences yet. I just want you to look. Together, we are going to see if we can figure out the pattern, or rule, that the informal possessive pattern follows. Then we will see if we can decide what the pattern, or rule, is for the formal possessive pattern.

ways of talking

Note the positive language: *Together, we are going to figure out, decide, and focus on the pattern*, not the "right" way.

Start by focusing the students' attention on the informal side of the chart. Identify and summarize the pattern.

We're going to focus on the informal side first. I'm going to read the sentences for you. On the informal side we have *We went to my aunt house, A giraffe neck is very long, My dog name is Princess, I made people beds,* and *Be good for Annie mom.* Let's just look at the informal sentences. How do you know that the house belongs to my aunt? How do you know *house* and *aunt* go together? How do you know it's not my grandma's house?

DAWNNELLA: **Because it says *my aunt house.***

You're right. It does say *my aunt house,* so we know the house doesn't belong to grandma or anyone else, don't we? The words *aunt* and *house* are right next to each other, so we have an owner and what that person owns.

Owner plus what is owned – do you think that might be the pattern? Let's check and see if that works. Is *aunt* the owner and the *house* what she owns? (The students should respond affirmatively.) Let's look at another sentence: *A giraffe neck is very long.* Who is the owner?

STUDENTS: **A giraffe.**

And what does the giraffe own?

STUDENTS: **His neck.**

So we have an owner, *giraffe*, right next to what it owns, *neck*.

(I read through each of the informal sentences in the same way.)

So it looks like the pattern for the informal side could be written as the owner plus what they own. (I write **owner + what is owned** under the informal side of the chart.)

Focus the students' attention on the formal side of the chart. Identify what is different, and summarize the pattern.

Let's see if the pattern is the same for the formal side of the chart. (I read through all of the sentences.) What changed? I underlined parts to show you what I really want you to pay close attention to, so look closely and see if you can figure out how the formal side is different from the informal side.

TYREEK: **You put an *-s* on the formal side.**

Is that the only difference? Just the *-s*?

TYREEK: **And that apostrophe thing.**

What was that *'s* on the end of? What had the *'s*? Was it the owner or what was owned?

STUDENTS: **The owner.**

Discovering the Pattern

Follow these key steps first for all the informal sentences, then for all the formal sentences.

1. Read the sentences.
2. Focus students' attention on how sentences show possession.
3. Describe the pattern.
4. Test the pattern in each sentence.
5. Write the pattern on the chart.

what if...

a student looks at the chart and says that the informal side is missing an *'s* or doesn't have an apostrophe?

Simply refocus the student's attention by saying, "I don't want to know what it doesn't have. I want to know how you know *aunt* owns the house."

So we have an **owner plus an *'s* plus what is owned**. Do you think that might be the pattern? Let's see if that works. We'll start with the first sentence: *We went to my aunt's house.* Do we have an owner plus an *'s*? Yes, we have *my aunt*, the owner, and there is an *'s* on the end of *aunt*. Then we have what my aunt owns – her house. Let's check the rest of the sentences to make sure our pattern, or rule, works for each sentence. *A giraffe's neck is very long.* Do we have an owner with an *'s* on the end?

STUDENTS: Yes.

Who is the owner?

note

Testing each sentence for whether it fits the pattern reinforces students' learning, helping them retain their new knowledge.

STUDENTS: A giraffe.

And what is owned by the giraffe?

STUDENTS: His neck.

Exactly, *giraffe* is the owner and has an *'s* on the end of it, and *neck* is what it owns. (I point to each word as I talk about it.) So this sentence follows our pattern for formal language because we have an owner plus an *'s* plus what is owned. (I read through each sentence, and we check to make sure there is an *'s* on the end of the owner in each sentence.) I think our rule works, so I'm going to write **owner + 's + what is owned** on the formal side of our chart because that is the rule for formal possessives. (I write the rule on the chart.)

SHOWING POSSESSION

INFORMAL	FORMAL
We went to my aunt house.	We went to my aunt's house.
A giraffe neck is very long.	A giraffe's neck is very long.
My dog name is Princess.	My dog's name is Princess.
I made people beds.	I made people's beds.
Be good for Annie mom.	Be good for Annie's mom.
THE PATTERN	THE PATTERN
owner + what is owned	owner + 's + what is owned

So we have our rules for informal and formal English. Which one do you think you will need to use most often in school?

STUDENTS: Formal.

You're right. Most of the time, formal is going to be the most appropriate choice for school.

Guided Practice

▶ **Lead students to create some example sentences as a group, and write them on a piece of chart paper.**

Now we are going to practice writing our own sentences. Let's pretend that we are talking with the principal of the school. Should we use the formal or informal pattern when we talk with the principal?

STUDENTS: **Formal.**

And what is the formal possessive pattern?

STUDENTS: **Owner plus *'s* plus what is owned.**

Let's pretend that we are going to tell the principal that Dajon is going to have a birthday party next week. We need an owner and what is owned. Who is going to be the owner, and what does this person own?

ONTIANA: **Dajon is the owner, and he owns his birthday party.**

How can we write that using the formal pattern?

GARRETT: ***Dajon's birthday party* – with an *'s* on the end of Dajon.**

Garrett, please write that on the chart paper. (Garrett writes "Dajon's birthday party" on the chart paper.) What do we want to say about Dajon's birthday party?

BOBBY: ***Dajon's birthday party is next week.***

Excellent. Go ahead and add that part to our sentence, Bobby. (On the chart paper, Bobby adds "is next week.")

Now we're going to pretend that we are telling a friend about the birthday party. Since we are talking to a friend, we can use formal or informal language. Which pattern would you like to use this time?

SEVERAL STUDENTS: **Informal!**

What is the informal pattern?

STUDENTS: **Owner plus what is owned.**

That's right, so what will our sentence look like now?

I'ANA: **Dajon birthday party is next week.**

Good! I'ana, you can write "Dajon birthday party is next week" under our formal sentence. (I'ana writes the sentence on the chart paper.)

Dajon's birthday party is next week.

Dajon birthday party is next week.

note

Since this is the students' first experience with comparing and contrasting language, the teacher is primarily responsible for giving the students the language necessary to discuss the pattern. In later lessons, the students will assume more of the responsibility.

ways of talking

Repeating the patterns – **owner + thing owned, owner + 's + thing owned** – helps remind students throughout the lesson that language is patterned.

note

Some students may use formal language when speaking with their best friends. This is perfectly acceptable. However, all students should choose formal language when speaking to the principal.

what if...

a child uses multiple vernacular patterns in his or her sentence?

Focus only on the student's use of the formal and informal possessive patterns. Do not address or change other vernacular patterns in the student example. If a student uses other vernacular patterns, simply jot down the example for future minilessons.

Independent Practice

Give students time to work independently to write sentences using the possessive patterns.

Now, I want you to write two sentences on your own. For the first sentence, pretend you are talking to your very best friend. You will need to decide if you should use formal or informal language when you talk to your best friend. For your second sentence, I want you to pretend that you are talking to the principal. You will need to decide if you should use formal or informal language when you talk to the principal. Make sure your sentences show the possessive pattern. (I write the scenarios – **1. best friend** and **2. principal** – on the chart paper or on the board for students for reference. As students return to their seats to write their own sentences, I circulate around the room to make sure students understand the possessive patterns.)

Pretend you are talking to . . .
1. your best friend
2. the principal

Sharing for Understanding

Allow the students to share some of the sentences they wrote.

I saw some excellent sentences as I walked around. Who would like to share their work? Dar'Asia, give us the sentence you wrote to your best friend first.

DAR'ASIA: **My mom car is broke down.**

Does Dar'Asia's sentence follow the formal or the informal pattern? How? Who is the owner, and what does that person own?

CHA'ZON: **She used the informal. Her mom is the owner, and she owns the car.**

Yes! Dar'Asia's sentence follows the informal pattern! I noticed that Dar'Asia's sentence to the principal followed the formal pattern. Dar'Asia, would you read the sentence to the principal?

DAR'ASIA: **My mom's car is broke down.**

What makes this sentence formal?

BOBBY: **It has an *'s* on the end of *mom*.**

Exactly, there is an *'s* on the end of the owner.

(I call on several students to read their sentences to their best friend and the principal. I lead the students to analyze the use of the patterns for each sentence.)

Lead the students to debrief the activity by discussing the ease or difficulty of the lesson.

I want you to think about the different things we did during today's lesson. We discovered the informal possessive pattern, and we discovered the formal possessive pattern. We also wrote sentences using the possessive patterns. What was the most difficult thing we did during this lesson? What was the easiest thing we did during this lesson? (I allow students to discuss the questions.)

I'm going to hang this chart on the wall so we can use it when we edit our writing. We will continue to work with the possessive patterns in short lessons for the next couple of weeks. And, of course, we'll use the chart in our editing for the remainder of the year.

Assessing the Lesson

When I assess this lesson, I observe how readily the students take on the task of writing their own sentences. As I walk around the room, I make a mental note of which students struggled to use the pattern. Since this is the students' first experience with code-switching, I know that the majority of the students will need additional practice and exposure to comparing and contrasting language before they are comfortable with the process. Therefore, my subsequent lessons offer a lot of support, so I do not worry too much about any difficulties the students are having at this point.

In addition to informally assessing the students' ability to write sentences using the patterns, I also note the students' responses as we debrief the lesson. Typically, they have varying thoughts about what was difficult and what was easy. Some students will say that the informal pattern is easier, while others will say that the formal pattern is easier. I try not to allow this to be the end of the conversation. What I am really looking for is the thinking behind their answers.

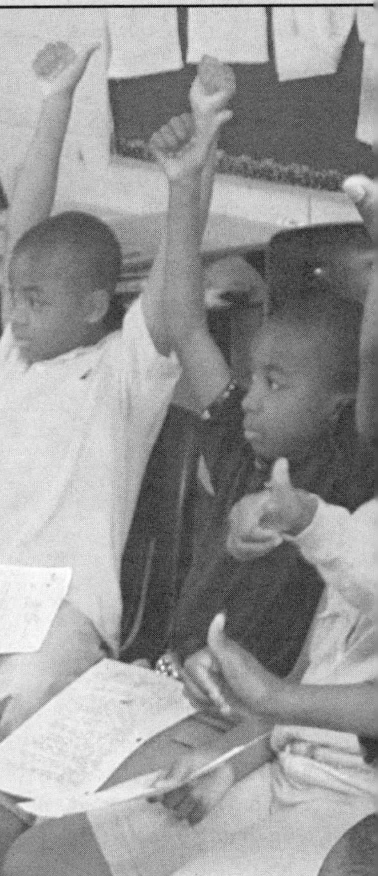

Lesson 2

Classifying Formal and Informal Possessive Patterns

Engagement

▶ **Have the students gather around the *Showing Possession* code-switching chart they created in the previous lesson. Review the terms *formal* and *informal* with the students.**

We have been talking about formal and informal, and we discussed that formal is dressed up and informal is not dressed up. Who can give me an example of someplace that you might go that would be formal, a place you would dress up for?

QUINTIN: **Church.**

ANDREW: **School.**

GARRETT: **Party.**

What about some places that would be informal, places you would not need to get dressed up for?

HEZEKIAH: **Chuck E. Cheese's.**

QUATASIA: **Store.**

SAMUEL: **Home.**

Sure, those are all great examples of places you don't really need to be dressed up to go to.

▶ **Review the term *possession*.**

Last week we made a chart, and we talked about possessive patterns. We talked about how a possession is something you own. For example, I said that I possess a blue truck. That means I own a blue truck. Then we talked about how people can show possession using informal English and formal English. We came up with some rules for how people use the possessive pattern in informal English and formal English. In informal English, we noticed that the pattern was **owner + what is owned**. For example, in the first sentence, my aunt is the owner and my aunt owns the house, so we have an owner plus what is owned. On the formal side, we decided that the pattern was **owner + *'s* + what is owned**. In the phrase *my aunt's house,* my aunt is the owner, with an *'s* on *aunt,* and the house is what is owned, so *my aunt's house* fits the formal pattern.

materials

- *Showing Possession* code-switching chart
- *Possessive Patterns* wall chart
- two sentence strips with sentences showing possessive patterns
- flip-chart paper
- one sentence strip for each student
- markers, pencils

goals

STUDENTS WILL:

- recognize possessive patterns inside informal and formal language.
- review possessive patterns inside informal and formal language.
- distinguish between formal and informal possessive patterns.
- write sentences using the formal and informal possessive patterns.
- classify sentences as formal or informal based on the possessive pattern.

Direct Instruction

Show the class a wall chart titled *Possessive Patterns,* with a column on the left labeled *Informal* and a column on the right labeled *Formal.* Set the purpose for the lesson.

Today we are going to be making a really big wall chart, and I'm going to have you help me out with this. We will be focusing on the possessive patterns and how we use them with informal English and how we use them with formal English.

Show the class a couple of sentence strips with sample sentences. As a group, determine whether the sentences use the formal or informal possessive pattern. Tape the sentences in the correct column of the wall chart.

I wrote two sentences, and I really need your help in deciding where they go on the chart, using the possessive pattern. (I reveal the first sentence, which I have written on a sentence strip.)

> **The teacher's book is on the shelf.**

Does this sentence use the informal or formal possessive pattern?

STUDENTS: **Formal.**

How do you know?

ONTIANA: **Because it sounds more formal.**

Is that what we said our pattern was for formal English, that it sounds more formal? What is the pattern that makes it formal?

I'ANA: **It has an *'s*.**

Is that the whole pattern?

DESTINY: **No, it has an owner plus an *'s* plus what is owned. The teacher is the owner, and she owns the book. And *teacher* has an *'s* on the end.**

Yes, that's our pattern, so I am going to tape the sentence strip on our chart under the formal English side because you are absolutely right – it follows the formal pattern.

Let's look at this sentence:

> **My brother bird is very noisy.**

(I lead the students to determine the pattern. We post the sentence on the wall chart.)

Guided Practice

As a group, build a sentence using a list of suggested words you have written on the board.

Now we're going to add some sentences to the wall chart. I have some owners and some things these owners could own that I wrote on the board. You are going to pick an owner and what is owned from this list.

OWNER	WHAT IS OWNED
the teacher	bird
my mom	shirt
that girl	car
my brother	bike
the principal	house

I want you to pretend you are talking to one of your friends on the playground, so in your mind, you will need to decide if you want to write a formal or informal sentence. Let's try writing a sentence together. Let's start by choosing an owner and what is owned. Which owner do we want to use? (Several students call out responses.) I heard several of you saying *the principal*, so we will use *the principal* as our owner. What should the principal own?

SAMUEL: **The car.**

Okay. Now, do we want to use the formal or informal possessive pattern? Since we're talking to a friend, we can use either one.

SEVERAL STUDENTS: **Formal!**

Okay, we'll use the formal possessive pattern. What will the formal possessive pattern look like?

DAR'ASIA: **The principal's car.**

Yes, *the principal* plus an *'s* plus *car*. Dar'Asia, would you please start our sentence by writing "The principal's car" on our sentence strip? (While Dar'Asia writes, I continue with the lesson.) We want our sentence to have some detail, so what can we say about the principal's car?

DESTINY: **It's parked behind the school.**

The principal's car is parked behind the school. What a great sentence! Destiny, go ahead and write the rest of our sentence on the strip and add it to the formal side of the chart.

Independent Practice

Give students time to write their own sentences using one of the possessive patterns. Remind them of the steps they need to follow.

Now you're going to write your own sentences. First, you will choose an owner and what is owned. You can use the words from the list on the board, or you can choose your own words. Then you will need to think about how you speak to your friends when you are on the playground. Do you use formal or informal language? After you think of a sentence, you are going to write it on the sentence strip. Make sure your sentences start with a capital and end with a period, exclamation point, or question mark. You'll want to write an interesting sentence because once everyone has finished, you will have a chance to come to the front of the class with your sentence. And each of you will get to be the teacher. Are there any questions? (I have students pass out supplies. As students write, I circulate around the room to monitor and aid as needed.)

Sharing for Understanding

Have the students take the teacher role to share their sentences.

I'm very excited to see your sentences. Now it's your turn to be the teacher. Who would like to share their sentence first? Andrew, you're raising a quiet hand. Why don't you come to the front of the class and read your sentence. Then you can see if the rest of us can figure out if your sentence is formal or informal.

ANDREW: **My sentence is *Andrew shark is powerful.* (Andrew holds up his sentence strip for the rest of the class to see.) Is it formal or informal? I'm going to pick a quiet hand. Garrett.**

GARRETT: **Informal. It don't have no *'s*.**

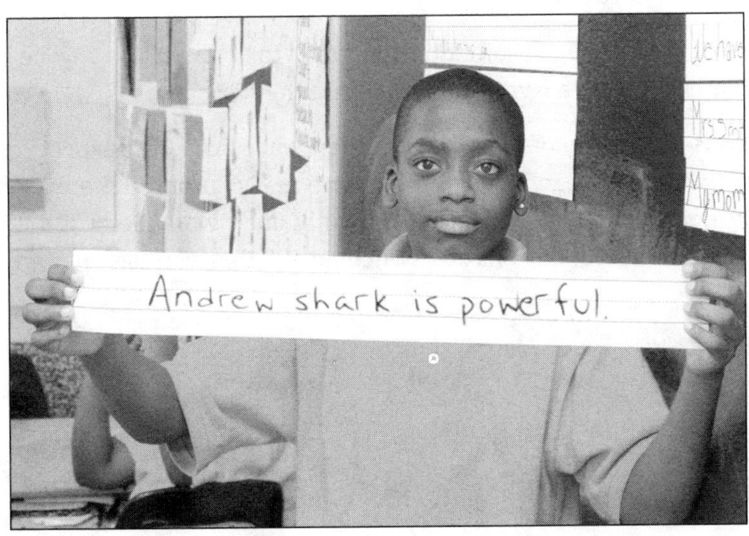

What is the informal pattern that Andrew's sentence is following?

> GARRETT: **Owner plus what is owned.**

Andrew, is Garrett correct?

> ANDREW: **Yes, and this is a fiction sentence because I really don't have a shark.**

Thank you for pointing that out. Okay, since your sentence is informal, you can tape your sentence on the Informal side of our chart. Dar'Asia, you're waiting patiently, so you can take the teacher role next.

> DAR'ASIA: **I wrote *Pumbo is Novelle's dad.* Do you think that is formal or informal?**

(Time permitting, I allow each student to share his/her sentence with the class. By the end of the lesson, the students have helped to create a wall chart illustrating the formal and informal possessive patterns.)

Lead the students to debrief the activity by explaining their choice of language when speaking to a friend on the playground.

I want you to think about the language you used when you wrote your sentence. Did you use the formal or informal possessive pattern? How many of you used the formal pattern? (Several hands go up.) Why did you decide to use the formal pattern for this assignment?

> SAMUEL: **I usually use formal, so I already know that pattern.**

Okay, you used the language you usually use with your friends. Does anyone have a different reason for using the formal pattern? (I allow several students to share.) How many people used the informal pattern? Why did you use the informal pattern?

> QUATASIA: **You can use informal when you talk to your friends. It's easier.**

So you picked the language choice that you found to be easier. Did anyone have another reason? (I allow a few students to share their responses.)

I know this is a new way of thinking about language, so I don't expect you to be experts with it right away. But you all have really surprised me with how well you're doing. If you are still having difficulty, don't worry because we'll be spending more time working on code-switching and the possessive pattern.

Assessing the Lesson

Since this is the students' first attempt at purposefully selecting formal or informal English and then following the rule for that language variety, I do not grade the assignment. Instead, I focus on the level of difficulty my students experienced with creating their own sentences and their ability to provide rationale for their language selection. During these early assignments, students tend to write sentences that reflect their own linguistic tendencies. This is perfectly acceptable as long as the students are able to articulate which pattern they used. At this point in our code-switching journey, I expect students to recognize that patterns govern how language is used and that language is a purposeful choice made by the speaker or author.

Since students typically write in the language variety with which they are most comfortable, I rarely find students struggling to write or classify their own sentences. There are, however, students who have difficulty describing the patterns of and classifying sentences written by their peers. To help minimize this problem, we constantly review the patterns as we discuss each sentence. This is a trend we will continue as we move through the remaining possessive lessons as well as future grammar lessons.

Lesson 3

Practicing the Formal Possessive Pattern

Engagement

▶ **Have students gather around the completed *Showing Possession* code-switching chart. Review the formal and informal possessive patterns.**

We have been working on formal and informal. Last time we worked on the possessive pattern. Remember that we talked about how possessives show ownership? We looked at how possession, or ownership, is used in the formal pattern and the informal pattern. Last week you helped me make a big chart on the board. Do you remember writing the formal and informal sentences on sentence strips for the chart? Who can tell me what the pattern is for the informal possessive? It's up on the chart if you need help remembering the pattern. Ontiana?

ONTIANA: **Owner plus what is owned.**

Owner plus what is owned. Does anyone have a sentence, an example, of the informal possessive pattern? Garrett?

GARRETT: **Can I use one that I wrote last week?**

Sure.

GARRETT: **My dad cat peed on the floor.**

The owner is *my dad*, and *cat* is what is owned, so that is an excellent example of the informal possessive pattern. Now let's look at the formal pattern. What is the formal possessive pattern? Remember you can use the chart if you need help. Dajon?

DAJON: **My mom's dress is blue.**

My mom's dress is blue. That's a good sentence. The formal possessive pattern is **owner + 's + what is owned**. (Many students say the pattern aloud with me.) And Dajon said *my mom's*, that's the owner, and *mom* has an *'s* on the end, and then *dress* is what she owns. So *My mom's dress is blue* fits the formal pattern.

Direct Instruction

▶ **Set the purpose for the lesson. Remind students of the reason for using the formal pattern.**

Today you are going to be taking sentences that are informal and making them formal. Why do you think I would be having you make all the sentences formal?

SAMUEL: **You want to.**

materials

- *Showing Possession* code-switching chart
- chart paper with a sample sentence using the informal pattern
- copy of the reproducible *Possessive Pattern practice* for every student
- markers, pencils, highlighters

goals

STUDENTS WILL:

- recognize possessive patterns inside informal and formal language.
- practice using the formal pattern on their own.
- rewrite sentences that contain the informal possessive pattern to sentences that contain the formal possessive pattern.

I'ANA: It's easy.

QUINTIN: Because we're in school.

Because we're in school and school is a formal place, we usually need to use formal English in our writing.

Lead students in the process of editing a sample sentence.

Let's take a look at a sentence. (I read the sentence I have written on the chart paper.)

Where is the possessive pattern in this sentence?

STUDENTS: Owner plus what is owned.

So who's the owner?

STUDENTS: Your mom.

Right, my mom. (I underline *My mom* in the sentence.)

STUDENTS: *Favorite color* is what she owns.

Favorite color is what she owns. (I underline *favorite color*.) So how can we make this sentence formal? Cha'zon?

CHA'ZON: Just add an *'s*.

Add an *'s* to what?

CHA'ZON: The end of *mom*.

Okay. So now we have

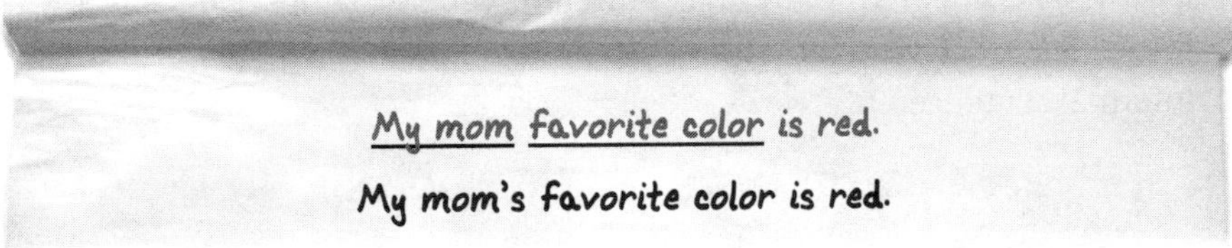

(I write the formal sentence under the informal sentence on the chart paper.) And now do we have a sentence with the formal pattern?

STUDENTS: Yes.

Yes, because now we have *My mom's*, the owner plus an *'s* plus *favorite color*, which is what she owns. Now our sentence fits the formal possessive pattern.

note

A customizable version of the *Possessive Pattern practice* reproducible is available on the CD-ROM.

Guided Practice

Hand out a copy of the reproducible for *Possessive Pattern practice* to each student. Guide students through the process of completing the first sentence.

When you go back to your seats to do your work, you're going to do exactly what I just did. You'll have a sentence, you're going to find the informal pattern for possession, and you're going to edit, or change, the sentence to make the possessive pattern formal. Then you're going to rewrite the whole sentence so that it is formal. Let's look at the practice sentence on your sheet. (I have written the first sentence from the reproducible on the chart paper.)

What time does Mrs. Smith class go to lunch?

(The students read along with me.) Where is the informal possessive pattern? Tajanta?

TAJANTA: **Owner plus what is owned?**

Okay, so who is the owner?

STUDENTS: **Mrs. Smith.**

And what does she own?

STUDENTS: **Her class.**

The class belongs to Mrs. Smith. (I underline *Mrs. Smith class.*) Now that you've found the pattern, you are going to change the sentence to show the formal pattern. What do we have to do to make it formal?

STUDENTS: **Add the *'s*.**

To what?

STUDENTS: **Mrs. Smith.**

(I add the *'s* in the original informal sentence.)

On the line under the informal sentence, you will write the sentence using formal English. (I write *What time does Mrs. Smith's class go to lunch?* under the informal sentence.)

What time does Mrs. Smith's class go to lunch?

What time does Mrs. Smith's class go to lunch?

Independent Practice

Give students time to practice editing sentences on their own.

Now your job is to find the informal pattern in each sentence and rewrite the sentence to make it formal. However, there is one very tricky sentence that has two informal possessive patterns in the same sentence. I'm going to see who's going to be tricked and who's not.

GARRETT: **You can't trick me.**

Maybe or maybe not. I'm going to be walking around, and I'll be looking to see who was fooled and who figured out which sentence has two informal possessive patterns.

DAJON: **Mrs. Swords, do you mean like one sentence has two patterns?**

Yes. Do you think you'll be tricked?

SEVERAL STUDENTS: **NO!**

(I circulate around the room as the students work on the assignment, giving assistance as needed.)

Celebrate student successes as they occur during the independent practice.

Hezekiah has found all of the informal patterns for the first three sentences, and he successfully changed them to formal.

I couldn't fool Ontiana! She found the sentence with two informal patterns — *What time does Mrs. Smith class go to Mrs. Spruill room?* — and changed both of them to formal:

(After giving students time to work on the assignment, I allow the students to share their feelings about the assignment.)

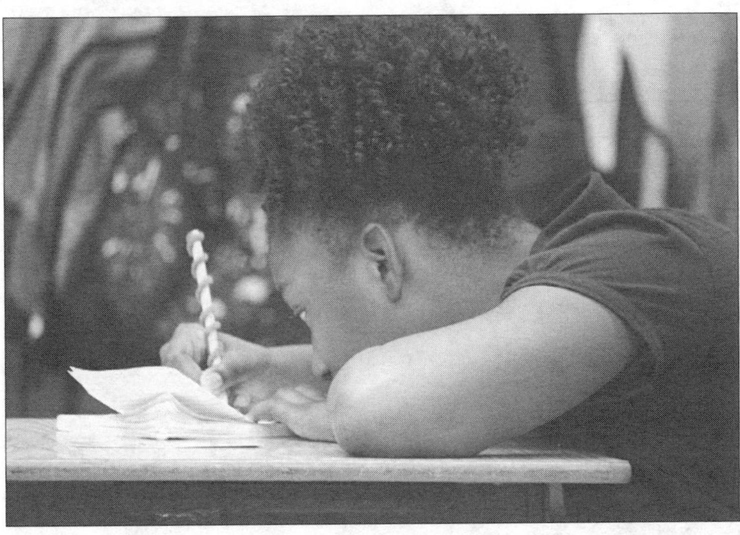

Sharing for Understanding

▶ **Ask students how they approached the assignment.**

How did you find the informal patterns in the sentences?

GARRETT: **I looked for an owner next to what they owned; then, when I rewrote the sentence, I just put an *'s* on the owner.**

Who else used this approach?

TAJANTA: **I did almost the same thing. I read the sentence and looked for the owner and what they owned. Then I underlined the pattern and put the *'s* on the owner like you did earlier. Then I wrote the sentence over.**

Raise your hand if you did something similar to what Garrett and Tajanta did. Did anyone do something different?

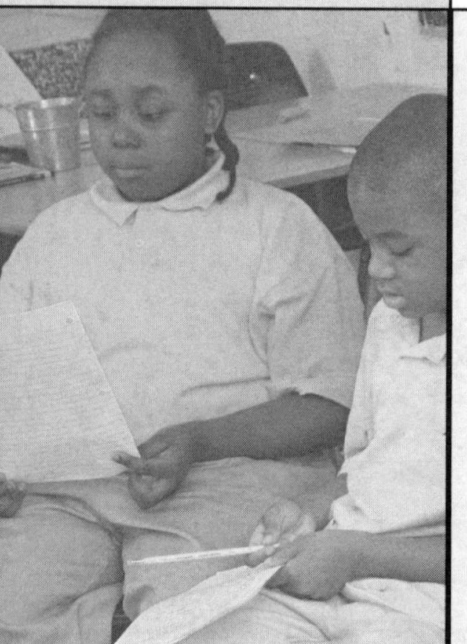

Assessing the Lesson

I collect the practice sentences completed by the students and use them to determine which students were able to successfully complete the assignment. Later, I work with students who had difficulty in a small-group setting. During my time with the small group, I go over the assignment by having the students talk through each sentence in much the same way I did during the Guided Practice portion of the lesson.

Possessive Pattern practice sentences

DIRECTIONS: Rewrite each sentence using the formal possessive pattern.

1. What time does Mrs. Smith class go to lunch?

2. I saw Quan mom buying milk at the grocery store.

3. Somebody wrote words on my brother homework.

4. The best thing about Mrs. Bright lesson was listening to the story.

5. I lost my friend book on my way to the bus.

6. Givonni voice was so soft that I did not hear him.

7. What time does Mrs. Smith class go to Mrs. Spruill room?

8. Dr. Poe fixed the bird broken wing.

Lesson 4

Editing Writing for the Formal Possessive Pattern

Engagement

Have the students gather around the *Showing Possession* chart. Review the terms *formal* and *informal*.

We have been talking about what it means to be formal and informal for several weeks. Who can tell me a place or a time when you might use informal language? A place or a time you could speak informally?

CHA'ZON: **At the mall.**

At the mall, you could use informal language.

TAJANTA: **With your mom.**

When you talk with your mom, you might use informal language. What about a time or a place you would need to use formal language? Who has an example of a place or a time when you would use formal language?

DESTINY: **Like when you're talking to your friends or your grandma. And when you're at school, you use formal.**

You could use formal or informal language when you're talking to your friends or your grandma. And, yes, we need to use formal language at school.

DAR'ASIA: **When you're about to be the President and you have to talk to a lot of people on TV.**

If you were going to be the President, you would want to speak formally, especially if you were on television.

Review the ways you have practiced using the formal and informal patterns for *Showing Possession* in previous lessons.

So far, we have looked at and described the formal and informal patterns for Showing Possession. You have written your own sentences showing the formal or informal possessive pattern. Since most of our school writing is formal, you have also practiced editing sentences by finding the informal possessive pattern and changing it to formal. So you have done quite a bit of work with the formal and informal possessive patterns.

materials

- *Showing Possession* code-switching chart
- chart paper with a short writing sample to practice editing
- student writing portfolios with previous writing assignments
- highlighters, pencils

goals

STUDENTS WILL:

- recognize possessive patterns inside informal and formal language.
- define possessive patterns inside informal and formal language.
- use formal possessive patterns in editing their own writing.

Direct Instruction

▶ Introduce the focus of the lesson.

Today you are going to look at your own writing, and you're going to be looking for the possessive pattern, since that is the pattern we have been talking about. Now, since this is writing for school, do you think we need to use the formal or informal possessive pattern?

STUDENTS: **Formal.**

Formal, and the formal pattern is **the owner plus an 's plus what is owned**. (I point to the chart on the wall, and the students chime in to read the pattern aloud.)

▶ Model locating possessive patterns in a piece of writing and editing for the formal possessive pattern.

So as you look through your writing portfolio, I want you to look for times when you used the possessive pattern. And if you used the possessive pattern formally – if you used **owner + 's + what is owned** – you're going to take your highlighter and highlight the pattern. If you used the informal pattern, you're going to change it to formal and then highlight it. Let's look at an example. This is a selection from a piece of writing that I wrote earlier:

BALIN

Balin is the name of Mrs. Smith's new baby. Balin's hands and feet are very small. Balin clothes are very small, too. He is a cute baby.

Now my job is to look for the times that I used the possessive pattern. Let me look carefully at my sentences. *Balin is the name of Mrs. Smith's new baby.* Oh, I used it right there (I point to the pattern). *Mrs. Smith's new baby* – *Mrs. Smith* is the owner; then I have the *'s*, and *new baby* is what she owns or has. Since it is already formal, I'm going to highlight that. (I highlight *Mrs. Smith's new baby.*)

Guided Practice

Engage the students' help in finding additional possessive patterns.

Now let's see if you can help me with the rest of this. Let's read the next sentence. (I point to the sentence as the students read.)

STUDENTS: **Balin's hands and feet are very small.**

Did I use a possessive pattern in there?

STUDENTS: **Yes! *Balin's*, and his hands and feet are what he owns.**

Did I use the formal or informal pattern?

STUDENTS: **Formal!**

Yes, I used the formal pattern again because I have the owner, *Balin,* plus an *'s* plus *his hands and feet,* which is what he owns. Tajanta, would you highlight the pattern for us? (Tajanta comes to the easel and highlights *Balin's hands and feet.*) Let's read the next sentence.

STUDENTS: ***Balin clothes are very small, too.***

Did I use a possessive pattern?

STUDENTS: **Yes!**

DESTINY: **But you used informal at school!**

You're right! I used the informal possessive pattern in this sentence. That is why it is so important to edit our writing before we write a final copy. What did I say I was going to do if I found an informal pattern in my writing?

STUDENTS: **Change it to formal!**

How am I going to do that?

SEVERAL STUDENTS: **Put an *'s* on *Balin.***

DORIS: **Put it on *Balin* because the clothes is what he owns.**

HEZEKIAH: **Balin is the owner.**

Balin is the owner, and he owns the clothes. The pattern for the formal is **owner + 's**, so you're right, the 's goes on the end of *Balin*. (On the chart paper, I add the *'s* to the end of *Balin*.) And now we can . . .

STUDENTS: **Highlight it! (I choose a student to highlight the pattern on the chart paper.)**

Let's look at the last sentence.

STUDENTS: ***He is a cute baby.***

Do I have a possessive pattern in this sentence?

STUDENTS: **No.**

Nope, not in this one. Let's reread the paragraph and see if all of our possessive patterns are formal now. (Have students read the paragraph with you.)

note

While one goal of this lesson is to teach students to edit informal English, turning it into formal, Standard English, that's not always the case. Sometimes, informal English is fully appropriate and even necessary in student writing, for example in narrative writing. As students build dialogue, of course they will use a range of styles of English to create voice and character.

Independent Practice

Have students find a selection from their own writing portfolio. Allow them to work independently, editing their own writing for the formal possessive pattern.

So when you get back to your seat, this is what you are going to do. You are going to read through your writing and look for possessive patterns. Some of your pieces of writing might not have any possessive patterns, and that's okay. If you don't have a possessive pattern, just try a different piece of writing. I want you to look very, very carefully for those patterns. If you do find a pattern and it is formal, you are going to highlight it. If it is informal . . .

DESTINY: **You're going to change it to formal.**

You're going to change it to formal – because this is a *school* assignment – and then you're going to highlight it. I'm going to give you twenty minutes to work on this. At the end of the assignment, each of you will have a chance to share one of the patterns that you found. You may go back to your seats very quietly and start highlighting your patterns.

note

For now, "school assignments" call for formal English. In later units, we will explore how different types of school assignments call for different styles of language.

Sharing for Understanding

Gather the students in a circle with their edited writing. Have them share examples of possessive patterns they found in their own work.

Okay, this is your chance to share the patterns you found. We're just going to go around the circle. When it is your turn, you may share one of the patterns you found. If you don't want to share today, just say "Pass," and we'll keep going. Since you are sharing a pattern you highlighted in your writing, all of the patterns should be what?

STUDENTS: **Formal.**

So your job, when you are not sharing, is to make sure the pattern being shared is formal. Andrew, let's start with you.

ANDREW: **Andrew's big brother.**

Do we have an **owner + *'s* + what is owned**?

STUDENTS: **Yes.**

Good job. Tehjia?

TEHJIA: **Tehjia's big sister.**

GARRETT: **Wow – that's just like Andrew's. Almost anyway.**

It is a lot like Andrew's. How does it fit the formal pattern? Nije?

NIJE: ***Tehjia* has a *'s*, and it is next to *big sister*.**

Tehjia is the owner, there is an *'s* on the end of her name, and *big sister* is what she owns, or what belongs to her. Exactly.

Have students use thumbs-up, thumbs-down, or thumbs to the side to do a quick assessment of which students had difficulties with the assignment.

Let's quickly show how you felt this assignment went. Thumbs-up if it was easy, thumbs-down if it was difficult, thumbs to the side if it was a little difficult.

From now on, when we work on editing, we will be looking for that formal possessive pattern.

Assessing the Lesson

I use the students' self-assessment of the difficulty of the assignment in conjunction with the observations I made as the students completed their independent work to determine which students need the most help. The most common difficulty among students during this assignment is locating the informal patterns in their own writing. When I notice a student who is unable to find the informal possessive pattern, I often have him/her read the work aloud to themselves or a classmate. This helps the student to focus on each word and helps eliminate skimming. I also help struggling students isolate the possessive pattern by prompting. I might say, "I see a pattern in the first paragraph." Sometimes, I simply read the work aloud to the student, emphasizing the possessive pattern as I read. I use the self-assessment portion of the lesson to see which students felt they were struggling through the assignment and which feel comfortable with editing for formal English. Students generally recognize when they have difficulties during an assignment and accurately self-assess. Thus, I am able to confirm which students will need the most attention in future lessons.

3

Plural Patterns

Lessons

THIS UNIT INCLUDES THE FOLLOWING LESSONS:

1. Defining Formal and Informal Plural Patterns
2. Classifying Formal and Informal Plural Patterns
3. Practicing the Formal Plural Pattern
4. Editing Writing for the Formal Plural Pattern

In this unit, we'll explore plural patterns, ways to show more than one. Since the first grammar unit (Showing Possession) dealt with nouns and noun phrases, it's natural to extend our focus to other noun patterns – those showing plurality. Also, this unit will deepen students' abilities in critical thinking as they work to discover a slightly more complex rule for informal English plural.

UNIT 3

Plural Patterns

The Pattern

In our students' papers, we noticed that vernacular-speaking students may show more than one by inserting a **number word** (*I have* two *dog*) or **another signal word** (*I have* many *friend*). At other times, no signal word appears in the sentence; instead, we know the student means more than one through **common knowledge** (*I should respect adult; In fall, people turn their clock back*). We will build on students' existing grammar knowledge to teach the formal pattern – *I have two dogs and two cats.* Thus, vernacular and Standard English both show plurality but follow different patterns.

Vernacular pattern:
number words
(*one, two, three*)
other signal words in the sentence
(*all, some, many, several*)
common knowledge
(we simply know that the sentence refers to more than one)

Standard English pattern:
noun + -*s*

The Code-Switching Chart

Identifying vernacular plural patterns in kids' work

Identifying vernacular instances of plurality in students' work is fairly straightforward. We just look for regular nouns that signal more than one and that would take -*s* to form the plural in Standard English.

These students have used the informal pattern for showing plurality:

In my family I have two dog and two cat. Duke is my favorite dog. He is a black lab. I just got him last week He is so cute and little but he

In my family I have two dog and two cat.

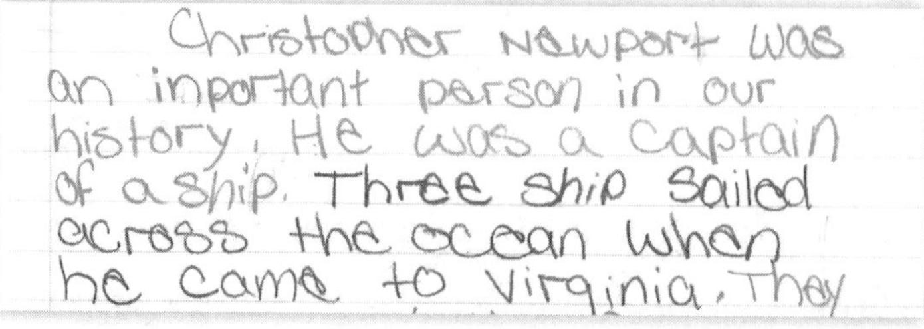
Christopher Newport was an important person in our history. He was a Captain of a ship. Three ship sailed across the ocean when he came to Virginia. They

Three ship sailed across the ocean when he came to Virginia.

Choosing the examples

The first step in building a code-switching chart is to collect a range of student papers in which students follow the vernacular, or informal, pattern for plurality. We use these to pull example sentences for our chart. For our *Plural Patterns* chart, we're looking for examples of *regular* nouns. In the previous two samples, we readily find two examples – *I have two dog and two cat* and *Three ship sailed across the ocean.* In each case, the corresponding plural equivalent in Standard English would take an *-s*. We will not put nouns that would take an irregular plural form in Standard English on the chart (*ox, deer, fish*, and so on).

Creating the code-switching chart

As with all our compare and contrast charts, we set up a T-chart. We title our chart *Plural Patterns.* As always, we list informal sentences from student writing on the left, writing the formal translations next to them on the right. We use four to six sentences, remembering to correct any errors of spelling or punctuation or capitalization and to shorten the sentences so they fit on one line. We also remember to return any other vernacular grammar patterns to the Standard English equivalent to help students focus on the plural patterns only. Finally, we write *The Pattern* under each column of the chart, leaving space to write the pattern during the lesson.

We've chosen examples that illustrate each vernacular rule: number words, other signal words, and common knowledge. We order the examples to facilitate students' discovery of the vernacular patterns. Since number words are the most prototypic and straightforward, we put two examples with number words early in our list, and then we include an example or two with other signal words (*all, several, a bunch*, etc.), followed by one example illustrating common knowledge as the pattern for vernacular plural.

In order to direct students' attention to the vernacular pattern, we underline the number words or other signal words. For the sentences illustrating common knowledge, we don't underline anything.

Next, we translate each vernacular example into Standard English. For these, we underline the plural *-s*, the pattern for showing plurality in Standard English.

PLURAL PATTERNS

INFORMAL	**FORMAL**
I have two dog and two cat.	I have two dogs and two cats.
Three ship sailed across the ocean.	Three ships sailed across the ocean.
All of the boy are here today.	All of the boys are here today.
Taylor loves cat.	Taylor loves cats.
THE PATTERN	**THE PATTERN**
number words other signal words common knowledge	noun + *-s*

Now we're ready for the lesson!

Lesson 1

Defining Formal and Informal Plural Patterns

materials

- *Plural Patterns* code-switching chart
- *Showing Possession* code-switching chart (on the wall)
- flip-chart paper
- markers, pencils, paper

goals

STUDENTS WILL:

- recognize plural patterns inside formal and informal language.
- define plural patterns inside formal and informal language.
- distinguish between informal and formal plural patterns.
- write sentences using informal and formal plural patterns.

Engagement

▶ **Gather the students in a central location around an easel with a T-chart that has been labeled *Plural Patterns* with *Informal* on the left and *Formal* on the right. Keep the chart covered for now. Briefly review the terms *formal* and *informal*.**

We have been talking about formal and informal language. We are going to review what it means to be formal and what it means to be informal. Who would like to share what formal means?

ANDREW: **It means something that is fancy.**

Something that is fancy or dressed up. What are some times that you would need to use formal language?

ONTIANA: **Church.**

When you're in church. Maybe some people thought that might be informal, so maybe some churches require formal language and some don't.

JALANAY: **School.**

School. Samuel?

SAMUEL: **When you're getting a job.**

Good. What about informal? What does *informal* mean?

QUINTIN: **Not dressed up.**

Okay, so where is a place you would not need to dress up?

GARRETT: **At home or on the street.**

At home or on the street. Sure, you could use informal language then.

▶ **Introduce the topic for the lesson and define key concepts. Review the possessive pattern covered in the previous unit and introduce the term *plural*.**

We have talked about possession and how we show possession (point to the *Showing Possession* chart). We discovered a formal possessive pattern in language and an informal possessive pattern. Today we are going to talk about another pattern. This pattern is called the *plural pattern*. What does *plural* mean?

GARRETT: **Plural is like there is more than one.**

Exactly. Plural means more than one. For example, there are nineteen students in this class. Because nineteen is more than one, the number of students is plural.

Who thinks they can give an example of a sentence that shows more than one?

ANDREW: **There were two teachers in my kindergarten class. That's a plural sentence.**

Yes, there is a plural number of teachers because two is more than one. What are some other things that you have more than one of, things that would be plural?

DESTINY: **There is more than one month in the year.**

Oh, there are twelve months in the year. Since twelve is more than one, there is a plural number of months in the year.

ONTIANA: **We have ten toes.**

JALANAY: **And fingers.**

Yes! Ten is more than one, so we have a plural number of toes and fingers, too.

Direct Instruction

▶ **Set the purpose for the lesson. Show students the *Plural Patterns* code-switching chart.**

Now we're going to look at some sentences that have plural patterns in them. I'm going to be looking for who's really thinking today. We're going to need some real brain power on this one. When you see the chart, you will notice that some of the sentences are in the Formal English column and some of the sentences are in the Informal English column. We are going to see if we can write a rule, or pattern, for formal and informal plurals. This is the same thing we did when we looked at the possessive patterns. (I reveal the Plural Patterns chart.)

Take a minute to look at the chart, but don't say anything. (Students begin whispering. Several students are convinced they see the pattern.)

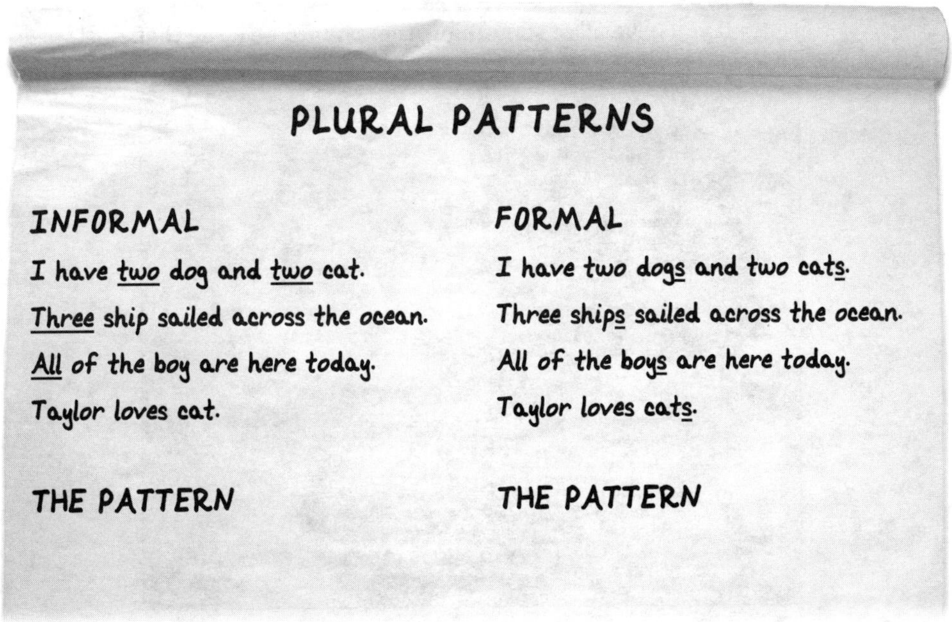

PLURAL PATTERNS

INFORMAL	FORMAL
I have two dog and two cat.	I have two dogs and two cats.
Three ship sailed across the ocean.	Three ships sailed across the ocean.
All of the boy are here today.	All of the boys are here today.
Taylor loves cat.	Taylor loves cats.
THE PATTERN	THE PATTERN

note

While Standard English also uses number words and other signal words, we don't underline these, since it's really the *-s* that Standard English *requires* in showing plurality.

Discovering the Pattern

Follow these key steps first for all the informal sentences, then for all the formal sentences.

1. Read the sentences.
2. Focus students' attention on how sentences show plurality.
3. Describe the pattern.
4. Test the pattern in each sentence.
5. Write the pattern on the chart.

note

Since the students are still learning the technique of comparing and contrasting language to discover patterns, the teacher is primarily responsible for supplying the students with the language they need to discuss the patterns.

Start with the Informal side of the chart. Identify and summarize the pattern.

Let's look at the informal sentences first. You're really going to have to listen as I read through the informal sentences because there is actually more than one rule for the informal plural pattern. Our informal sentences are *I have two dog and two cat, Three ship sailed across the ocean, All of the boy are here today,* and *Taylor loves cat.*

Let's really focus on that first sentence. How do we know that there is more than one dog and cat?

> SEVERAL STUDENTS: **It says *two!***
>
> DAWNNELLA: **And two is more than one!**

You're right! The word *two* shows us that there is more than one, so a number word tells us that *dog* and *cat* are plural. Maybe that's the pattern for informal plurals. Let's check to see if that pattern works for any of our other sentences. *Three ship sailed across the ocean.* Does this sentence follow the pattern?

> STUDENTS: **Yes!**

How? Ontiana?

> ONTIANA: **It says *three*, and *three* is a number word.**

Three is a number word, so we know that *ship* is plural. Let's go ahead and add the rule **number words** to our chart. (I write **number words** in the Informal English column.)

Let's look at the next sentence. *All of the boy are here today.* How do we know that there is more than one boy?

> I'ANA: **It says *all.***

The word *all* isn't a number, so how do we know that there is more than one?

> NIJE: **If you have all of something, there has to be more than one.**

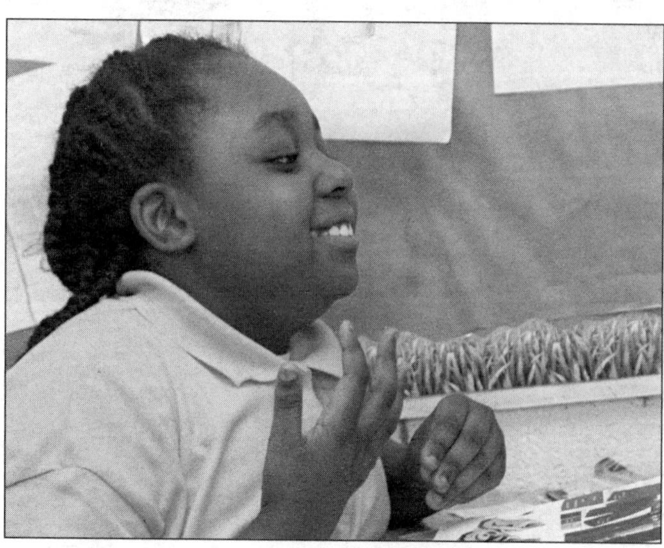

The word *all* is telling us there's more than one. It's *signaling* to us: "hey, there are plural things here!" So I'm going to add the rule **other signal words** to the chart. (I write **other signal words** in the Informal English column.) Can anyone think of some other words like *all* that signal there's more than one?

I'ANA: ***Many?***

Yes, if there are *many* of something, there must be more than one.

DAWNNELLA: ***Lots.***

The words *lots*, or *lots of*, or *a lot of* signal to us that there are plural things. Good! OK, let's take a look at our last sentence. *Taylor loves cat.* Does this sentence follow either of our patterns?

SEVERAL STUDENTS: **No!**

Well, I told you this chart would be tricky. If there isn't a number word, and there isn't a signal word, how do we know that Taylor loves more than one cat?

DESTINY: **Everyone know Taylor love all cats.**

Now Destiny said that we all just know that Taylor loves all cats. How do we know that, Destiny?

DESTINY: **She be talking about cats and writing about cats, and she have a lot of cats.**

I think we can write a rule that says all of that. Let's call it **common knowledge**. Common knowledge means that we know the sentence is plural because we all know something about the sentence that isn't actually written down. We all know how much Taylor likes cats, so we know that the sentence about her is probably about her loving more than one cat. Let's go ahead and add **common knowledge** to our rules. (I add this to the chart.)

what if...

a student thinks that the *-s* on *loves* signals more than one?

If so, remind students that the noun, or naming word, is the only word that can show plurality. You might say, "let's think about this for a minute, is the sentence saying there is more than one love?" Students should recognize that it doesn't make sense for *loves* to be plural. You could then say, "since *loves* does not show more than one, what is there more than one of?"

Focus the students' attention on the Formal English side of the chart. Identify and summarize what is different.

Now let's look at the Formal English side of the chart. (I read through all of the sentences.) What has changed? How is the formal side different from the informal side?

SEVERAL STUDENTS: **It has an *-s*.**

What has an *-s*? Destiny?

DESTINY: **Cats and dogs.**

GARRETT: **Whatever there is more of.**

Oh, so there is an *-s* on the end of *dog* to show more than one dog, and there is an *-s* on the end of *cat* to show more than one cat. The pattern must be that there is an *-s* on the end of the naming word, or noun, that is plural.

SEVERAL STUDENTS: **Yes!**

ways of talking

As always, we ask students "What changed?" or "What's different inside Formal English?" These positive ways of speaking recognize that all language varieties follow systemic rules.

Let's check this pattern and see if it works for our other sentences. *Three ships sailed across the ocean.* Does this sentence follow our pattern?

STUDENTS: Yes.

How? Samuel?

SAMUEL: There's an -*s* on the end of *ship*, and there are three ships.

So *ship* has an -*s* on the end, and there is more than one ship. (I go through each sentence in this way.) Well, it looks like this rule works, so I'm going to write **noun + *s*** on the Formal English side of our chart. (I write the rule on the chart.)

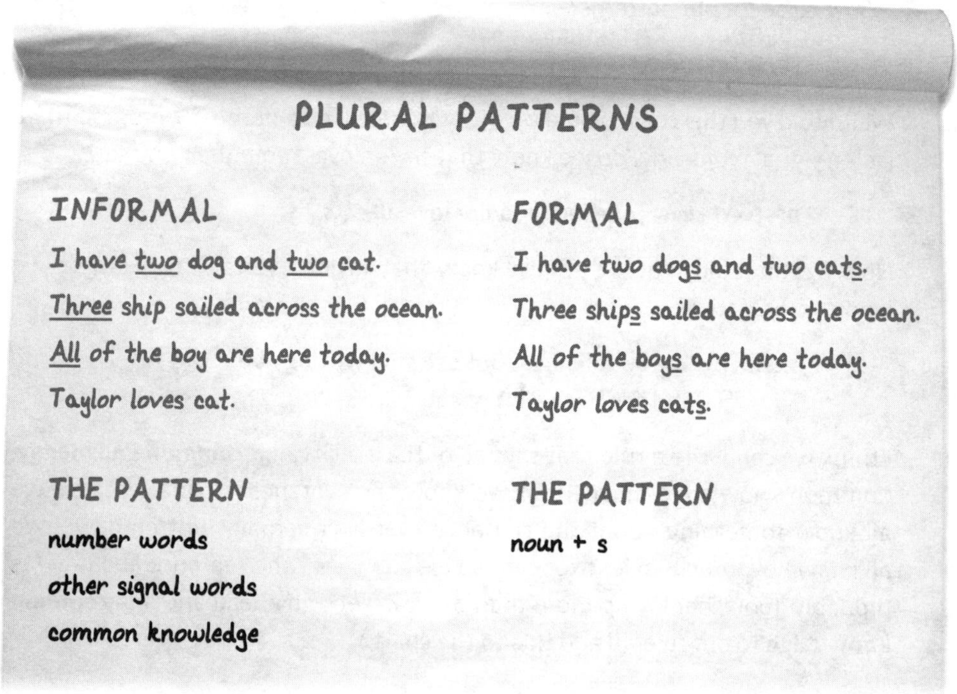

PLURAL PATTERNS

INFORMAL	FORMAL
I have two dog and two cat.	I have two dogs and two cats.
Three ship sailed across the ocean.	Three ships sailed across the ocean.
All of the boy are here today.	All of the boys are here today.
Taylor loves cat.	Taylor loves cats.
THE PATTERN	THE PATTERN
number words	noun + s
other signal words	
common knowledge	

Now that we have our rules for formal and informal plurals, I will leave this chart up in our classroom for you to use when you write. Which one, formal or informal, do you think you will usually use in school?

STUDENTS: Formal.

Yes, we will be practicing writing formally in school.

Guided Practice

Lead students to create some example sentences as a group, and write them on a piece of chart paper.

Now that we have decided the patterns for using plurals, let's practice writing some sentences. Let's pretend that we are talking to a teacher in the building.

Should we use formal or informal language when we talk to teachers?

STUDENTS: **Formal.**

What is the formal plural pattern? (I point to the rule as the students say it aloud.)

STUDENTS: **Noun plus *-s*.**

Let's look around the room. What is something we have more than one of?

TAJANTA: **Books!**

Okay, how can we write a sentence about how many books we have? We need to make sure we use the formal plural pattern of naming word plus *-s*.

QUINTIN: **We have a lot of books in our class.**

Which word is plural in the sentence *We have a lot of books in our class*?

I'ANA: **Lot.**

You're right that *a lot* shows us that there is more than one, but what do I have a lot of?

I'ANA: **Oh, books.**

Yes. So Quintin was right. We are going to write **book + *-s*** when we write our sentence because that is the formal plural pattern. Quintin, would you please write our sentence on the chart paper. (Quintin writes *We have a lot of books in our class* on the chart paper.)

Now let's pretend that we are talking to a family member. We can speak formally or informally to our family. Which pattern would you like to use?

TAJANTA: **Informal. We already did a formal one.**

We did already write a sentence using the formal pattern, but remember that you can choose formal or informal when you are talking to your family. So when you write your own sentences, keep that in mind. What do we have more than one of in our classroom?

ANDREW: **Desks.**

What is the pattern for showing plurality in informal language?

ANDREW: **Number words, signal words, and common knowledge.**

So how can we let our family member know that we have more than one desk using the informal pattern?

NIJE: **We can say how many we have.**

Exactly. We can use a number word or some other signal word. Who thinks they have an informal sentence for the number of desks we have in our room?

BOBBY: **We have twenty-one desk in our room.**

Very nice. Bobby, you can go ahead and add that sentence to our chart paper.

ways of talking

Note the positive language used to guide the student in identifying the plural noun.

Independent Practice

Give students time to write sentences using the plural patterns.

Now it is your turn to write two sentences on your own. For the first sentence, let's pretend that you are talking to another teacher in the school. You will need to decide whether you should use formal or informal language. For the second sentence, let's pretend that you are talking to a family member. Again, you will need to make the decision to use formal or informal language. I want you to look around the room and find something that we have more than one of and then use that in your sentence. This way, you can make sure you're using the plural pattern in each of your sentences. (I write the scenarios: *1. teacher* and *2. family member* on the chart paper or on the board.) After sending the students to their seats to complete the assignment, I walk around the room to make sure students understand the plural pattern and to offer assistance when it is needed.

Say that there is more than one of something in the class.

Pretend you are talking to . . .
1. a teacher
2. a family member

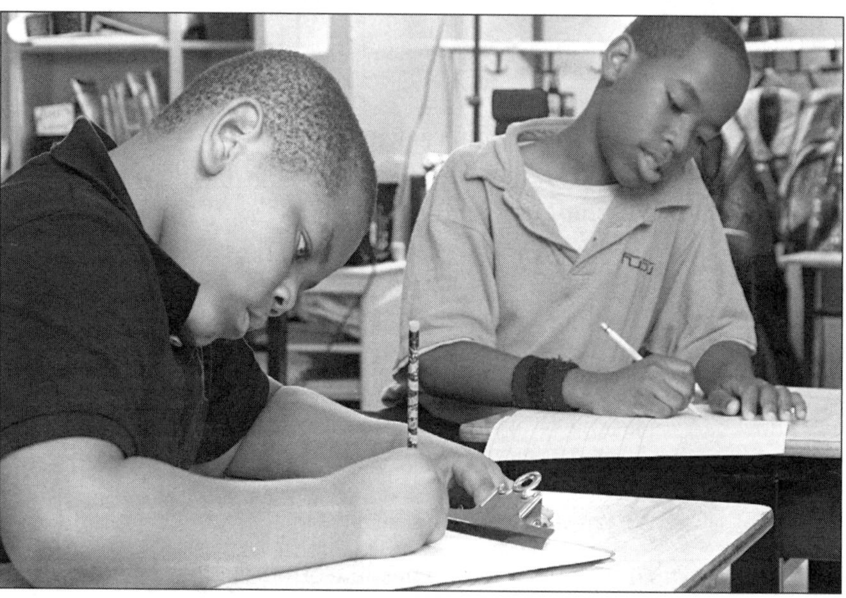

Sharing for Understanding

Give the students a few minutes to share their sentences.

Wow! I am so impressed with some of the wonderful sentences you wrote. Who would like to share their sentences? Samuel, would you share the sentence you wrote to the teacher first?

SAMUEL: **There are eight boys in my class.**

Is Samuel's sentence formal or informal, and how do you know?

I'ANA: **Formal because boy has an *-s* on the end of it.**

You're exactly right! Samuel, would you read the sentence that you wrote to a family member?

SAMUEL: **It's the same.**

That's okay. Go ahead and read it.

SAMUEL: **There are eight boys in my class.**

So Samuel wrote a formal sentence to a family member. Samuel, why did you choose formal language for the second sentence?

SAMUEL: **That's how I talk at home.**

Is there anybody who wrote an informal sentence to show how they would speak to a family member? (I allow a child to share his/her informal sentence.)

Lead the students to debrief the activity by discussing their choice of language when speaking with a family member.

How many of you used formal language when you wrote the sentence that shows how you talk to your family members? Why did you choose formal language?

How many of you used informal language when you wrote the sentence showing how you talk to family members? Why did you choose informal language?

(I encourage students to discuss these questions.)

Our *Plural Patterns* chart will stay on the wall throughout the year so we can use it to edit our writing.

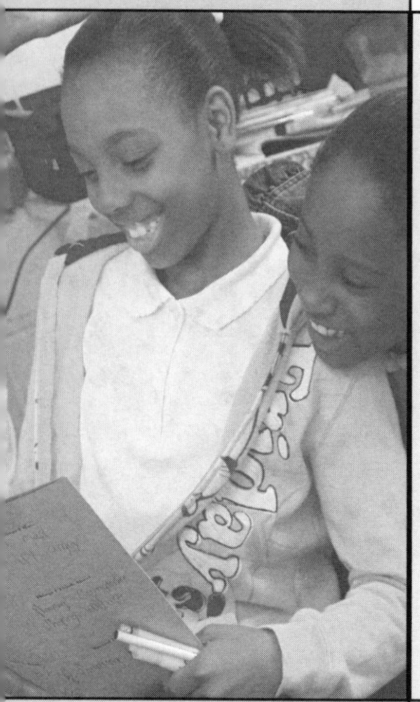

Assessing the Lesson

I encourage students to discuss the debriefing questions. Typically, students respond that they choose formal or informal language based on how they actually speak to family members. A few students will say that they just wanted to write an informal sentence. There aren't any right or wrong answers to these questions. The debriefing gives me an opportunity to take an informal poll of those students who typically use this informal pattern at home, and I make a mental note of these students because they may have more difficulty using the formal pattern. The debriefing also gives students the opportunity to discuss and respect diversity in the classroom.

Classifying Formal and Informal Plural Patterns

Engagement

Have the students gather around the *Plural Patterns* code-switching chart they helped to create in the previous lesson. Review the terms *formal* and *informal*.

We have been talking about the terms *formal* and *informal* for several weeks now. How is formal language different from informal language?

CHA'ZON: **Formal is more dressed up, and informal is like "Yo, what up?"**

So formal language is dressed up, and informal language is more casual. Who would like to remind us of a time we would want to use formal language?

I'ANA: **Someplace important – like when you go to get a job.**

DAWNNELLA: **Or when you give an important speech at school.**

Yes, you would want to speak formally when you go for a job interview or when you are giving a speech at school. When might you choose to speak informally?

GARRETT: **At a ball game or at home.**

TYREEK: **Yeah, when you with your homies!**

Sure, you could choose to use informal language with your friends.

Review the term *plural* as well as the formal and informal plural patterns.

We recently talked about plural patterns. What does the word *plural* mean? Garrett?

GARRETT: **Plural means more than one.**

Plural means more than one. What is the informal plural pattern?

ANDREW: **There are number words in the sentence or sometimes we just know.**

Andrew just told you that for the informal pattern, you need number words, signal words, or common knowledge to let you know that there is more than one. For example, in the sentence *I have two dog* (I write the sentence on chart paper), the number *two* shows there is more than one. How could we make the sentence *I have two dog* formal?

TEHJIA: **I have two dogs. Put an *-s* on *dog*.**

Exactly. For formal English, we are going to add an *-s* to the word that there is more than one of. There is more than one dog, so we are going to add an *-s* to *dog* to show it is plural.

Lesson 2

materials

- *Plural Patterns* code-switching chart
- *Classifying Plural Patterns* wall chart
- one sentence strip for each student
- markers, pencils

goals

STUDENTS WILL:

- recognize plural patterns inside formal and informal language.
- distinguish between formal and informal plural patterns.
- define plural patterns inside formal and informal language.
- write sentences using formal and informal plural patterns.
- classify sentences as formal or informal based on the plural patterns.

Direct Instruction

Show the class a wall chart titled *Plural Patterns,* with a column on the left labeled *Informal* and a column on the right labeled *Formal.* Set the purpose for the lesson.

Today I am really going to need your help because we are going to build a really big wall chart for plural patterns. We will be writing sentences that show the formal plural pattern and the informal plural pattern. Then we will put our sentences on the wall chart.

Show the class a couple of sample sentences. As a group, determine whether the sentences use the formal or informal plural pattern.

Let's start with a sentence I wrote. Can you help me decide if this sentence shows the formal or informal plural pattern?

> I finished twelve math problem last night.

Is this sentence formal or informal?

STUDENTS: **Informal.**

Tehjia?

TEHJIA: **It's informal.**

Why is it informal? What's the pattern?

TEHJIA: **There is no *-s* on the end.**

There isn't an *-s* on the end, but what does it have? (Tehjia does not answer.) How do you know there is more than one? *I finished twelve math problem last night.*

DESTINY: **It's a number word.**

What is the number word?

DESTINY: ***Twelve.***

The sentence says *twelve*, and *twelve* is a number word that shows more than one. So Tehjia was right; this sentence shows the informal pattern. Let's look at another sentence.

> It takes me twenty minutes to get to school.

STUDENTS: **Formal.**

Why?

DAJON: **Because *minutes* has an *-s* on the end of it.**

ways of talking

Help students talk about the pattern in positive terms, rather than describing the pattern as lacking or missing something.

what if...

a student thinks that a plural word is simply any word that ends in an *-s*, such as *takes*?

Simply ask students if the word is plural by asking if there is more than one. You might ask, "Is there more than one take?" Students should quickly realize that *takes* is not plural.

Our naming word is *minutes*, and there is an *-s* on the end of *minutes*. The *-s* is what tells you this is the formal plural pattern.

Add the sample sentences to the wall chart in the correct column.

So we have one informal sentence and one formal sentence. I'm going to tape each sentence on our wall chart under the correct column: Informal or Formal.

Guided Practice

Lead the students to create a sentence that shows either the formal or informal plural pattern.

Today you are going to write your own sentences using the plural pattern. We are going to be writing sentences as though we were speaking to our friends. Then I will need your help in making a big Plural Patterns chart for our wall. Which pattern, formal or informal, should we use when we talk to our friends?

DAR'ASIA: **You can use formal or informal, right?**

When you talk with your friends, you can choose to use formal or informal. It is completely up to you!

Now we're going to write a sentence together using the plural pattern. Pay close attention because you are going to write your own sentences in just a few minutes. First, we have to think of something we have more than one of. What do we have more than one of?

SAMUEL: **Math games.**

Okay, let's write a sentence about the number of math games we have. How many do we have?

QUATASIA: **Fourteen.**

Now we need to decide if we want to make our sentence formal or informal. What do you think? (Several students state their opinions.)

I heard a lot of you saying the formal plural pattern. So what will our sentence look like? Quatasia?

QUATASIA: **We have fourteen math games.**

Quatasia, would you please write our sentence on the sentence strip. (Quatasia writes "We have fourteen math games" on the sentence strip.)

We have fourteen math games.

what if...

your students say that you use informal language when speaking to your friends?

Remind students that in informal situations, it is up to them to decide whether to use formal or informal language. Say, "you get to decide for yourself whether you want to use formal or informal language when you talk with your friends."

Independent Practice

Have students work independently to create sentences that show the formal or informal plural pattern.

Now it's your turn to write a sentence using the plural pattern. Who remembers what we did first when we wrote our sentence?

> ONTIANA: **We decided something we had a lot of.**

Yes, we looked around the room and found something we had more than one of, something that was plural. Then what did we do?

> DAJON: **We made it formal.**

We had to decide if we wanted to write a formal or informal sentence. What was the last thing we did?

> I'ANA: **We wrote a formal sentence.**

You are going to pretend that you are talking to your friends, so your sentence can show either the formal plural pattern or the informal plural pattern. Make sure you think about what you want to write BEFORE you start writing. Samuel will hand out the sentence strips. (I walk around the room as the students write their sentences, offering assistance as needed.)

Sharing for Understanding

Have the students share their understanding by helping to create the large wall chart.

I am so impressed by all of the wonderful sentences I saw you writing. Let's get started on our wall chart by sharing our sentences. This is the part where you get to be the teacher. Dawnnella, would you like to go first?

I'll help Dawnnella model what you are going to do. You will read your sentence aloud and then ask the class if the sentence shows the formal or informal plural pattern. Dawnnella, would you model this for us?

> DAWNNELLA: **My sentence says *We made cupcakes for my birthday*. (She shows her sentence to the class.) Is it formal or informal?**

> STUDENTS: **Formal.**

Now Dawnnella will ask how you know it's formal.

> DAWNNELLA: **What is formal?**

> BOBBY: ***Cupcakes* ends with *-s*.**

> DAWNNELLA: **Yep.**

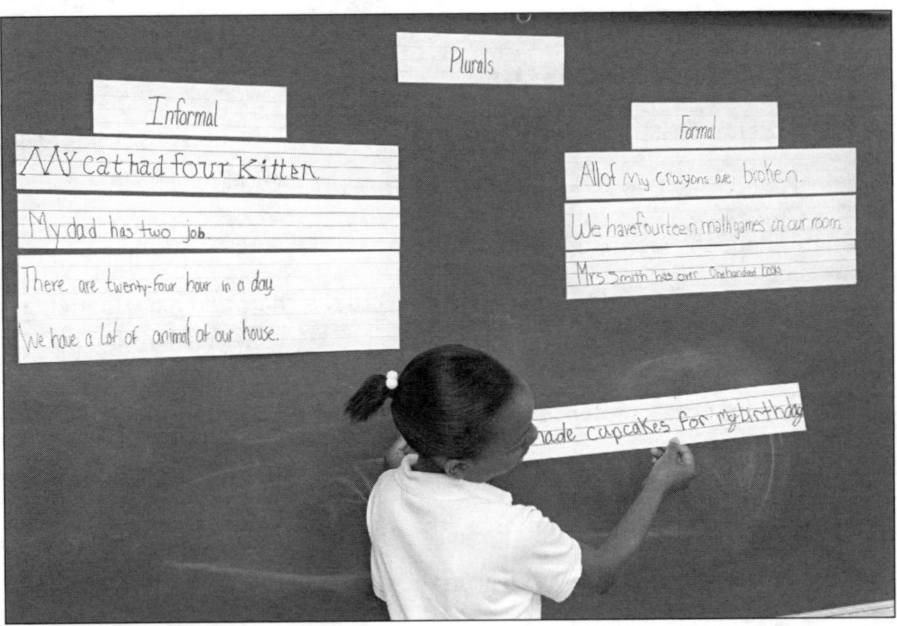

Yes, the *-s* on the end of *cupcakes* shows the sentence is formal. Dawnnella, would you please tape the sentence on the Formal side of the chart? (Dawnnella tapes the sentence on the Formal side of the chart.)

(All the students take turns adding their sentences to the wall chart.)

We'll leave this chart up for a little while, and you can use it, along with the chart showing the patterns, to help you when you are editing your writing.

Allow students to discuss the purpose of today's lesson.

Why do you think we created this big chart? What was the purpose?

BOBBY: **So we could see what formal and informal sentences look like.**

DORIS: **So we could say if the sentence was formal or informal.**

The purpose of today's lesson was to practice using the formal and informal plural patterns and to decide if sentences contain the formal or informal pattern. Thumbs-up if you think you know the difference between the formal and informal plural patterns, thumbs-down if you don't know the difference, and thumbs to the side if you're a little unsure.

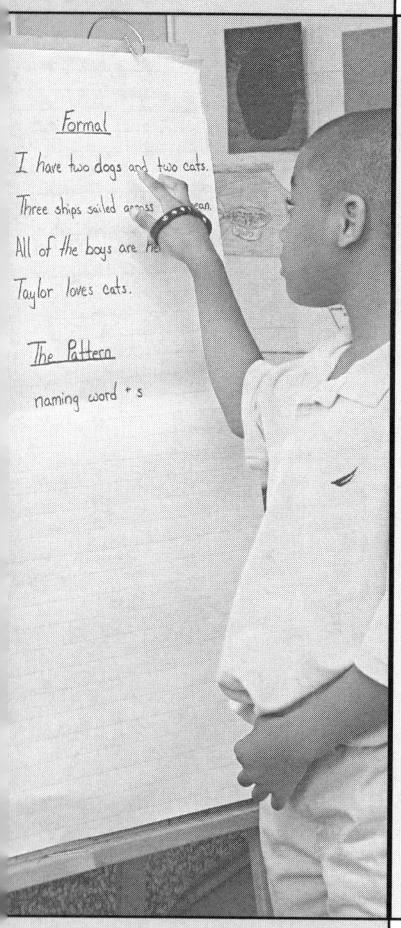

Formal
I have two dogs and two cats.
Three ships sailed
All of the boys are
Taylor loves cats.
The Pattern
naming word + s

Assessing the Lesson

As the students write their own sentences, I make sure they are using a plural pattern. Periodically, I find students who confuse the plural and possessive patterns. When this happens, I remind the students that we are working on showing plurality, or more than one. Then I direct their attention to the chart and have them read the rules for showing formal plurality. I help them edit their sentence by having them check to see that their sentence matches the formal pattern. I often jot down notes about students who seem to struggle as well as those who seem to understand the concept. I add additional notes as the students create the large wall chart. I specifically look for students who rely on their peers before determining if a pattern is formal or informal. I also take note of the students who, by showing a thumbs-down or thumbs to the side, indicate they are uncomfortable with distinguishing between the formal and informal plural patterns. I focus on these students during subsequent lessons.

Practicing the Formal Plural Pattern

Lesson 3

Engagement

▶ **Have students gather around the *Plural Patterns* code-switching chart. Review the formal and informal plural patterns. Have students provide example sentences of each.**

We have spent several weeks working on formal and informal language. For the past several days, we have worked on the plural pattern. Remember that the word *plural* means more than one. Let's review the formal and informal plural patterns. What is the informal plural pattern? Andrew?

ANDREW: **Umm, there is a number word or other words in the sentence that show more than one.**

Number words, other signal words in the paragraph or sentence, and common knowledge are used to show the plural pattern. Who would like to give us an example of a sentence that shows the informal plural pattern?

QUINTIN: ***I got three book from the library.***

Right, *three* shows there is more than one, and *book* is the noun. What is the formal plural pattern? Samuel?

SAMUEL: **The word that's more than one has an *-s* on the end.**

The naming word, or noun, has an *-s* on the end. Who has an example of a formal plural sentence?

DORIS: ***My mom has two jobs.***

The *-s* on the end of *jobs* tells us there is more than one.

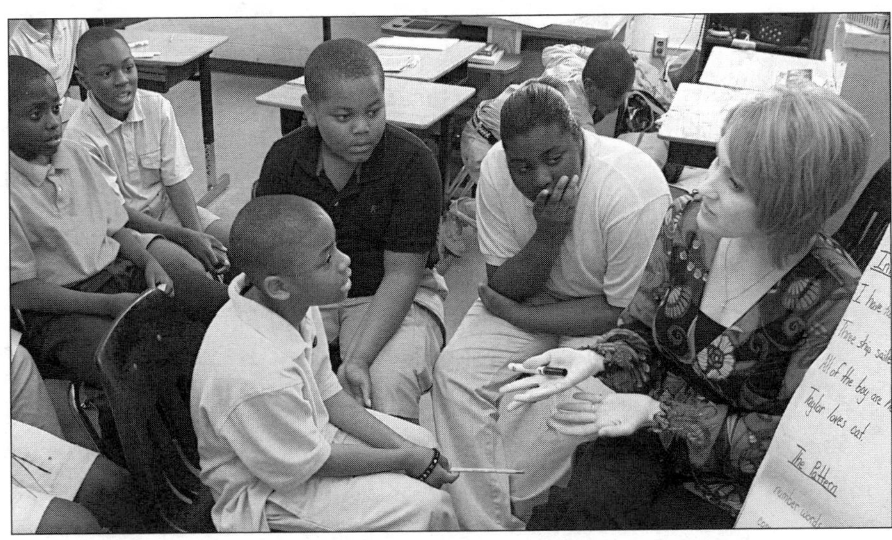
Taylor loves cat.
The Pattern

materials

- *Plural Patterns* code-switching chart
- chart paper with a sample sentence using the Informal pattern
- a copy of the reproducible for *Plural Pattern practice* for every student
- markers, pencils, highlighters

goals

STUDENTS WILL:

- recognize plural patterns inside informal and formal language.
- practice using the formal pattern on their own.
- rewrite sentences that contain the informal plural pattern to sentences that contain the formal plural pattern.

Direct Instruction

Set the purpose for the lesson. Remind students the reason for using the formal pattern.

Today we are going to be looking at several sentences and changing informal plural patterns to formal ones. Why would we want to make our writing formal?

> ONTIANA: **School is formal.**

School is a formal place, and when we complete a writing assignment, we usually need to use formal language.

Model the process of editing a sentence for the formal pattern.

Let's look at this sentence I found in a student's paper last year. (I reveal a sentence written on chart paper.)

We played outside for twenty minute.

What is the informal pattern used in this sentence?

> HEZEKIAH: **Twenty.**

There is a number word in this sentence that shows plurality, or something that is more than one. What do we need to do to make this sentence formal?

> STUDENTS: **Add an *-s*.**

To which word?

> STUDENTS: ***Minute.***

Okay, so I'm going to add an *-s* to the word *minute* to make it formal. (I add an *-s* to *minute* on the chart paper.) Now I am going to rewrite the sentence using the formal pattern. (I read the sentence aloud as I rewrite it.)

We played outside for twenty minutes.

Now my sentence is formal. I have a noun, or a naming word, plus an *-s*, and that is the formal plural pattern.

Guided Practice

Hand out a copy of the reproducible for *Plural Pattern practice* to each student. Lead students through the process of completing the first sentence.

Your job today is to do exactly what I just did. You will have several sentences to edit. You will read each sentence, find the informal plural pattern, and then

ways of talking

Reiterate the pattern as you talk about the sentences. This reminds students that language is described in terms of patterns.

note

An editable version of the *Plural Pattern practice* reproducible is available on the CD-ROM.

edit the sentence to make the plural pattern formal. Once you do that, you will rewrite the sentence using the formal pattern.

Let's read the first sentence and edit it together. (I have written the first sentence from the reproducible on the board; the students read it along with me.)

We have a lot of book in our class library.

How do we know there is more than one book?

SAMUEL: **We can look at the shelves.**

Okay, common knowledge is one way. We can look at the shelves in the class library. Are there any clues in the sentence that let us know there is more than one book?

QUINTIN: **It says *a lot*.**

We have a signal word. We know that *a lot* is more than one. What do we need to do to make the sentence formal?

TAJANTA: **Put an *-s* on the end of *book*.**

So on your paper, you will put an *-s* on the end of the plural word. (I add the *-s*.) Then you will rewrite the sentence using the formal pattern. (I write "We have a lot of books in our class library.")

We have a lot of books in our class library.
We have a lot of books in our class library.

Independent Practice

Give students time to practice editing the rest of the sentences on their own.

The first sentence on your sheet should look like this (I point to the sentence on the board). The second sentence says, *Christopher Newport brought three ship with him to Jamestown.* Your job is to find the informal pattern in each sentence and rewrite the sentence to make it formal. There is one very tricky sentence that has two informal plural patterns in the same sentence. I wonder whom I will trick this time. (I circulate around the room as the students work on the assignment, giving assistance as needed.)

Announce student successes as they happen.

Nije couldn't be fooled! He found the sentence with two informal patterns — *Do you wear glove or mitten when it's cold outside?* — and changed both of them to formal!

Sharing for Understanding

Ask students how they approached the task.

As you edited the sentences, how did you decide which word to make plural?

DAR'ASIA: **I looked for whatever there was more than one of.**

Could you give us an example of how you did that using one of the sentences?

DAR'ASIA: **Like in the first sentence, *Christopher Newport brought three ship with him to Jamestown,* I added an *-s* to *ship* because there were three.**

And three is more than one, so you knew that *ship* was plural?

DAR'ASIA: **Yes.**

Did anyone do it a different way?

GARRETT: **I looked for the nouns. Then I picked which one was plural. Like in *Most of the girl went to the library, girl* and *library* are the nouns. Since it says *most*, I know that *girl* needs an *-s* to be formal. It doesn't make sense for there to be more than one library.**

So you looked for the naming words, or nouns, first. Then you decided which word was plural. Very nice. Why do you think we took the time today to edit sentences?

ANDREW: **Probably so we can edit our writing sometime.**

QUATASIA: **Yeah, like when we write, we can use formal plurals.**

Exactly. It's important to practice editing for the formal plural pattern because that is something we will be doing with our own writing.

Assessing the Lesson

I collect the editing practice sheets completed by the students and use them to determine which students were able to successfully complete the assignment. I use our discussion during the sharing portion of the lesson, in addition to the practice sheets the students complete, to determine how successful individual students are in using the formal plural pattern. I work with students who had difficulty in a small-group setting. During my time with the small group, I go over the assignment by having the students talk through each sentence in much the same way I did during the guided practice portion of the lesson.

Plural Pattern practice sentences

DIRECTIONS: Rewrite each sentence using the formal plural pattern.

1. We have a lot of book in our class library.

2. Christopher Newport brought three ship with him to Jamestown.

3. Most of the girl went to the library.

4. I helped my mom bake cookie.

5. We had twenty-four math problem for homework.

6. Do you wear glove or mitten when it is cold outside?

7. Brianna sharpened all of the pencil.

8. I saw many animal at the zoo.

Lesson 4

materials

- *Plural Patterns* code-switching chart
- chart paper with a sample paragraph to practice editing
- student writing portfolios with entries or previous writing assignments
- highlighters, pencils

goals

STUDENTS WILL:

- recognize plural patterns inside formal and informal language.
- define plural patterns inside formal and informal language.
- use formal plural patterns in editing their own writing.

Editing Writing for the Formal Plural Pattern

Engagement

▶ **Have the students gather around the *Plural Patterns* chart. Review the formal and informal plural patterns.**

We have now spent several days working on plural patterns. Let's review the formal and informal plural patterns. Who would like to tell us about the informal plural pattern?

TYREEK: **There is a number word and other words to say more than one.**

That's right, number words, other signal words, and common knowledge tell us if something is plural. What is the formal plural pattern?

DAR'ASIA: **There is an *-s* on the end of the word that is more than one. Like *I like books. Books* has an *-s* on the end because I like more than one book.**

Exactly, the *-s* on the end of the noun, or naming word, shows there is more than one.

Direct Instruction

▶ **Introduce the topic for today's lesson.**

Today you are going to be editing your own writing. You're going to be editing the writing you've been working on for the past week. Remember that once you publish this piece, you will have it on display in the classroom. Which pattern do you think you should use in your writing?

STUDENTS: **Formal!**

Why do we want to use the formal pattern? Quintin?

QUINTIN: **Because it is a formal writing that other people might see.**

Thumbs-up if you agree with Quintin; thumbs to the side if you disagree.

Model locating plural patterns in a piece of writing and editing for the formal plural pattern.

I have a paragraph written by a student a few years ago. The paragraph has both formal and informal plural patterns in it. However, since school writing usually needs to be formal, *all* of the plural patterns need to be formal, so I will need your help in making the entire paragraph formal by changing the informal plural patterns to formal. Let's start by reading the paragraph together. (I run my finger under the words as we read the paragraph together.) Let's look at each sentence, one at a time, and make sure the formal pattern was used. Every time we find a formal plural pattern, we are going to highlight it. If we find an informal plural pattern, we are going to make the pattern formal and then highlight it.

Jamestown

Last week all of the third-grade student took a trip to Jamestown. The student were divided into groups of two boys and two girl. All of the groups were given lists of thing to look for in Jamestown. There were twelve items on each list. My group only found some of the thing on the list. We saw two canoe and six longhouse that looked like the kind the Powhatan Indians used long ago. We were excited because both the canoes and the longhouses were on our list. However, we didn't see all three crop that the Powhatan Indians planted. Next time when we have a task on a field trip, I hope my group is able to finish.

Let's look at the first sentence. *Last week all of the third-grade student took a trip to Jamestown.* I see the word *all*, and I know that is a signal word, so there must be more than one student. Now I need to make the sentence formal by changing *student* to *students*. I'm going to add an *-s* to the end of it and highlight the word *students*. We'll do the rest of the paragraph together.

note

A customizable version of the paragraph "Jamestown" is available on the CD-ROM.

note

Our sample paragraph illustrates *only* vernacular examples of the grammar pattern we're exploring — here, plural patterns.

ways of talking

Note the positive language: we're not "correcting" *student;* we're "changing" it to formal English.

Guided Practice

Engage the students' help in locating and editing the remaining plural patterns.

Let's look at the next sentence. *The student were divided into groups of two boys and two girl.* Are there any plural patterns in this sentence?

JALANAY: **Two boys and two girl.**

That is actually two patterns. Let's look at the first one, *two boys.* Is that formal or informal?

STUDENTS: **Formal.**

JALANAY: **There is an *-s* on the end.**

Right, since *boys* ends with an *-s*, it is formal. Jalanay, would you highlight the formal pattern for us? (Jalanay highlights the word *boys.*)

What about *two girl*? Is that formal or informal?

STUDENTS: **Informal.**

How do you know?

DAWNNELLA: **It says *two* and that's it.**

The number word tells us that it is plural. What should we do to make it formal?

STUDENTS: **Add an *-s*!**

Andrew, would you please put the *-s* on the end of *girl.* (Andrew adds the *-s.*) Now you can highlight it because we made it formal. (Andrew highlights *girls.*) Let's read the sentence again and see if we found all of the patterns. *The student were divided into groups of two boys and two girls.* Did we find all of the patterns?

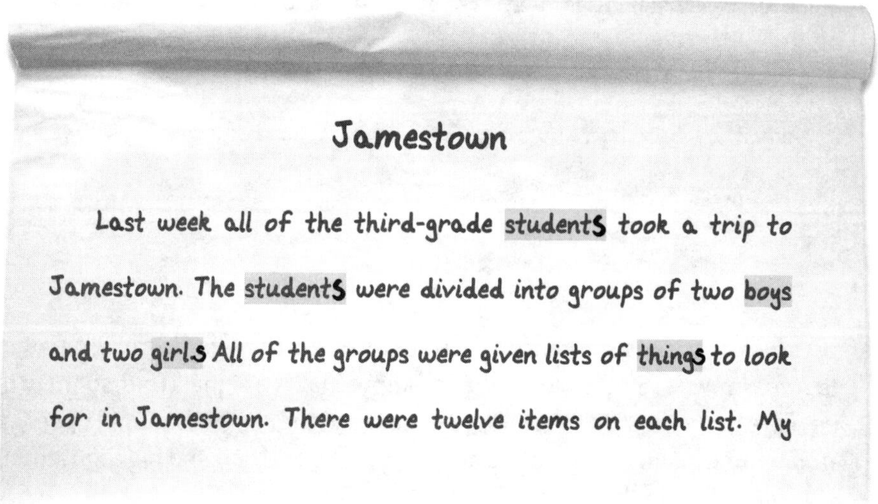

Jamestown

Last week all of the third-grade studentS took a trip to Jamestown. The studentS were divided into groups of two boys and two girlS All of the groups were given lists of thingS to look for in Jamestown. There were twelve items on each list. My

(I continue reading through the paragraph until all of the plural patterns are found. Students will highlight formal patterns and locate informal patterns, change them to formal, and then highlight them. Once students have located all of the patterns, I reread the entire paragraph.)

Good job, everyone. I'm going to hang this paragraph in the classroom as an example of editing for formal plural patterns.

Independent Practice

▶ **Have the students work independently to edit their own writing for the formal possessive pattern.**

Now that we have edited a paragraph together, you are going to edit some of your own writing. You are going to read through your writing and do exactly what we just did with the Jamestown paragraph. Take your time. As you read through your work, look for examples of the plural pattern. If you find a formal plural pattern, highlight it. If you find an informal pattern, change it to formal and then highlight it. (I give students five to ten minutes to edit their own writing. I walk around the room as they complete the assignment and assist students who are having trouble with the assignment.)

Sharing for Understanding

▶ **Have the students gather in a circle to share examples of plural patterns they found in their own work. Make sure they bring their writing with them.**

Now it's your turn to share some examples of the plural patterns that you found in your own writing. We're going to go around the circle, and each of you will share one sentence that contains a plural pattern. You'll need to pick one of your highlighted patterns. That means that all of the examples we share in the circle will be . . .

STUDENTS: **Formal.**

QUATASIA: **That's just like when we did possessives!**

It's exactly the same. Let's get started. If you would rather not share, just say "Pass," and we'll go on to the next person. Nije, would you like to get us started?

NIJE: **On Saturday my cousins spent the night at my house.**

Which word is plural?

NIJE: ***Cousins.* I put an *-s* on the end.**

Nice job. Quintin? (I continue around the circle in this fashion until everyone has a turn or until we run out of time.)

what if...

it is taking too much time to complete the Guided Practice portion of the lesson?

Due to the length of the Jamestown paragraph, it may be necessary to complete only part of the paragraph during this lesson. You can then finish the paragraph during a subsequent lesson.

note

As the students share their sentences, periodically ask students how their sentence fits the plural pattern.

Conclude the lesson by having students use thumbs-up, thumbs-down, or thumbs to the side to do a quick assessment of which students had difficulties with the assignment.

Let's do a quick thumbs-up, thumbs-down, or thumbs to the side to show how you felt about this assignment. Thumbs-up if you thought it was easy, thumbs-down if you thought it was difficult, and thumbs to the side if it was a little difficult.

I see a lot of thumbs up and a few thumbs to the side and thumbs down. Would anyone like to share why you felt the assignment was difficult? Bobby?

BOBBY: **It was hard to find the patterns.**

Did anyone else feel that finding the patterns was difficult? (Several students raise their hands.) Anyone have any other difficulties? (I allow a few students to share.) Try not to worry if you had a difficult time today. As you have more opportunities to practice, you will find that editing for formal language will become easier to do.

Assessing the Lesson

In addition to using the students' self-assessments (thumbs-up, thumbs-down, or thumbs to the side), I also assess as I walk around the room during the independent practice portion of the lesson. During this time, I note which students are struggling with the assignment. I work with these students individually or in small groups during writing time. To help these students, I have them edit their work with me. I have them orally read each sentence and look for plural patterns in the same way we did during the guided practice portion of the lesson.

Reviewing Possessive and Plural Patterns

Lessons

THIS UNIT INCLUDES THE FOLLOWING LESSONS:

1. Comparing and Contrasting Possessive and Plural Patterns
2. Practicing Possessive and Plural Patterns
3. Editing for Formal Possessive and Plural Patterns

Now that we've completed our lesson units on showing possessive patterns and plural patterns, it's time for review. Standard English possessive and plural patterns are so similar that students often confuse them for a time. Indeed, we used to find apostrophes sprinkled generously over students' papers in places where they don't belong – even on verbs (*She walk's to the store*). So now is the time to firm up our students' understanding of Standard English possessives and plurals.

Over the next three lessons, we'll focus on formal English singular nouns: singular possessives, singular plurals, and the difference between the two.

Reviewing Possessive and Plural Patterns

The Pattern

To highlight and distinguish the patterns of singular possession and plurality for students, we'll use a Venn diagram. This will help students firm up their knowledge. They'll be able to see the similarities between possession and plural. (Here's where the confusion lies: **noun + *s*** vs. **noun + *'s* + noun.**) Students will also see the differences between possessive and plural forms.

For our review, we have our possessive and plural wall charts nearby for easy reference. Here are the key components of the possessive chart and the plural chart:

SHOWING POSSESSION

INFORMAL	**FORMAL**
We went to my aunt house.	We went to my aunt's house.
A giraffe neck is very long.	A giraffe's neck is very long.
My dog name is Princess.	My dog's name is Princess.
I made people beds.	I made people's beds.
Be good for Annie mom.	Be good for Annie's mom.
THE PATTERN	**THE PATTERN**
owner + what is owned	**owner + *'s* + what is owned**

PLURAL PATTERNS

INFORMAL	**FORMAL**
I have two dog and two cat.	I have two dogs and two cats.
Three ship sailed across the ocean.	Three ships sailed across the ocean.
All of the boy are here today.	All of the boys are here today.
Taylor loves cat.	Taylor loves cats.
THE PATTERN	**THE PATTERN**
number words **other signal words** **common knowledge**	**noun + *s***

Creating the Venn Diagram

This is the only time that we'll use a Venn diagram. In doing so, we draw circles that give us plenty of space so that we have room to write out a range of contrasts. Of course we ensure that there's some room in the intersection area to write the few commonalities between formal possessive and formal plural.

We like to make the circles different colors, just to catch the students' attention. Finally, we write the label *Formal Possessive* under the left-hand circle and the label *Formal Plural* under the right-hand circle.

We make sure that the items in our list for formal possessives match up with our items in our list on formal plurals. For example, the meaning of possessive ("shows ownership") matches up with the first item in our formal plural list, the meaning of plural ("shows more than one"); the second line for possessives, "two nouns side by side" matches up horizontally with the second line for plurals, "takes only one noun."

Here's the finished Venn diagram listing the similarities and differences between possession and plurality.

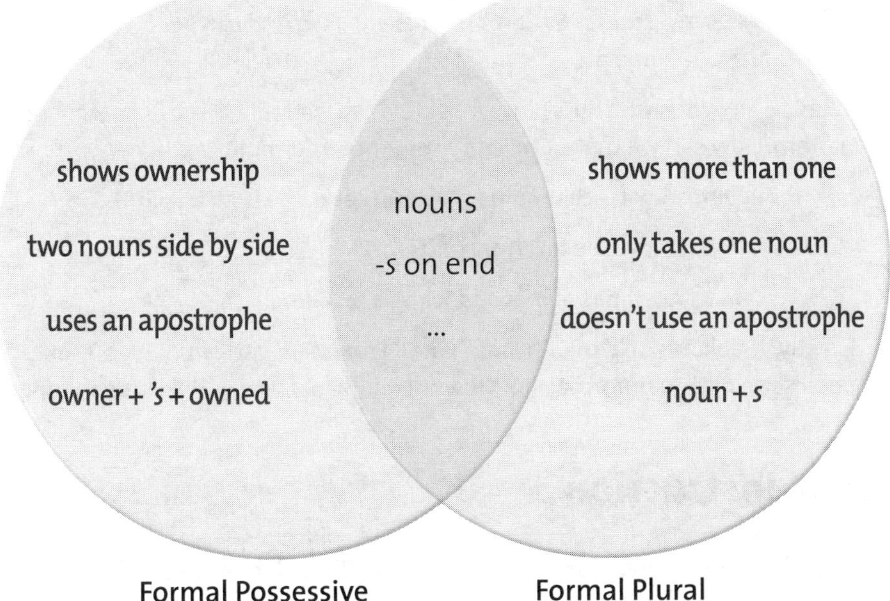

Lesson 1

Comparing and Contrasting Possessive and Plural Patterns

Engagement

Gather the students around an easel with a drawing of two circles forming a Venn diagram. Keep the drawing covered for now. Review the possessive and plural patterns.

We have spent several weeks talking about formal and informal language. So far, we have talked about two different kinds of patterns. First, we discussed the formal and informal possessive patterns; then we described the formal and informal plural patterns. Let's review the possessive patterns. Who has an example of a sentence that shows the formal possessive pattern?

CHA'ZON: **My teacher's name is Mrs. Swords.**

How does Cha'zon's sentence fit the formal possessive pattern? Destiny?

DESTINY: ***Teacher* has an *'s* on the end of it. And *teacher* owns the name.**

We have an **owner plus an 's plus what is owned**, and that is the formal possessive pattern. How can we make Cha'zon's sentence informal?

BOBBY: **Say teacher name. "My teacher name is Mrs. Swords."**

How does that follow the informal pattern?

QUATASIA: **It has owner and what is owned.**

Exactly. It follows the **owner plus what is owned** pattern, which makes the possessive pattern informal. (I review the plural pattern in the same manner.)

materials

- initial *Venn Diagram for Plurals and Possessives* on chart paper
- one sheet of paper for each small group (or use preprinted Venn diagram from the CD-ROM)
- markers, pencils, highlighters

goals

STUDENTS WILL:

- review the formal possessive and plural patterns.
- compare and contrast the use and purpose of the formal possessive and plural patterns.

Direct Instruction

Introduce the topic for today's lesson. Reveal the Venn diagram and explain how it works.

Today we are going to compare and contrast language using a Venn diagram like the one I have here. (I reveal a Venn diagram drawn on chart paper.) A Venn diagram is a chart that helps us keep our ideas organized.

The first thing we need to do is label the two circles in our diagram. Today we are going to work together to compare and contrast the formal plural and formal possessive patterns because sometimes students confuse these. So I am going to label one circle *Formal Possessive* and the other circle *Formal Plural*.

We're going to do part of the Venn diagram together; then you will work in groups to finish it on your own. In a Venn diagram, we put all of the things that the two sides have in common in the middle, where the two circles overlap, so we

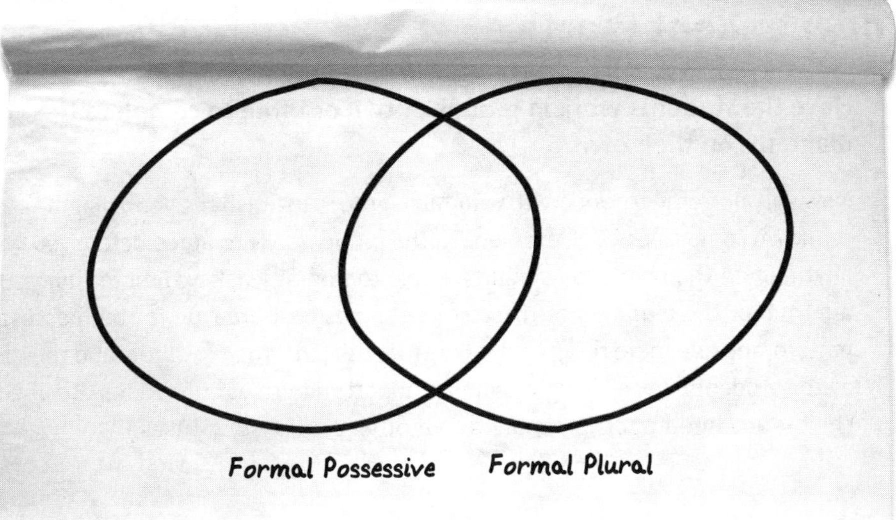

Initial *Venn Diagram for Plurals and Possessives*

will write all the ways that the formal plural pattern and the formal possessive pattern are *alike* here in the middle. Things that are true *only* for the formal plural pattern will go under that plural heading where the plural circle does not overlap with the possessive circle. Things that are true *only* for the formal possessive pattern will go under that heading where the circles do not overlap.

Guided Practice

Ask the students to help complete the Venn diagram on formal plural and possessive patterns.

Let's start by looking at how formal plural patterns and formal possessive patterns are alike. What is something that formal plural and formal possessive patterns have in common? How are they alike?

TYREEK: **They both have an *-s* on the end of the word.**

Yes, they both end in *-s*. (I add this to the chart.) When you work with your group, you are going to be looking for other ways the formal plural and formal possessive patterns are alike, and you will write these right here (I point to the center of the Venn diagram) where the two circles overlap. Now let's look for ways that they are different. What is something that is true for formal plurals but not for formal possessives?

DESTINY: **It doesn't have an apostrophe.**

Oh, that's a good one. I'm going to write "no apostrophe" in the circle labeled *Formal Plural*. Now let's look at the possessive side and add things that are only true about the formal possessive pattern. I'ana?

I'ANA: **The possessive pattern does use an *'s*.**

Good. The possessive pattern uses an apostrophe. Let's add that to the chart under the Formal Possessive heading.

note

If your students are having trouble drawing the circles for a Venn Diagram, there is a printable blank Venn Diagram available on the CD-ROM.

what if...

the majority of your students are having difficulty with this assignment?

Bring the class back together and complete the Venn Diagram as a group. This allows you to clear up any misconceptions as they occur while you steer the conversation in the right direction.

Independent Practice

Have the students work in groups of two or three to complete the Venn diagrams on their own.

Now you are going to work with your table groups to finish the Venn diagram. Let's set down some rules. First, everyone in the group needs to agree before you write anything on the chart. You should be able to find at least two more things that are true for the plural pattern, two more things that are true for the possessive pattern, and one more thing that is true for both patterns. (I walk around the room as the students work. This gives me an opportunity to ask questions about their choices and initiate conversations about other possible responses.)

Sharing for Understanding

Have the students gather in a circle on a carpet or a central location to help complete the class Venn diagram you began during the Guided Practice portion of the lesson. Make sure they bring their Venn diagrams with them.

Now that you have had a chance to work with your group on completing your own Venn diagrams, you are going to get to share your work. As we talk about the ways formal possessives and formal plurals are alike and different, I will add them to our class Venn diagram that we started earlier. What did you write in the circle that shows how formal possessives and formal plurals are alike?

HEZEKIAH: **They're both nouns.**

Nice job. They are nouns. (I write "nouns" on the diagram.) Anything else they have in common? (I record all appropriate responses, which often include

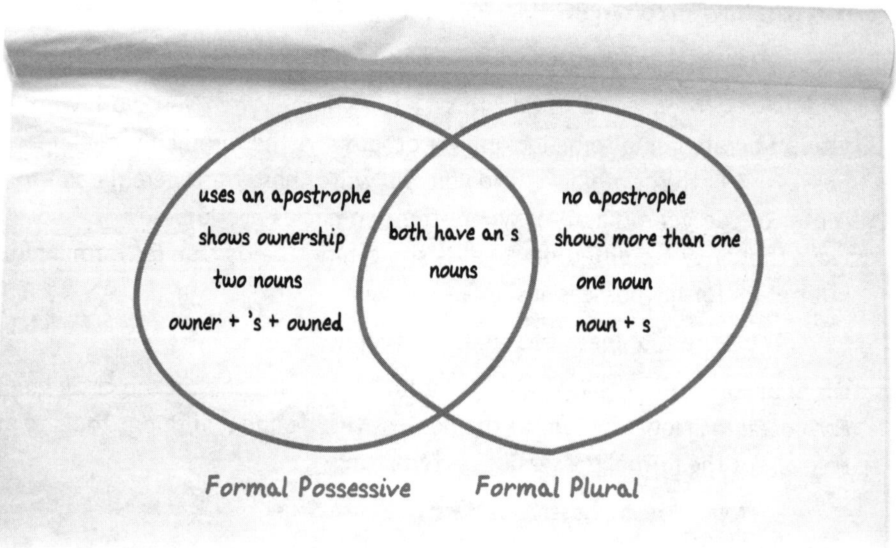

Final *Venn Diagram for Plurals and Possessives*

"They're both nouns," "We use them in school writing," and "We edit for them." I then ask students what they wrote under the *Formal Possessive* and *Formal Plural* headings. I also record these responses. Typically, students respond that the possessive pattern shows ownership and the plural shows more than one, the possessive pattern uses two nouns and the plural pattern only takes one, and that the possessive pattern is **owner + *'s* + what is owned** and the plural pattern is **noun + *s*.**)

Great job listing things about the formal possessive and plural patterns. I'm going to hang this chart on the wall. If you are editing and you are unsure whether something is possessive or plural, you can refer to the chart.

Assessing the Lesson

As I visit the various groups during the independent practice portion of the lesson, I want to distinguish between students who are having difficulty with using the Venn diagram and those who are struggling with the plural and possessive patterns. I have found that students who have trouble completing the Venn diagram often think too broadly. Typically, these students simply write the formal patterns under each heading and do not know what to do next. Of course, there is a wealth of information in the patterns themselves, but the struggling student is not adept to being that specific. I often ask struggling students questions such as "What do you know about the formal possessive pattern?" As the student begins to recite the pattern, "noun plus . . . ," I stop him/her. I might say something like "Wait! You said the formal possessive pattern has a noun. Does the formal plural pattern have anything to do with nouns?" Generally, the student is able to affirm that the plural pattern includes nouns. At this point, I am able to aid the student in adding the information in the appropriate place on the Venn diagram. Once students realize how to be more specific, they are able to complete the assignment in their groups with relatively few problems.

Lesson 2

materials

- completed *Venn Diagram for Plurals and Possessives*
- chart paper with a sample sentence using the Informal pattern
- markers, pencils, highlighters
- a copy of the reproducible for *Plural and Possessive Patterns practice* for every student

goals

STUDENTS WILL:

- practice using the formal possessive and plural patterns on their own.
- identify patterns as possessive or plural.
- edit sentences that contain the informal possessive or plural patterns to sentences that contain the formal possessive or plural patterns.

Practicing Possessive and Plural Patterns

Engagement

▶ **Gather the students around the Venn diagram completed in Lesson 1. Review the formal possessive and plural patterns.**

Let's look at the Venn diagram we created to compare and contrast the formal possessive and formal plural patterns. How are the two patterns different?

> BOBBY: **One has a -s and one has a *'s*.**

Which one has an -s and which one has an *'s*?

> BOBBY: **The plural has a -s and possessive has a *'s*.**

The plural pattern uses an -s and the possessive pattern uses an *'s*. How else are they different?

> DESTINY: **Plural means more than one.**

> I'ANA: **And the possessive pattern shows how someone owns something.**

Excellent! The plural pattern shows more than one, whereas the possessive pattern shows ownership.

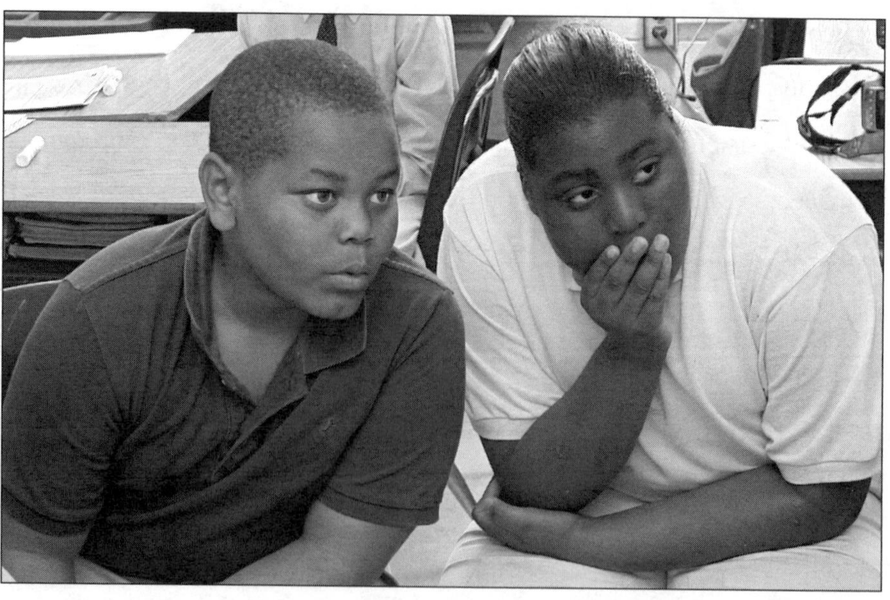

Direct Instruction

Explain the purpose of today's lesson. Remind students that when editing they need to determine whether a sentence contains a possessive pattern or a plural pattern.

Today we are going to change informal sentences to formal sentences. Why are we changing all of the sentences to formal English?

> STUDENTS: **School is formal!**

Right! However, before we can change any of the sentences, we will have to decide if the informal pattern in the sentence is a possessive pattern or a plural pattern.

Show students a sample sentence. Model the editing process by doing a think aloud.

Let's look at this sentence I wrote on the chart paper:

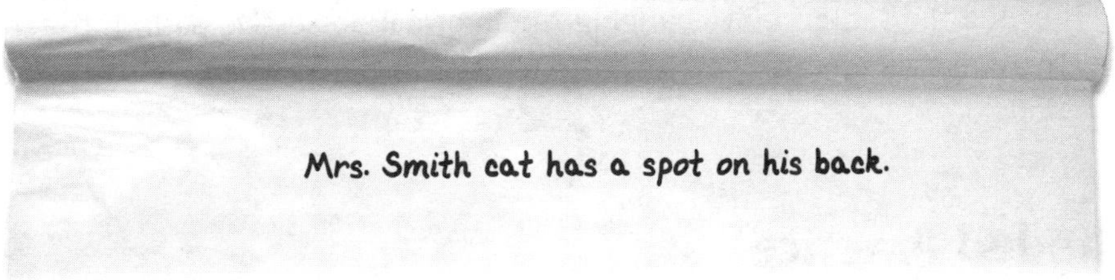
Mrs. Smith cat has a spot on his back.

I am going to do this sentence on my own. I want you to listen to my thinking as I go through this sentence. Then when I'm finished, I'm going to ask you what you noticed about how I thought about this sentence, so pay close attention.

Mrs. Smith cat has a spot on his back. First, I have to decide if there is an informal pattern in this sentence and whether that pattern shows plurality or possession. When I read the words *Mrs. Smith cat,* I know that the cat belongs to Mrs. Smith. If something belongs to someone, that shows ownership. That means that the informal pattern in this sentence is possessive — remember that the informal possessive pattern is **owner + thing owned**. I'm going to write "possessive" on the line in front of the sentence. (I write "possessive" on the chart paper.) Now I need to change the sentence to make it formal. I am going to look at the possessive chart to make sure I'm using the right pattern. I see that the formal possessive pattern is **owner + *'s* + what is owned**. Okay, if Mrs. Smith is the owner, then I need to add an *'s*. *Cat* is what she owns, so let me highlight *Mrs. Smith's cat* to show that I now have a formal pattern.

possessive
Mrs. Smith's cat has a spot on his back.

Okay, so let's review the steps. What did I do first?

ONTIANA: You read the sentence.

Okay, first I read the sentence. What did I do next?

ANDREW: Umm, you looked to find a pattern that was more than one or possessive. And you wrote "possessive" on the line.

I looked for the informal pattern, and once I decided it was a possessive pattern, I wrote "possessive" on the line. Then what did I do?

TYREEK: You changed it to formal and highlighted it.

I edited the sentence by changing the informal possessive pattern to formal. Then I highlighted the formal pattern just like we do when we edit our own work.

Guided Practice

Hand out a copy of the reproducible for *Plural and Possessive Patterns practice* to each student. Lead students through the process of completing the first sentence.

note

An editable version of the *Plural and Possessive Patterns practice* reproducible is available on the CD-ROM.

Now you are going to edit some sentences. I'm handing out a sheet with some student writing samples that use the informal pattern for possessive and plural. I have written the first sentence here on the chart; we'll do this one together.

Most of the girl knew the answer to that question.

Do we have an informal plural or possessive pattern in this sentence?

STUDENTS: Plural!

What is plural in this sentence? Garrett?

GARRETT: *Most of the girl.*

So what do we have more than one of?

GARRETT: *Girls* because it says "most of."

We know it is plural because *most of* tells us that there is more than one. So, Garrett, would you come up and write the word *plural* on the line in front of the sentence? Now, what do we need to do to make it formal?

STUDENTS: Add an -*s*.

Tehjia, would you please edit this sentence for us. (Tehjia adds an -*s* to the end of *girl*.) Did she choose the correct word to add an -*s* to?

STUDENTS: Yes!

Okay, Tehjia, go ahead and highlight the formal plural pattern. (Tehjia highlights the word *girls*.)

plural   Most of the girls knew the answer to that question.

Independent Practice

Have the students work on their own or with a partner to practice plurals and possessives.

For the rest of the sentences, you will be doing exactly the same thing that we did together. Read each sentence carefully, decide if the informal pattern is plural or possessive, and write plural or possessive next to the sentence. Then you need to make the sentence formal and highlight the edited pattern. The second sentence reads *Juwan sweater is blue*. Let's do a thumbs-up if you think this sentence has an informal plural pattern and thumbs to the side if you think the informal pattern is possessive. (I use this quick assessment to determine which students need help.)

Sharing for Understanding

Have the students gather in a circle on a carpet or a central location to share how they completed the assignment.

I want you to think about how you determine if a sentence contains a plural or possessive pattern in it. As you completed the assignment, how did you decide if the informal pattern was plural or possessive?

DAWNNELLA: I read all the sentences and did the ones that were plural first because they were easier.

How were they easier?

DAWNNELLA: Because it was easy to tell there was more than one of something and then I just put the -*s* on.

Thumbs-up if, like Dawnnella, you looked for plural patterns first. Dajon, why did you look for plural patterns first?

DAJON: Most of the sentences with plural patterns had number words, and they was easy to find.

ways of talking

When students use vernacular grammar while answering a question, we do not correct them. Correction isn't effective in teaching Standard English. Instead, we silently make note of any grammar issues for later code-switching lessons.

So the number words showed which sentences contained a plural. You used one of our informal plural patterns to edit the sentences – very smart thinking! Who did something different? (I allow several students to explain their approach to editing the sentences. I also continue to have the rest of the class use thumbs-up to show if they used a similar method.)

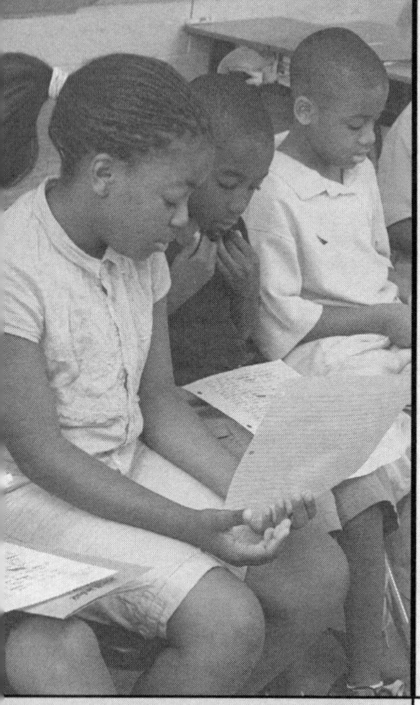

Assessing the Lesson

I use the practice sentences to determine which students are having problems distinguishing between plural and possessive patterns. I also use the discussion during the sharing time to informally assess students' ability to explain what they did and why they did it.

The most common mistake students make during the individual practice time is to confuse the formal possessive and plural patterns. When I address this issue, I refer to our charts. I have them look at the pattern and decide if the word requires an *-s* or an *'s*. I often have them explain the pattern to me, as this aids the students in making sense of the patterns for themselves.

Plural and Possessive Patterns practice sentences

DIRECTIONS: Write whether the sentence uses the informal plural or informal possessive pattern. Rewrite each sentence using the formal plural or possessive pattern.

1. Most of the girl knew the answer to that question.

2. Juwan sweater is blue.

3. How many pairs of shoe do you have?

4. What time is Kayla appointment?

5. Mrs. Smith cats are named Trinity and Tristin.

6. There are sixty minute in an hour.

7. Some of the boy are playing basketball.

8. The baby name is Braedon.

Lesson 3

materials

- sample paragraph "The Wall" on chart paper
- markers, pencils, highlighters
- one copy of the writing sample "Kasey and Jake" for each student

goals

STUDENTS WILL:

- identify patterns as possessive or plural.
- practice using the formal possessive and plural patterns on their own.
- edit a paragraph that contains informal possessive and plural patterns, changing these patterns to formal language.

Editing for Formal Possessive and Plural Patterns

Engagement

Review the previous lesson. Practice identifying plural and possessive sentences.

Let's take a moment to review what we did yesterday with the plural and possessive patterns. We looked at several sentences, determined if the informal pattern in each sentence was plural or possessive, and then edited the sentences to make them formal. Let's try that with a couple of sentences.

There are many parent in the school today.

Does this sentence contain an informal plural pattern or an informal possessive pattern?

SEVERAL STUDENTS: **Plural!**

How do you know?

DESTINY: **It has *many parent*, and *many* is more than one. Right?**

You're exactly right. Destiny, please write "plural" on the line in front of the sentence. Now what do we need to do to make the sentence formal? Bobby, would you please edit this sentence for us? (Bobby adds an *-s* to *parent.*) Thumbs-up if you agree with Bobby, and thumbs to the side if you disagree. Good, we're going to put an *-s* on the end of *parent* because there is more than one parent. Bobby, you can go ahead and highlight our plural pattern now that it is formal.

plural There are many parents in the school today.

Let's look at the next sentence.

My mom name is Shari.

Does this sentence contain an informal plural or possessive pattern?

SEVERAL STUDENTS: **Possessive.**

How do you know?

QUINTIN: **Mom owns her name.**

How does that follow our informal pattern?

STUDENTS: **Owner plus what is owned.**

I'ana, would you please edit our sentence and make it formal? (I'ana adds an *'s* to *Mom.*) Thumbs-up if you agree, and thumbs to the side if you disagree. You're right, I'ana. You can highlight *Mom's name* because now it follows the formal pattern of **owner + 's + what is owned**.

Direct Instruction

Introduce the topic for today's lesson.

Today you are going to help me edit a paragraph I wrote. We are going to pretend that this paragraph was written as part of a school assignment, so we are going to edit this paragraph to make sure it is written using formal language. Why would that be important?

DAR'ASIA: **You have to have professional language in school so you can practice it and get a job one day. Also school is formal.**

School is a formal place, so we need to use formal, or professional, language. Let's read the paragraph together. (I read out loud the following chart.)

The Wall

One of the wall in our classroom looks like a farm. There is a big red barn, and there are many animal on the wall. The cow bell really rings, the sheep fur is made of cotton ball, and the haystack is made out of real piece of hay. There is even a mouse tail peeking out of the hay! There are little flower all over the grass. There is also an apple tree with lots of red apple. I like to look at all of the colorful thing on our wall.

Now we need to make sure formal language is being used in every sentence. Let's look at that first sentence: *One of the wall in our classroom looks like a farm.* Well, I don't see an owner in this sentence, but I know we have more than one wall in here. It looks like we have an informal plural. I'm going to make it formal by adding an *-s* to *wall.* Let me reread the sentence to make sure it's formal: *One of the walls in our classroom looks like a farm.* Yep, it's formal. Let me highlight the word *walls* since that's the plural word I edited. Now I'm going to have you help me finish editing this paragraph. It's important that we look at each sentence in order as we edit. We want to make sure we find all of the informal patterns.

note

We make sure our paragraph includes only those vernacular patterns we have covered in class – at this point, possessive and plural.

note

A customizable version of "The Wall" is available on the CD-ROM.

note

In some of the phrases in this paragraph – *cow bell, sheep fur,* and *mouse tail* – the first noun (*cow, sheep, mouse*) might be considered a simple modifier of the second noun (*bell, fur, tail*). However, in this lesson, we treat these examples as possessives: *cow's bell, sheep's fur, mouse's tail.*

Guided Practice

Help students select the informal patterns.

Are there any other informal patterns in this paragraph?

QUINTIN: **You need an *-s* on *animal*.**

You're right! *Animal* follows the informal plural pattern. How do we know the sentence refers to more than one?

How do you know? Quatasia?

QUATASIA: **The word *many*.**

The word *many* is a number word that tells you there is more than one animal. And what do we do to make this formal?

HEZEKIAH: **You add *-s* to the end of *animal*.**

Good! Hezekiah, please add an -s to the end of *animal*, and read the sentence for us.

HEZEKIAH: **"There is a big red barn, and there are many animals on the wall." Can I highlight it, too?**

Yes, now that we have made the pattern formal, go ahead and highlight it. (Hezekiah highlights the word *animals*.) Who sees another informal pattern?

(I continue reading through the paragraph until all of the plural and possessive patterns are found. Students highlight formal patterns and locate informal patterns, change them to formal, and then highlight them. Once students have located all of the patterns, I reread the entire paragraph.)

Independent Practice

Have the students practice editing informal plural and possessive patterns on their own.

Now that we have edited a paragraph together, I can see that you are ready to edit a paragraph on your own. You are going to practice editing informal plural and possessive patterns using a paragraph about my two dogs. Their names are Kasey and Jake. You will do exactly the same thing we did together. You will look for informal possessive and plural patterns, change the patterns to formal, and then highlight the pattern. (I help individuals who seem to be struggling during this time.)

Mrs. Swords has two dog named Kasey and Jake. Jake fur is red, and Kasey fur is black and brown. They have many toy. Kasey favorite toy is a pink pig. The pig fur is very soft. Jake likes to play with a stuffed rabbit. The rabbit fur is green and white. Mrs. Swords loves to buy toy for her dog.

note

A customizable version of the paragraph "Kasey and Jake" is available on the CD-ROM.

Sharing for Understanding

Have students check their work in small groups.

Today we are going to check our work in small groups. You are going to work with other people who sit at your table. I want you to take turns and read one sentence at a time. Make sure you read the edited sentence, the one with the formal pattern. If everyone at the table agrees that the sentence is formal, the next person will take a turn. To get started, let's have the person whose first name is alphabetically last in each group go first. Then the person on his or her left will go second. You will continue going around the circle until all of the sentences have been read and all of you agree on the editing. (As I circulate around the room during this time, I ask the students why they made the choices they made and how they determined if the pattern was plural or possessive.)

Assessing the Lesson

Since the students check their work with one another, I do not collect their work. I informally assess the students as I walk around during both the independent practice and the sharing time. By this time I am aware of which students are struggling with the concept of formal and informal language, and I check on them first.

I often find a few students struggling with plural and possessive patterns, even at this point in our studies. Generally, these students are unsuccessful at editing for both patterns at once. To simplify the task of editing for both patterns within a piece of writing, I often advise struggling students to edit for one pattern at a time. Therefore, they might edit for plural patterns first and then turn their focus to possessive patterns. Most importantly, I want my students to understand that editing is a skill that takes practice, and that with time, they will become more efficient with this portion of the writing process.

5 Showing Past Time

Lessons

THIS UNIT INCLUDES THE FOLLOWING LESSONS:

This unit addresses showing past time in vernacular and Standard English: *Last week, we play a game* versus *Last week, we played a game*. The patterns for showing past time are interestingly similar to the patterns for showing plurality. In vernacular English, we show both plurality and past time through context (with words such as *six, several, many/yesterday, last month*, and *before*) and through common knowledge (the fact that we know there's more than one of something or that something happened in the past). Similarly, for both plurality and past time, Standard English uses redundant word endings (*-s* and *-ed*).

UNIT 5

Showing Past Time

The Pattern

The pattern for showing past tense in Standard English is easy – we show past tense with the *-ed* ending when there is one and only one regular verb in a clause.

In vernacular English, we notice signals in other places in the sentence that indicate past time. Perhaps the student uses **time words and phrases** to show past time (e.g., *yesterday, last week, last summer, earlier this year*). Perhaps there are other past time verbs – *said, went*, or *flew* – or even other verbs that do use *-ed* – such as *walked* or *wondered* – in the sentence or paragraph. If there are no explicit signals in a sentence, perhaps we simply know based on the meaning of the sentence that the events were set in the past: *Martin Luther King talk to the people.* We know that's set in the past because we know that Martin Luther King, Jr., lived and died decades ago. We call that **common knowledge**.

Vernacular pattern:
time words and phrases
(*yesterday, last week*)
common knowledge
(we just know the event happened in the past)

Standard English pattern:
verb + *-ed*

In working with past time patterns, we focus on affirmative, regular verbs (e.g., *Yesterday I watch Looney Tunes* and *Last summer, my brother squirt me with the water gun*). The sentences we will explore have only one main verb – no auxiliaries. This ensures that we're dealing with regular past time and not other forms of the verb that take an *-ed* in Standard English (perfect: *had entered;* passive: *was encouraged*). That means that examples like *I had enter_ the room* or *She was encourage_ to run* will not be part of this unit. We will address these in the resource CD with this book and on our website at www.heinemann.com.

The Code-Switching Chart

As always, a compare and contrast chart containing informal patterns and their formal equivalents is the main tool in this lesson.

Choosing examples

Again, the first step in building a code-switching chart is to collect a range of papers in which students follow the vernacular, or informal, pattern for showing past time.

Choosing examples for our *Past Time Patterns* chart turns out to be somewhat tricky. We know that the past time contrast between vernacular and Standard English has to do with an *-ed*. Whereas the Standard English verb takes an *-ed* ending (*She walked to the store yesterday*), the vernacular sticks with the bare, or root, form of the verb (*She walk to the store yesterday*).

These students have followed the informal pattern for showing past time: **time words and phrases, common knowledge:**

Looking for the Hat
There was a boy, he allways wore a hat
ever when he was sleep. One day he woke up
and could not find his hat and his friends
want to see his new hat on his birthday.
He call his friends to help find the hat.

One day ... his friends want to see his new hat.

name of the book was camp rock.
So I ask her Can I trade her
Book for my Bratz doll. She Said
it was not enough So I trade
her for my mp3 player So we

She said it was not enough so I trade her for my MP3 player.

Additionally, we often find examples in student writing like these:

1. **I have already turn on the TV.**
2. **I had enter the room.**
3. **Aaliyah should be acknowledge for all of the wonderful thing she did.**
4. **She was delight to come.**
5. **She have a friend name Raven.**

While each of these sentences has an equivalent in Standard English that does sport an *-ed*, not a single one of these examples will go on our past time chart. None represents the simple past tense. Sentences 1 and 2 correspond to the Standard English perfect (*I have turned; I had entered*). Sentence 3 corresponds to the Standard English passive (*Aaliyah should be acknowledged*), and sentences 4 and 5 use the form corresponding to the Standard English past participle as an adjective.

We want to focus our kids' attention on only one very specific contrast between vernacular and Standard English: the case in which a clause has one and only one verb (no auxiliaries) and that verb is regular in Standard English – it takes *-ed* to make past tense (e.g., *She walk yesterday* vs. *She walked yesterday*).

Why do none of those examples go on our past time chart? Examples 1–4 all have auxiliary verbs, and the word that would take an *-ed* in example 5 isn't even functioning as a verb – it's functioning as an adjective describing a noun (*a friend name Raven*) – so just being sensitive to which forms take an *-ed* in Standard English isn't enough.

In the meantime, we will look for a very specific kind of example to go on our *Past Time Patterns* chart. We will choose a sentence with the following:

- No auxiliaries (*can/could, will/would, shall/should, may/might, have, be*, etc.)
- Only one verb
- That verb would be regular in Standard English (uses *-ed* to form past tense)

What if student writing contains a sentence like *She never went to school because her mom said she cannot go*? It may feel like *cannot* should be put into a past tense form (*couldn't go*), and that's true. However, the example does not go on the past time chart. Why? Because there are two verbs in its clause (*She cannot go*) and because *cannot* is not regular in Standard English (it does not take an *-ed* to make past tense).

Creating the code-switching chart

For this code-switching chart, we'll choose five to seven vernacular sentences showing past time from student writing. As always, we edit the sentences to make sure they fit on one line and that the only vernacular pattern is the one we're focusing on – past time.

Then we want to order the sentences to help lead students in pattern discovery, so we make sure to put sentences with explicit time words and phrases (*yesterday, this morning, last Saturday*, etc.) first and early in the list. That will let our students discover the main pattern: **time words and phrases show past time**. Then we can proceed to the exception – **common knowledge** – in the last sentence or two in the chart.

PAST TIME PATTERNS

INFORMAL	FORMAL
Yesterday I trade my MP3 player.	Yesterday I trad<u>ed</u> my MP3 player.
We walk all around the school last night.	We walk<u>ed</u> all around the school last night.
Last Saturday we watch that movie.	Last Saturday we watch<u>ed</u> that movie.
I call my grandma two days ago.	I call<u>ed</u> my grandma two days ago.
Martin Luther King talk to the people.	Martin Luther King talk<u>ed</u> to the people.
THE PATTERN	**THE PATTERN**
time words and phrases **common knowledge**	**verb + *-ed***

Now we're ready for the lesson!

Defining Informal and Formal Past Time Patterns

Engagement

Gather the students in a central location around an easel with a code-switching T-chart that has been labeled *Past Time Patterns*. Keep the chart covered for now. Review previous lessons.

We have been talking about formal and informal language patterns. We learned that formal language is dressed up, and we usually use formal language at school. We know that informal language can be used at home because informal language is more casual. So far, we have talked about formal and informal language with two types of patterns: plurals and possessives.

Introduce the idea of *action verbs*.

Today we are going to focus on formal and informal language patterns that deal with action verbs. Does anyone know what an action verb is?

SAMUEL: **Something that you do?**

That's exactly what it is. An action verb is a word that shows action, like *jump*. *Jump* is something you can do, that makes it an action verb. Let's make a list of some action verbs.

DORIS: **Sing.**

ONTIANA: **Dance.**

(As the students say the words, I write them on flip-chart paper.)

Direct Instruction

Introduce the topic for today's lesson. Show students the *Past Time Patterns* code-switching chart.

I'm so glad you remember what action verbs are because you are going to need that knowledge to define the patterns for our chart. Today we are going to be discovering the formal and informal patterns that show past time. When we talk about past time, we are talking about actions that have already happened.

Show students the *Past Time Patterns* code-switching chart. Give students a minute to look for patterns that show actions in the past.

As you take a look at the chart, I want you to focus on how you know that the action has already happened, or taken place. Let's see what you notice. (I reveal the chart.)

Lesson 1

materials

- *Past Time Patterns* code-switching chart
- flip-chart paper
- one sentence strip for each student
- markers, pencils, paper

goals

STUDENTS WILL:

- recognize past time patterns inside formal and informal language.
- define past time patterns inside formal and informal language.
- distinguish between formal and informal past time patterns.

Discovering the Pattern

Follow these key steps first for all the informal sentences, then for all the formal sentences.

1. Read the sentences.
2. Focus students' attention on how sentences show past time.
3. Describe the pattern.
4. Test the pattern in each sentence.
5. Write the pattern on the chart.

Start with the informal side. Ask students to describe how they know an action already happened in the informal sentences. Underline the words that indicate past action.

Let's start with the informal side of the chart. *Yesterday I trade my MP3 player.* How do you know the action has already taken place? How do you know the author isn't trading the MP3 player right now or that he's not going to trade tomorrow?

> QUINTIN: **It says *yesterday.***

The word *yesterday* tells us that the action already happened. (I underline *yesterday* in the sentence.) Let's look at the next sentence. *We walk all around the school last night.* Hmmm, I don't see the word *yesterday* in this sentence. How do we know the action has taken place?

> DAJON: **It says *last night.***

So *last night* is another way we know that the action has already happened. (I underline *last night* in the sentence.)

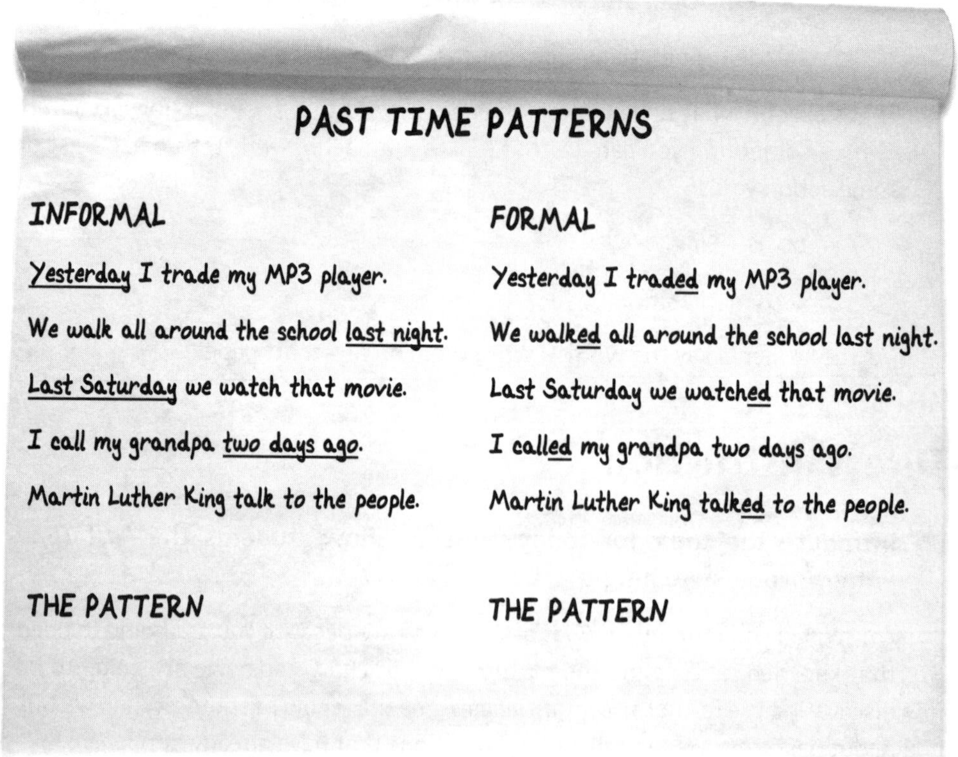

PAST TIME PATTERNS

INFORMAL	FORMAL
Yesterday I trade my MP3 player.	Yesterday I traded my MP3 player.
We walk all around the school last night.	We walked all around the school last night.
Last Saturday we watch that movie.	Last Saturday we watched that movie.
I call my grandpa two days ago.	I called my grandpa two days ago.
Martin Luther King talk to the people.	Martin Luther King talked to the people.
THE PATTERN	THE PATTERN

Guided Practice

Aid students in taking over the teacher role for the next couple of sentences.

Who would like to take over the teacher role for this next sentence? Tehjia?

TEHJIA: **How do you know it already happened in *Last Saturday we watch that movie*?**

QUINTIN: **It says *Last Saturday*.**

TEHJIA: **Yep.**

Go ahead and underline *Last Saturday.* (Tehjia underlines the words.)

Andrew, would you take over the teacher role for the next sentence?

ANDREW: ***I call my grandpa two days ago.* How do you know the action already happened?**

ONTIANA: ***Two days ago.***

ANDREW: **Yes, the words *two days ago* show the action already happened.**

(Andrew underlines *two days ago.*)

Ask students to create a rule that describes the informal past time pattern.

Let's focus on the first four sentences for right now. I want you to take a minute and see if you can come up with a rule to describe the informal past time pattern. Who thinks they have a way to describe the pattern?

QUATASIA: **Maybe other words in the sentence.**

Other words in the sentence. Can we be more specific? What kind of other words show that the action already occurred?

DAR'ASIA: **We could say time words, like *yesterday, morning, last Saturday*, and *two days ago*. Those tell time.**

So **time words** tell us that an action happened in the past. Okay, let's make sure that works for our first four sentences. *Yesterday I trade my MP3 player.* Do we have a time word?

STUDENTS: **Yes!**

What is it?

TEHJIA: ***Yesterday.***

Yesterday, and we already underlined it. Let's look at the next sentence. (We go through each of the first four sentences in the same way.)

what if...

the students are unable to articulate *time words*?

If the students are unable to come up with the term *time words.*, I supply the words as a suggestion. I might say, "all of these words have something to do with time. I wonder if we could come up with a rule about that."

Well, it looks like our rule works for the first four sentences, so we can go ahead and add that to our chart. (I write **time words** under "The Pattern" in the *Informal* column.) Now let's look at the last sentence. *Martin Luther King talk to the people.* How do we know the action already took place?

> ANDREW: **Martin Luther King died, so he can't talk to people anymore.**

You're right, since Martin Luther King died, we know that the action must have already taken place sometime in the past when he was still alive. I'm wondering if we can call this **common knowledge**. Most people know that Martin Luther King is no longer alive, so it is simply common knowledge that this sentence refers to a past time. (I add **common knowledge** below **time words**.)

Independent Practice

Break the students into pairs, and hand out sentence strips. Ask students to determine a formal past time rule and write it on a sentence strip.

Now that we've determined the rule for showing past time in informal language, you're going to work with a partner to see if you can figure out the rule for showing past time inside formal language. I want you to look very closely at the formal sentences to see if you can find how they're different from the informal sentences. What changed? Once you and your partner agree on a pattern, check to make sure it works in every sentence. Then you can write the pattern on your sentence strip. I'll give you six minutes to work on the pattern before we all meet back at the carpet. Any questions? Okay, you may get started! (I circulate around the room and offer assistance to students who are having difficulties. I also question the students' thinking in determining the formal rule.)

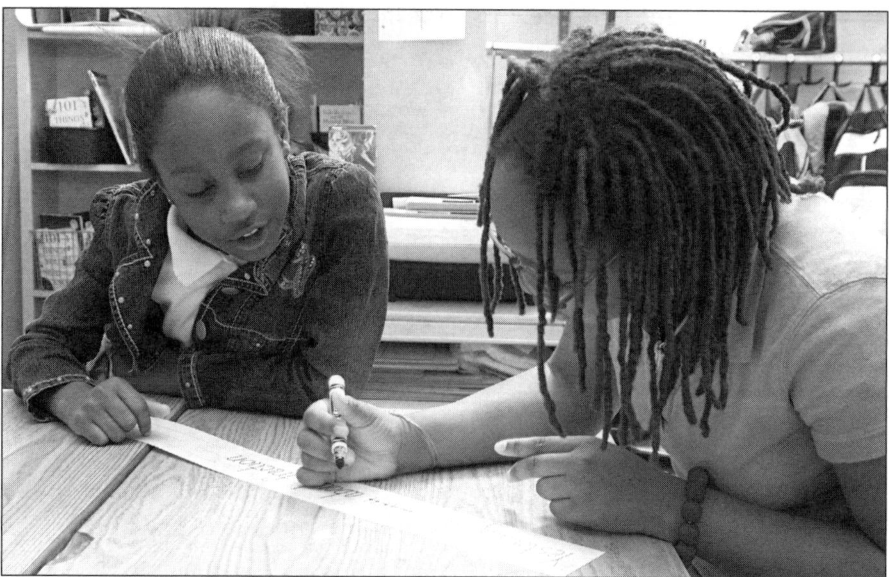

Sharing for Understanding

Have the students gather around the partially completed *Past Time Patterns* chart. Discuss the rules that different pairs of students wrote, and tape the sentence strips on the board.

Let's take a look at what you came up with. Who would like to share?

QUINTIN: **My partner was Garrett. We said "word + *-ed*."**

Did anyone have anything else?

HEZEKIAH: **We put "verb + *-ed*."**

I see a couple of people wrote "word + *-ed*," and some people wrote "verb + *-ed*." Which one is more specific, or more exact?

QUINTIN: **I think *verb* is better than *word*.**

Thumbs-up if you agree with the rule **verb + *-ed***. Okay, Quintin, you can write our rule on the chart. (Quintin writes **verb + *-ed*** under *The Pattern* in the Formal column on the chart.)

Conclude the lesson by allowing several students to share their thoughts about the lesson.

Very quickly, thumbs-up if you thought this lesson was easy, thumbs-down if you thought it was difficult, and thumbs to the side if you thought it was sort of easy. Who would like to share why they voted the way they did?

TEHJIA: **I said it was easy because we been doing charts for a long time.**

So it's become easier for you to find the pattern?

TEHJIA: **Yes.**

Anyone else want to share?

ANDREW: **It was a little hard because you have to think about how to say the rule.**

You found it difficult to find the right words to describe the pattern?

ANDREW: **Yeah because I knew what the pattern was, but I didn't know how I could say it.**

It will continue to get easier. (I allow a few more students to share.) You all did an awesome job today!

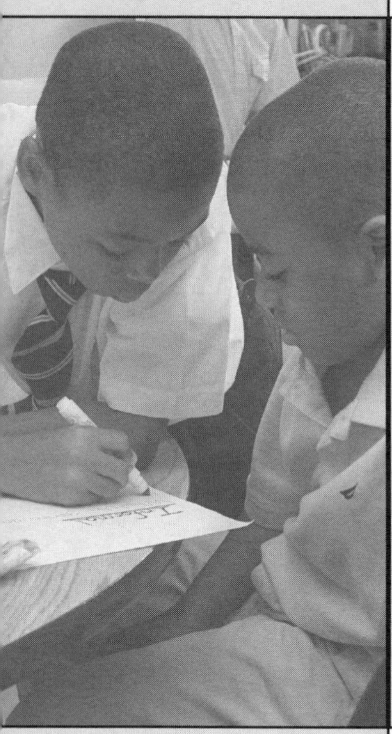

Assessing the Lesson

I rely on teacher observation to assess this lesson. I'm looking to see that the students are engaged, that they work well with their partner, and that they're able to defend their thinking. During Independent Practice, I challenge the students to prove their rule. The students usually state their rule and then apply it to each sentence, thus mimicking the process we use as a group. This is what I expect to see. I have concerns when students are unable to use the process. I coach students who are unable to prove their rule. I might say, "How does the first sentence fit your pattern?" Then I ask, "What about the next sentence? How does it fit the pattern?" I want my students to think about the process, not just the end result.

Classifying Informal and Formal Past Time Patterns

Engagement

Gather the students around an easel with the *Past Time Patterns* code-switching chart nearby. Review the formal and informal past time patterns by reading some sample sentences.

Yesterday we discovered the formal and informal patterns for showing past time. Let's take a look at a few sentences and decide if they follow the formal or informal pattern. Once we decide if the pattern is formal or informal, I'm going to ask you to describe the pattern. (I reveal the sentences.)

Jacob earn twenty dollars from mowing lawns last month.

We waited quietly for the movie to start.

George Washington serve as the first President of the United States.

Let's look at the first sentence. *Jacob earn twenty dollars from mowing lawns last month.* Is that formal or informal? Thumbs-up if you think it's formal, thumbs to the side if you think it is informal. (The students show their thumbs to the side.) Good. How does it follow the informal rule?

DAR'ASIA: **The time words show it's informal. It says *last month*.**

Exactly. What about the second sentence? *We waited quietly for the movie to start.* Thumbs-up for formal, thumbs to the side for informal. (The students show thumbs-up.) How does it follow the formal rule?

DAJON: ***Waited* is a verb with an *-ed* on the end.**

You all are on fire today! How about the last sentence? *George Washington serve as the first President of the United States.* Thumbs-up or thumbs to the side? (The students show their thumbs to the side.) What makes it informal?

ANDREW: **It talks about George Washington, and we know he's dead.**

So which rule does this sentence follow?

ANDREW: **Common knowledge.**

Right, so in informal language we can show past time using **time words** or **common knowledge.** In formal language, the rule is **verb + *-ed*.**

Lesson 2

materials

- *Past Time Patterns* code-switching chart
- chart paper with sample sentences using informal and formal past time patterns
- one sheet of flip-chart paper with a blank *Past Time Patterns* T-chart for each small group
- two small sentence strips for each student
- markers, pencils, paper

goals

STUDENTS WILL:

- define past time patterns inside formal and informal language.
- distinguish between formal and informal past time patterns.
- write sentences using formal and informal past time patterns.

Direct Instruction

Introduce the topic for today's lesson. Show the class a *Classifying Past Time Patterns* T-chart drawn on easel pad paper.

Now that we've defined the patterns for showing past time, we need to practice writing sentences that show past time. Today you are going to write two sentences using either the formal or informal pattern. Then in your groups, you will create your own chart showing formal and informal past time. The chart starts out looking like this (I hold up the chart). See how it's similar to the *Past Time Patterns* chart we worked on earlier, except there aren't any sentences yet? You'll be adding the sentences in your small group by looking at the sentences each of you wrote and then deciding as a group whether the sentences belong in the *Informal* column or the *Formal* column.

Demonstrate writing a sentence using the past time pattern by choosing from a list of different scenarios.

I have small sentence strips for each of you to write your sentences on and a piece of chart paper that is already labeled. To write your sentences, you will pick two different audiences from this list I have written on the board.

Pretend you are:

1. talking to your best friend
2. writing a paper you plan to publish
3. giving a speech to the whole school
4. talking to your mom
5. talking to the principal

Once you decide which scenario you are going to use, you will need to decide if you should use formal or informal language. I'm going to pretend I am talking to my mom. I could use formal or informal language to talk to my mom, but since I usually use formal language, I'm going to make my sentence formal. First, I need to choose an action verb. I'm going to use *walk*. The formal pattern is **verb + *-ed***, so I need to use the word *walked* in my sentence. I'm going to tell my mom about my trip to the store. My sentence is going to start with *I walked to the store.* (I write this on the sentence strip.) Now I need to add a detail to make it more interesting: *I walked to the store to buy a gallon of milk.* (I finish writing the sentence on the sentence strip and show it to the class.) Here is my sentence, and I used the formal past time pattern of *verb* plus *-ed*. This is what you will do on your own in a few minutes.

I walked to the store to buy a gallon of milk.

Guided Practice

Guide the students in writing their own formal or informal sentences showing past time.

Let's try a sentence together. Which scenario should we use?

QUATASIA: **Giving a speech.**

Okay, let's pretend we're giving a speech to the whole school. Are we going to use formal or informal language?

SEVERAL STUDENTS: **Formal!**

Why do we want to use formal language?

GARRETT: **Because we're giving a speech and it's in front of the school, so the principal might be there and other teachers.**

Since this is a speech, we want to make sure we use formal language. We are also in a formal setting – in front of the whole school – which, as Garrett said, includes the principal and teachers. Let's choose an action verb.

GARRETT: **Explore.**

Okay, let's make sure we follow the formal past time pattern.

GARRETT: **Explored.**

How does that follow the pattern?

TEHJIA: **Verb plus *-ed*.**

So what do we want our sentence to say?

DAR'ASIA: **We explored the different planets.**

Okay, would you start the sentence on the sentence strip? (While Dar'Asia writes, the rest of the class finishes the sentence.) Let's see if we can add a detail to our sentence.

I'ANA: **We explored the different planets so we could pass the science test.**

What a great sentence! I'ana, please finish writing the sentence on the sentence strip. (I'ana finishes the sentence.)

We explored the different planets so we could pass the science test.

what if...

students choose an irregular action verb?

Here, while *explore* is slightly irregular, it's close enough to the regular pattern. If a student chose *study*, we might say "Good choice! That one is a little harder so we'll address verbs like *study* later this year. Anyone have a simpler verb?"

The next part of the assignment is to put these sentences into our group's past time chart. Let's start with the sentence I wrote. *I walked to the store to buy a gallon of milk.* Will this sentence go on the informal or formal side?

STUDENTS: Formal!

Ontiana, would you please tape this sentence on the formal side? What about the sentence you wrote? *We explored the different planets so we could pass the science test.* Does this sentence follow the formal or informal past time pattern?

STUDENTS: Formal!

Right, we wrote two formal sentences. Now you will try this on your own.

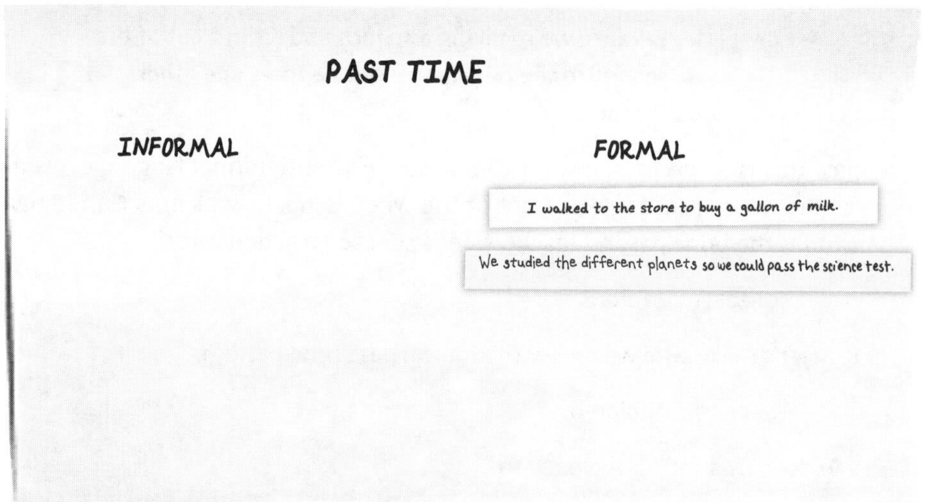

Independent Practice

Have the students write their own sentences and construct their own past time chart.

Your job is to pick two different scenarios and write a sentence for each of those audiences. You will need to decide if your sentences are going to be formal or informal. Once you've written your sentences on the sentence strips, you are going to read your sentences aloud to your group. As a group, you need to agree on whether the sentences are formal or informal. Once you all agree on which past time pattern each sentence contains, you can tape the sentences in the appropriate columns on your group's past time chart. Are there any questions about your job today? (I answer any questions and dismiss the students to complete the assignment. As the students work, I visit each group and talk to them about the audiences they chose and why they decided to use the particular pattern they chose. As the groups complete their charts, I hang them in the room.)

what if...

the students want to use an irregular verb?

There are many verbs that do not follow the formal pattern of verb + *-ed*, and it is likely that at some point your students will want to use these verbs. If students suggest an irregular verb, such as *run*, I might say, "Run is actually an irregular verb. It doesn't follow the regular formal pattern. The formal past time form of *run* is actually *ran*. So you'll need to use *ran* if you want to use the formal past time form." I also keep a list of irregular verbs, such as *flew, drove,* and *wrote,* on a piece of chart paper on the wall.

Sharing for Understanding

Give the students a few minutes to look at the other groups' charts and write comments.

Now that each group has completed their own charts, I am going to give you sticky notes so that you can comment on the charts. Your comments should start with *I notice* if you have a comment or *I wonder* if you have a question. Let's take five minutes for *I notice/I wonder.* (The students use the sticky notes to write *I notice/I wonder* comments. They put the notes on the charts.)

Who would like to share an *I notice/I wonder*?

QUINTIN: **I noticed that there were more formal sentences on all the charts except Quatasia's group.**

Good observation. Who else would like to share?

DAR'ASIA: **Mine goes with what Quintin said. I wrote *I wonder why group four had more informal sentences.***

Group four. That's Quatasia, Andrew, Tehjia, and Garrett. Would one of you tell us why you think you had so many informal sentences?

GARRETT: **Well, I wrote two informal sentences because that's how I talk to my friends and my mom.**

So you used the patterns that you use in your speech when your friends or your mom is your audience. (We spend about five minutes discussing *I notice/I wonder* statements.) All of you did a great job creating your own charts. Let's just get three things you liked about this lesson. Raise a quiet hand if you'd like to share.

I'ANA: **I liked that we could write informal sentences for some of our choices.**

(I allow two more students to share.)

note

The *I notice/I wonder* technique is something I do with my students during the editing process. It was not introduced during this lesson. I would suggest introducing the concept in a separate lesson where understanding and using the *I notice/I wonder* technique is the goal of the lesson.

Assessing the Lesson

To assess this lesson, I rely primarily on the discussions I have with the students during the Independent Practice portion of the lesson. During this part of the lesson, I ask the students which scenarios, or audiences, they chose. Then I ask if they decided to write sentences that contain the formal or informal past time pattern. This gives me some insight into their understanding of selecting language based on place, audience, and communicative purpose. As I speak with each group, I ask the students to defend their decisions to use the formal or informal past time pattern. Since time is limited, I focus on those students who chose to write informal sentences. I want to make sure that they chose a scenario for which informal language was an appropriate choice. I also look to see that the students are following the patterns correctly. I address students who are confused immediately. I also keep a close eye on these students during subsequent lessons.

Practicing the Formal Past Time Pattern

Engagement

Have the students gather around the Past Time Patterns chart. Review using the formal past time pattern.

For today's lesson, I want us to focus on using the formal past time pattern. Yesterday we practiced writing sentences in which you chose whether to use the formal or informal pattern. You made that decision based on your audience. Today we are going to focus on the formal pattern because most of our school writing is for an audience that requires formal language. Let's come up with a formal sentence for each of these two verbs. (I write two verbs on the board.)

grab
dance

Raise your hand when you think you have a formal sentence for the verb *grab*.

HEZEKIAH: **I grabbed a pencil out of my desk.**

How do we know the action is in the past?

ANDREW: ***Grabbed.***

What rule is *grabbed* following?

ANDREW: ***Verb* plus *-ed*.**

It follows our formal past time rule of *verb* plus *-ed*. Now let's have someone share a sentence for the verb *dance*.

ONTIANA: **When I was three, I danced in a ballet.**

When I was three, I danced in a ballet. How do we know the action has already happened?

I'ANA: ***When I was three.***

Ontiana did give some time words, but she also used the formal past time pattern. How did she use the formal past time pattern?

I'ANA: ***Danced.***

She used a verb with an *-ed* on the end of it.

Lesson 3

materials

- chart paper with a sample paragraph to practice editing
- copies of five different pieces of student work
- highlighters, pencils, paper

goals

STUDENTS WILL:

- Recognize past time patterns inside formal and informal language.
- Define past time patterns inside formal and informal language.
- Distinguish between formal and informal past time patterns.
- Edit sentences to make sure they contain the formal past time pattern.

Direct Instruction

Explain the purpose for today's lesson.

Since formal English is so important when you write formal papers, give speeches, and – when you're older – go for job interviews, we are going to focus on making sure you understand the formal past time pattern. Today we are going to practice peer editing. Our goal is for everyone to be able to edit a piece of writing to make sure that *all* the verbs follow the formal past time pattern. Let's look at a paragraph from a piece of writing a student wrote a few years ago. Then we'll edit it together before you work on your own.

note

A customizable version of the paragraph "Saturday" is available on the CD-ROM.

Saturday

Last weekend I ask my mom if I could go to the skating rink. My mom asked if I already clean my room. I pretended I did so I could go to the skating rink. But then my mom look in my room and yell, "Destiny clean your room NOW!" I work all morning to get my room nice and clean. When I was finished, I ask my mom if I could go to the skating rink. My mom said no because I lie to her. I cried because all my friends were going skating. I was so bored at my house on Saturday.

We're going to use the same strategy we've been using when we edit for formal patterns. First, we're going to read the entire paragraph. (I read through the paragraph.) After we read the piece of writing, we're going to go back through and read each sentence slowly, paying close attention to those past time patterns. If we find a formal past time pattern, we're going to highlight it. If we find an informal past time pattern, we're going to change it to formal and then highlight it.

Guided Practice

▶ **Lead the students to edit the paragraph to make sure the formal past time pattern is used throughout.**

Let's start with the first sentence. *Last weekend I ask my mom if I could go to the skating rink.* Do we have any past time patterns in this sentence? (Several students nod their heads.) Where is the pattern?

GARRETT: ***Ask.***

How do you know that *ask* is a past time verb?

GARRETT: **It says *Last weekend.***

Okay, we have some time words that show the action has already happened. Does that follow the formal or informal past time pattern?

SEVERAL STUDENTS: **Informal.**

What do we need to do to make it formal?

DAR'ASIA: **Add an *-ed.***

Dar'Asia, would you please make our pattern formal and then highlight it? (Dar'Asia changes *ask* to *asked* and highlights it as we go on with the next sentence.) Let's look at the next sentence. *My mom asked if I already clean my room.* Do we have any past time patterns in this sentence?

STUDENTS: **Yes.**

Where?

GARRETT: ***Asked* and *clean.***

Oh, we have two. Let's start with the first one. Is *asked* formal or informal?

STUDENTS: **Formal!**

Garrett, would you please highlight our formal pattern? (Garrett highlights *asked.*) What about *clean*? (We continue editing the paragraph as a class.)

Independent Practice

▶ **Have the students work on their own to edit authentic pieces of writing.**

I'm so impressed by how well you all did editing this paragraph! Now it's your turn to show what you can do on your own. I have five different pieces of writing authored by different people in our class. I have typed these pieces of writing and edited them so that all the words are spelled correctly and the only informal patterns are past time. I am going to give each of you one piece of writing to edit on your own. You are going to do exactly what we did as a group. What is the first thing you will need to do?

TAJANTA: Read it.

Yes, you're going to read the entire piece of writing. Then you will edit one sentence at a time, starting at the beginning. What will you do if you find a formal past time pattern?

BOBBY: I'm gonna highlight it.

What will you do if you find an informal past time pattern?

NIJE: Change it to formal and highlight it.

Okay, I think you're ready to start. (I hand out the papers and send the students back to their seats. I give them about ten minutes to edit the pieces of writing. As the students work, I circulate the room to answer questions and offer assistance.)

Sharing for Understanding

Have the students gather in groups according to which piece of writing they received.

Okay, let's see how we did. I want you to listen very carefully to the directions. You are going to sit with people who have the same piece of writing that you have. If you have a number one written on the top of your paper, you are sitting at the back table. (I place all of the groups.) You are going to check your work together.

Each group will have a leader. The leader's job is to read each sentence and pick a group member to explain the past time pattern or patterns in that sentence. So if you highlighted a past time pattern because it was already formal, that is what you will tell your group. If you had to change an informal past time pattern to formal before you highlighted it, that is what you will tell the group. You can discuss any disagreements, and I will be here to help if you need me. Turn your papers over. If you have a star on the back of your paper, you are the group leader. You may get started. (I give the students a few minutes to share. As they share, I listen to their conversations, intervening only when I am asked or see a need.)

Have students evaluate whether or not they met the goal for today's lesson.

Let's look back at our goal for this lesson. Our goal was to edit a piece of writing so that its verbs all showed the formal past time pattern. I want you to think about how you personally did with the lesson. Thumbs-up if you think you met our goal of editing the paper for all the past time patterns, thumbs-down if you feel you were not able to meet the goal and need some more practice, and thumbs to the side if you sort of met the goal. (The students show their thumbs.) Good. We'll continue to work with the past time patterns as we edit our own work during writing time.

Assessing the Lesson

To assess the success of this lesson, I rely on teacher observation of both the writing the students are editing and the conversations they are having during the sharing time. As the students are editing the pieces of writing, I walk around the room and write down what I notice. I try to write a quick note about each student. I might even just put a smiley face or a check next to the name of a student who is working quickly and accurately. For struggling students, I try to make short but specific comments. For example, I might write "slow to find patterns" or "misses informal patterns." I often notice a student or two who quickly highlight all of the verbs that end in *-ed* but then have difficulty locating the informal patterns. To help these students, I remind them of the strategy of editing each sentence, one at a time, starting at the beginning of the paper. I will often have them read the first sentence aloud. Then I will ask, "Does this action take place in the past?" If the student says yes, I refer to the chart on the wall to help him/her successfully determine if the pattern is formal or informal. If the student fails to recognize that the sentence shows past time, I point out the cue words. For example, I might say, "I notice the words *last year*." The student will most likely realize that the past time is being used. It is not uncommon for a few students to struggle with code-switching the past time pattern, and that is okay. This is only the third lesson about past time, so the students need time to practice their new skill.

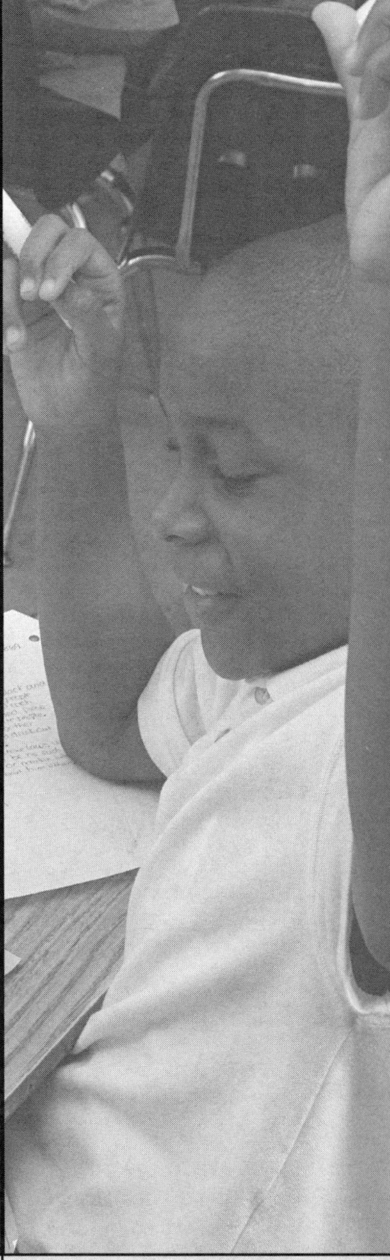

Lesson 4

Editing for the Formal Past Time Pattern

Engagement

Have the students aid in editing two or three sentences that contain past time patterns.

You all have been doing a wonderful job with the past time patterns. We have described formal and informal past time patterns, classified formal and informal past time patterns, and edited for past time patterns. Let's review our procedure for editing past time patterns. I have three sentences on the chart. (I reveal the chart.)

Last summer I stay with my grandparents.
Christopher Newport sail to Jamestown.
My mom cried at my sister's wedding.

Take a moment to read the three sentences to yourself. You should be noticing if they are formal or informal. (I give the students a minute to look over the sentences.) Are any of the sentences already formal?

ANDREW: **The last one is.**

What is the past time pattern in *My mom cried at my sister's wedding*?

DAWNNELLA: ***Cried.***

Since it is already formal, we'll just have Dawnnella highlight it for us. Are there any other sentences with the formal past time pattern? (The students shake their heads.) Okay, then let's look at the first sentence. *Last summer I stay with my grandparents.* How do we know the action took place in the past?

GARRETT: **It says *Last summer.***

A time word shows that the action is in the past. So what do we need to do to make the sentence formal?

I'ANA: **Add an *-ed* to the end of *stay.***

Go ahead and add that for us. Anybody disagree with I'ana? Okay, I'ana, you can highlight, too. (We edit the second sentence.)

materials

- paper, markers, pencils, highlighters
- current or previous formal writing assignments

goals

STUDENTS WILL:

- Recognize past time patterns inside formal and informal language.
- Define past time patterns inside formal and informal language.
- Edit their work for formal past time patterns.

Direct Instruction

Explain the purpose for today's lesson.

Today you are going to be editing your own work. You will be doing the exact same thing we did yesterday except today you will be looking at your own work, so your goal for today is to successfully edit your own writing. Before you get started, we'll warm up by practicing together. We'll use a paragraph a former student wrote to practice editing. Here is the paragraph. (I show the students the paragraph written on chart paper.)

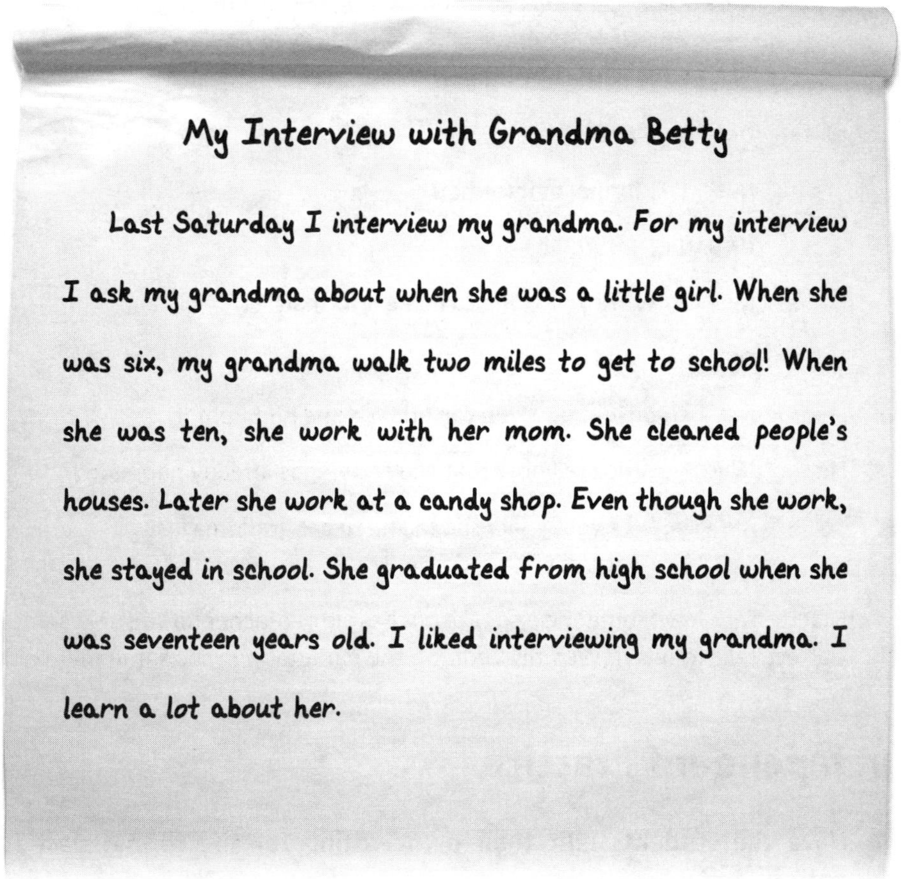

My Interview with Grandma Betty

Last Saturday I interview my grandma. For my interview I ask my grandma about when she was a little girl. When she was six, my grandma walk two miles to get to school! When she was ten, she work with her mom. She cleaned people's houses. Later she work at a candy shop. Even though she work, she stayed in school. She graduated from high school when she was seventeen years old. I liked interviewing my grandma. I learn a lot about her.

Let's read the paragraph aloud together. (We read the paragraph.) Okay, let's go back to that first sentence. Remember that we are looking for the past time patterns. We're going to highlight the formal patterns. If we find an informal pattern, we're going to change it to formal and then highlight it. Let me model that for you with the first sentence. *Last Saturday I interview my grandma.* I don't see a word with *-ed* on the end. But as soon as I read the words *Last Saturday,* I knew the author was talking about past time. This is the informal past time pattern because there are **time words** used to show past time. Now I need to find the verb. Okay, the verb is *interview.* To make *interview* formal, I need to add an *-ed* to the end. (I add the *-ed* to make the word *interviewed.*) Since the pattern is now formal, I can highlight it. (I highlight the word *interviewed.*)

Guided Practice

Allow the students to take over the role of teacher to finish editing the piece of writing.

Now that I've shown you how to think through a sentence and look for the past time pattern, we're going to finish editing the paragraph as a class. I'm looking for someone who thinks they can take on the teacher role for the next sentence. Nije, would you please read the next sentence and lead us through the editing process?

NIJE: **Okay. Let's look at this sentence. *For my interview I ask my grandma about when she was a little girl.* Who sees a past time pattern? Ontiana?**

ONTIANA: ***Ask.***

NIJE: **Is it formal or informal?**

ONTIANA: **Informal.**

NIJE: **How are you going to make it formal?**

ONTIANA: **Add an *-ed.***

NIJE: **Good job. Now you can add *-ed* and highlight it.**

Nice job, Nije! How do we know that the action has already happened?

ANDREW: **It already said she talked to her grandma last Saturday!**

Exactly! Let's have someone else take on the role of teacher for the next sentence. Garrett, take it away! (We finish editing the paragraph in the same manner.)

Independent Practice

Have the students edit their own writing for the formal past time pattern.

You all did an excellent job editing "My Interview with Grandma Betty"! I was especially impressed with our teachers! Now it's your turn to show what you know. You are going to be using the piece of writing we worked on last week. Use the process we used as a group today. Read your entire piece of writing before going back and looking at each sentence one at a time. What are you going to do when you come across an informal past time pattern?

QUINTIN: **Add the *-ed* to make it formal and highlight it.**

Make it formal and then highlight it. What if you find a formal past time pattern? What will you do with that?

I'ANA: **Highlight it.**

what if...

a student says that *was* is a past time pattern?

Tell the student they're right. *Was* does signal past time. However, in this lesson we're working with action words like *ask, walk,* or *like.* So redirect the students' attention to any action words we know show past time.

what if...

students have irregular verbs in the pieces of writing they are editing?

These are often the most difficult for students because they don't always identify the word as an irregular verb. When this happens, they may add the *-ed* as they would for a regular verb. As students come across irregular verbs, I orally comment on the verb. I might say, "Andrew remembered that *grew* is one of those irregular past time verbs! Nice job. Make sure you ask if you are unsure about one of your verbs." Since these verbs do not follow the stated pattern, I simply tell students the past form if they have added an *-ed.*

You're ready! You may go back to your seats and get started! (I help students on an individual basis as I see a need. The students work on editing for about ten minutes.)

Sharing for Understanding

Allow students to share one sentence they found that contains a past time pattern.

Let's come on back to the carpet and form a circle. Bring your edited work with you. We're going to take a few minutes to share some of the sentences with the past time patterns that you found. Since these are edited sentences, all of the past time patterns should be...

STUDENTS: **Formal!**

Exactly! Okay, we're just going to go around the circle. You may share one sentence that contains a past time pattern. If you would prefer not to share, you may pass. Who would like to start? Tyreek, you can get us started.

TYREEK: **Joe scored two points for our team.**

What is the formal past time pattern in Tyreek's sentence?

BOBBY: **Scored.**

That *-ed* on the end of *score* lets us know it follows the formal past time pattern. Ontiana?

ONTIANA: **The last time I went to my cousin house we played the Wii all day.**

Andrew? (The students continue to share their sentences until everyone has had the opportunity to share. I stop random students to ask how their sentence follows the past time pattern.)

Conclude the lesson by having students share something they found helpful about the lesson.

Let's have just a few people share something they found helpful about this lesson.

ANDREW: **I liked that we got to edit our own writing because I finished editing for the past time pattern.**

You liked that you were able to complete some of your own editing during the lesson. Okay. Who else would like to share? (I allow a few students to share.)

what if...

a student uses other vernacular patterns (e.g. *my cousin house*) in their answers?

We always stick to the lesson at hand – here Past TIme Patterns. We'll privately note that Ontiana is using vernacular possessive patterns and we'll work with her on that when we edit papers for multiple patterns in one sentence (Unit 10).

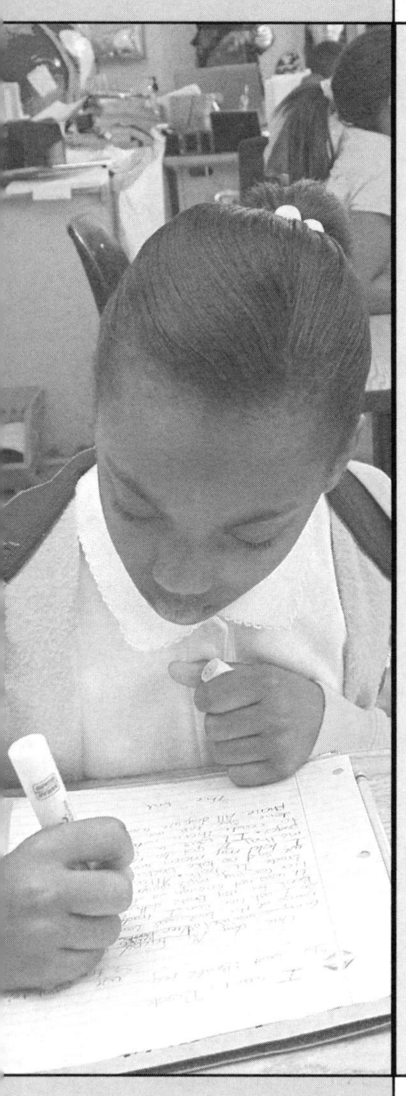

Assessing the Lesson

As I watch the students editing their own work, I look to see how proficient they are at finding past time patterns. While I want them to be able to locate examples of the formal past time pattern, I am most concerned about their ability to identify informal patterns and change them to formal. I have found that most students look for the *-ed* on the end of words to identify formal past time patterns, so they find these fairly quickly. The informal pattern is more difficult because students must consider the context in which the verb is used before determining if it is part of a past time pattern. For this reason, I usually have several students who struggle with this. To help these students, I start by conferencing with them about their work. I model the editing process using a sentence or two from their own work. Then I have them talk their way through a few sentences while I guide them with questions. Following the student-teacher conference, I pair them with a peer editing partner who has demonstrated an understanding of editing for the past time pattern. With time and practice, my students are able to effectively edit for and use the formal past time pattern.

Subject–Verb Agreement

Lessons

THIS UNIT INCLUDES THE FOLLOWING LESSONS:

1. Defining Informal and Formal Subject–Verb Agreement Patterns
2. Classifying Subject–Verb Agreement Patterns
3. Practicing Subject–Verb Agreement Patterns
4. Editing for Formal Subject–Verb Agreement Patterns

In our papers, we notice that vernacular-speaking students often use the vernacular pattern for subject–verb agreement: *Waxing mean to get bigger. Waning mean to get smaller.* Indeed, we find that is perhaps *the* most frequent informal pattern in our students' writing. Even so, we still wait to teach it until students have explored two or three other code-switching patterns first (typically using possessive, using plural, and showing past time). These are the more straightforward grammar patterns, enabling students to learn the ropes of contrastive analysis and code-switching. With that experience, students can move on successfully to subject–verb agreement, which is a more difficult pattern.

UNIT 6

Subject–Verb Agreement

The Pattern

The subject–verb agreement pattern occurs with verbs that would add *-s* for the third-person singular subjects in Standard English: *She helps people, She gives us treats, He respects other people.*

In vernacular English, we notice students often write sentences like *She love to go to church, She cook my favorite food, The rule say be nice to others.* These students are following a different pattern with the use of verbs:

Vernacular pattern:
any subject + bare verb

Standard English pattern:
he/she/it* subjects + verb + *s
any other subject + bare verb

Note this pattern applies to lone regular present-tense verbs – no helping verbs and no negatives. That's because only the first verb agrees with the subject. If we had helping verbs or irregular verbs like *be* or *have,* it would be those that agree (*She is walking, She has a good dog*). In this unit we will be focusing on the pattern in which third person singular verbs take *-s.*

We use the term *bare verb* with elementary students instead of the term *root* or *infinitive* (*infinitive* is actually ambiguous, referring potentially to the word *to* or to the verb form itself). The *bare verb* is the form of the verb without any endings or changes in shape. Another term we use is *dictionary form of the verb* – the form of the verb one would see as a column header in the dictionary.

The Code-Switching Chart

Identifying vernacular subject–verb patterns in kids' work

The pattern we're focusing on here occurs with a single affirmative, present-tense, regular verb – verbs that take *-s* for the *he/she/it* style of subjects in Standard English.

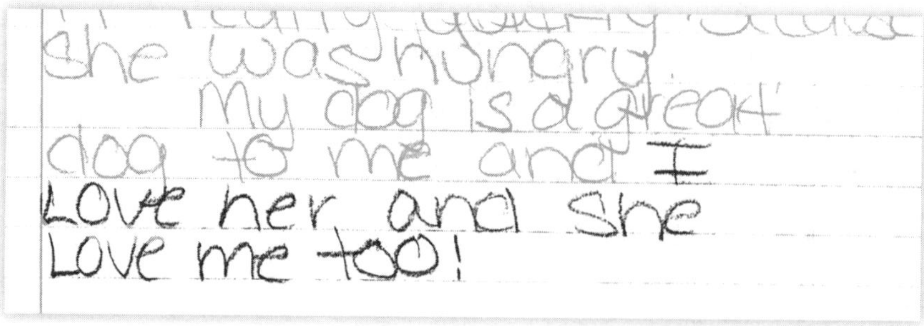

I love her and she love me too!

While other verbs like *do* and *have* show vernacular patterns contrasting with Standard English (*She always do nice things for us, My family always have a big feast*), these are not regular, so they won't go on this subject–verb agreement chart.

Choosing/creating examples

Usually in other code-switching lessons, we collect a range of sample sentences in which students use the vernacular, or informal, pattern we're examining and then build our chart from these student sentences. However, because students often find the subject–verb patterns difficult, we simplify the examples in our first subject–verb lesson, which will ensure that children really hone in on the pattern. And so, to begin, we choose a single sentence showing a third-person singular vernacular subject–verb agreement: *She work quickly.* We want the sentence to be short enough to fit on one line and the verb to be very familiar to the children. We will then build the full chart using only that one verb (you can use *give, walk, bake*, or whatever verb you want).

Once students have studied subject–verb agreement, we sometimes make a more complex chart in which we use a number of different *he/she/it* styles of sentences. We look for regular present-tense verbs, and we seek a range of different subject types: *My other brother walk to school, Valentine's Day mean to care for someone, It mean you love somebody. She help people when they are in trouble, He respect other people.* We want to make sure to have examples of each pronoun type – *he, she* and *it* – and we want one or two examples of full noun phrases – *my other brother*; *Valentine's Day*. This range of examples will allow students to discover the full subject–verb pattern.

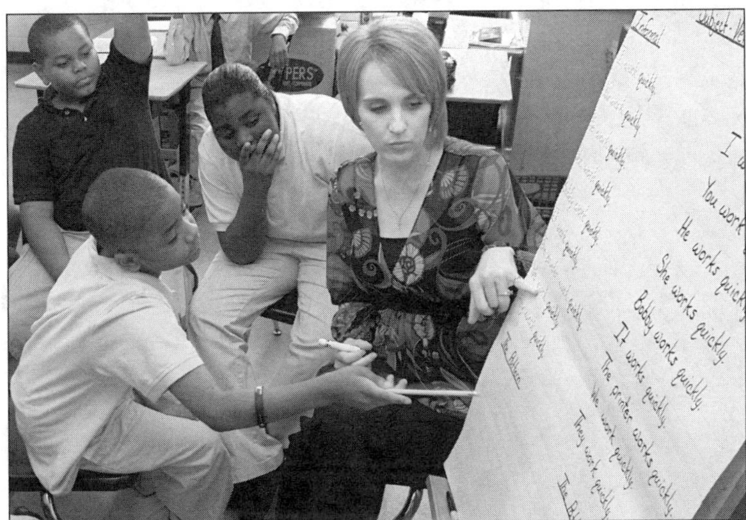

Creating the code-switching chart

As with all our compare and contrast charts, we set up a T-chart, or tree map. We title this one *Subject–Verb Agreement* and list our informal sentences on the left, writing their formal translations next to them on the right. As we have done with earlier lessons, we underline the contrasting parts of each sentence to help direct students' attention to the salient contrasts.

The *Subject–Verb Agreement* chart is a little different from our noun charts and even from our past time charts. Verb agreement charts will have more examples than the other code-switching charts because we need to show the whole verb paradigm – all the persons and numbers of subjects (*I, you, he/she/it, we, you, they*). Then we always put the examples in the same order – singular first, second, and third person: *I, you, he/she/it*; plural first, second, and third person: *we, you, they*. This forms the verb paradigm and becomes part of the overall structure in which students will find regular and recurring verb contrasts.

Although the contrast between formal and informal lies with third-person singular subjects (nouns and noun phrases for which we can substitute the pronouns *he/she/it*), we want our chart to include *all* the different persons and numbers of subjects. If we only included third-person singular subjects, students might conclude (erroneously) that *all* Standard English verbs have *-s* on the end (*We works, They works*). In constructing the examples for the *he/she/it* styles of subjects, we make sure to build examples that use a mixture of full noun phrase subjects (*My dad walks fast*) and pronoun subjects (*She walks fast*). This mixture of subjects that are full noun phrases and those that are pronouns will play an important role as students discover the pattern for third-person singular subject–verb agreement.

To help students discover the Standard English pattern, we put two examples of third-person singular pronoun subjects first after an example with *you* as subject. That lets students discover the pattern for *he/she/it* subjects inside Standard English: ***he/she/it* subject + verb + *s***. Then we put examples of a full noun phrase subject: *Bobby* and *The computer printer.* This will let students discover that when we can substitute *he/she* or *it* for the subject, the verb will take *-s* in Standard English.

Finally, we write *The Pattern* under each column of the chart, leaving space to write the pattern during the lesson.

SUBJECT–VERB AGREEMENT

INFORMAL	**FORMAL**
I work quickly.	I work quickly.
You work quickly.	You work quickly.
He work quickly.	He works quickly.
She work quickly.	She works quickly.
Bobby work quickly.	Bobby works quickly.
It work quickly.	It works quickly.
The printer work quickly.	The printer works quickly.
We work quickly.	We work quickly.
They work quickly.	They work quickly.
THE PATTERN	**THE PATTERN**
any subject + bare verb	***he/she/it* subject + verb + *s*** **any other subject + bare verb**

Now we're ready for the lesson!

Defining Informal and Formal Subject–Verb Agreement

Engagement

Have the students gather around the *Subject–Verb Agreement* code-switching chart. Keep the chart covered for now. Review *action verbs.*

OK, the last few lessons we have been talking about past time patterns. When we looked at past time patterns, we focused on action verbs. Does anyone remember what an action verb is?

DAR'ASIA: **A word that shows action.**

A word that shows action, or something that you can do. What are some examples of action verbs?

GARRETT: **Dance.**

HEZEKIAH: **Laugh.**

DAJON: **Read.**

Let's get a few more. (Three or four more students give examples of action verbs.)

Direct Instruction

Introduce the focus of today's lesson. Demonstrate subjects and verbs in sentences.

Today we are going to be describing how action verbs and subjects work together in a sentence. The subject is who or what the sentence is about. Let's look at this sentence.

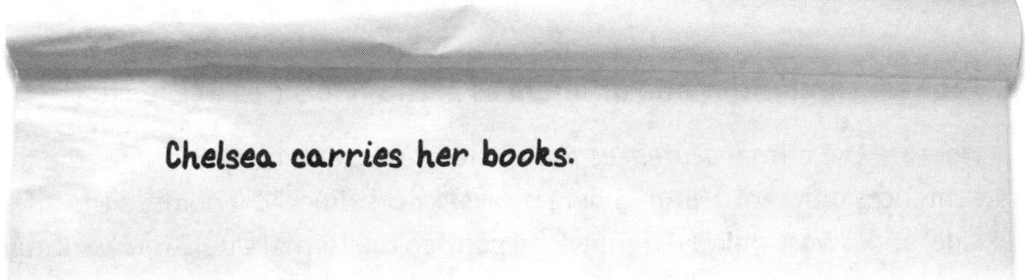
Chelsea carries her books.

Chelsea carries her books – this sentence is about Chelsea. It tells what Chelsea does, so *Chelsea* is the subject. The word *carries* tells what she does. It shows action, so *carries* is the verb.

Up until now, when I created the charts I used sentences you wrote yourselves. However, to help us focus on the pattern for subject–verb agreement, we are going to look at very simple sentences.

Lesson 1

materials

- *Subject–Verb Agreement* code-switching chart
- chart paper
- markers, pencils

goals

- recognize subject–verb agreement patterns in formal and informal language.
- define subject–verb agreement patterns in formal and informal language.
- distinguish between formal and informal subject–verb agreement patterns.
- write sentences using the formal subject–verb agreement pattern.

what if...

this is the first time your students are learning about subjects or action verbs?

You might want to teach this lesson in two separate sessions and spend the first session focusing on identifying subjects and verbs. Students should have some prior knowledge of these concepts before they begin describing subject–verb patterns.

note

Our *Subject–Verb Agreement* charts are the only code-switching charts in which we use constructed sentences. By looking at the changes in the shape of just one word, we help students home in on the patterns – *I work, you work, she work* vs. *I work, you work, she works* etc.

Show the students the *Subject–Verb Agreement* code-switching chart. Ask them to study the chart and look for patterns.

Don't say anything yet! Just take a moment to look at the sentences on the chart. Let's see if we can figure out how subjects and verbs work together to form patterns in informal and formal language. (I give the students a few minutes to look at the chart.)

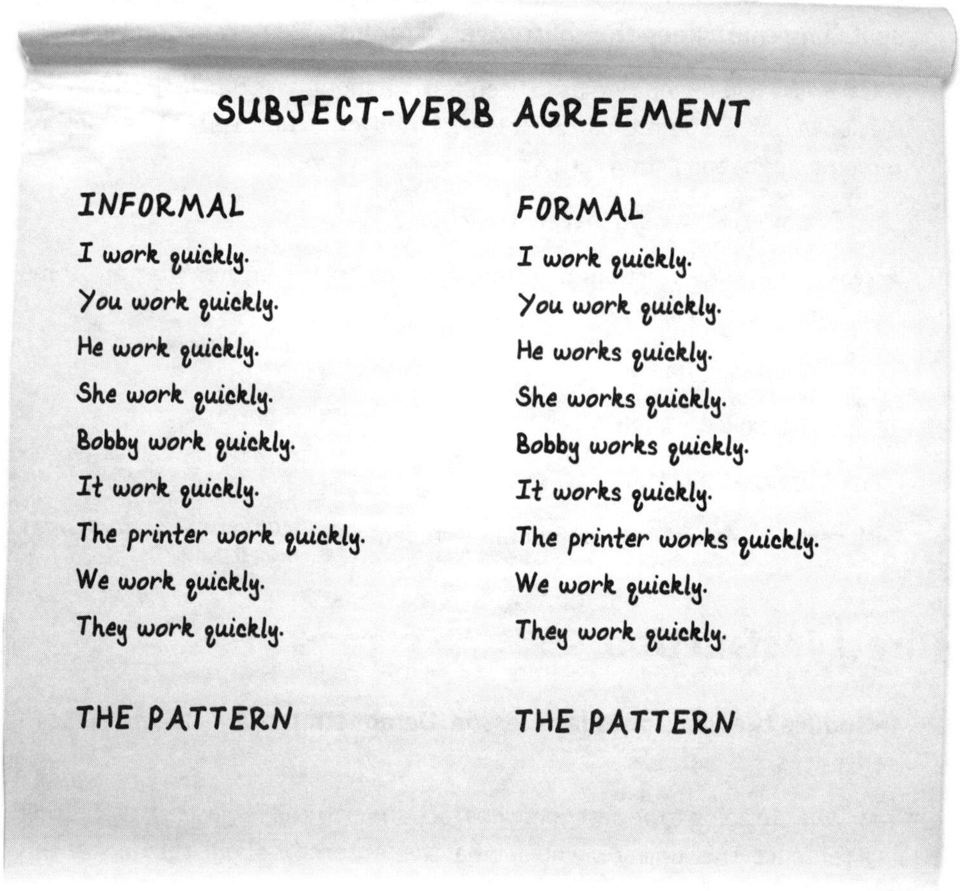

SUBJECT-VERB AGREEMENT

INFORMAL	FORMAL
I work quickly.	I work quickly.
You work quickly.	You work quickly.
He work quickly.	He works quickly.
She work quickly.	She works quickly.
Bobby work quickly.	Bobby works quickly.
It work quickly.	It works quickly.
The printer work quickly.	The printer works quickly.
We work quickly.	We work quickly.
They work quickly.	They work quickly.
THE PATTERN	THE PATTERN

Look for similarities and differences in the two sides of the chart.

How are the formal sentences like the informal sentences? How are the formal sentences different? Hmm... here it says "I work quickly" (I point to the informal side) and "I work quickly" right here (I point to the formal side). "You work quickly" (I point to the informal side). "You work quickly" (I point to the formal side). What do you notice?

TYREEK: **Some of the sentences are the same!**

Yes! Some of the sentences are the same for formal and informal subject–verb agreement. That should make them pretty easy to write!

Identify which formal sentences are different from the informal sentences. Look for a pattern of what those sentences have in common.

Let's focus on how some of the formal sentences are different from the informal sentences.

I'ANA: **Some of them have an *-s*.**

I wonder what the formal pattern is for using an *-s* on the end of a verb. Since the title is Subject–Verb Agreement, I know that the subject must be an important part of this pattern. Let's look at the sentences that contain verbs with an *-s* on the end of them and see what type of subject they use. In the sentence *He works quickly, he* is the subject. In *She works quickly, she* is the subject. Which other sentences have verbs that end in *-s*?

DESTINY: ***Bobby works quickly.***

What is the subject in that sentence?

STUDENTS: **Bobby.**

Bobby is the subject. And isn't *Bobby* a he? (The students nod their heads.) So here is another sentence where *he* is the subject. Any other sentences?

I'ANA: ***It works quickly.***

And what is the subject?

STUDENTS: **It.**

Okay, so far, we have *he, she,* and *it* that use verbs that end in *-s*. Do we have any other sentences with verbs that end in *-s*?

GARRETT: ***The printer works quickly.***

And the subject is...?

STUDENTS: **The printer.**

Okay, *the printer* is the subject. Can *the printer* be a *he, she,* or *it*?

GARRETT: **You can say *it*.**

Yes, *it* can take the place of *the printer*. So how can we write this pattern? Which subjects did we decide are paired with a verb ending in *-s*?

ONTIANA: **You mean like *he*?**

He is one of them.

DAR'ASIA: **She.**

She is another one.

SAMUEL: ***It?***

Okay, so we have ***he, she,* and *it* plus a verb plus an *-s***. Let's check this pattern. *He works quickly.* Do we have a *he, she,* or *it* as the subject?

STUDENTS: **He!**

What about the sentence *She works quickly*? Do we have a *he, she,* or *it* as the subject?

STUDENTS: **She!**

tip

Pronouns play a very important role in this lesson. Students will discover that if they can substitute *he, she,* or *it* for a subject, then in Standard English the verb will take *-s*.

what if...

a student names *Bobby* or *the printer* as subjects that fit the pattern?

Remind students that another way to describe *Bobby* is with the word *he*, and another way to describe *the printer* is with the word *it*. You might say, "Let's not describe the pattern using *Bobby* or *the printer*. Let's just say *he, she,* and *it* since those words can stand for so many different subjects."

Test the pattern and then write it under *The Pattern* on the formal side of the chart.

(I go through each of the sentences in this manner.) Okay, this rule works, so I'm going to write **he/she/it + verb + *-s*** under the Formal column on our chart.

Focus on the formal sentences that are the same as the informal sentences. Look for a contrasting way of describing the pattern for those sentences.

Well, we still have several sentences left in the Formal column that do not fit our pattern. How are the verbs in the rest of the sentences different from the ones in this pattern? (I point to the pattern on the chart.)

> TYREEK: **None of 'em have the *-s*.**

Another way to say that would be to call the verbs *bare verbs*. A bare verb is the dictionary form of the verb. You know how a verb looks when you look it up in the dictionary? That is a bare verb. It doesn't have any endings on it. So which subjects go with our bare verbs?

> I'ANA: **I.**

What else?

> BOBBY: **You.**

We have *I* and *you*. Anything else?

> QUATASIA: **We.**

And one more.

> SEVERAL STUDENTS: **They.**

So we could say ***I, you, we,* and *they* plus a bare verb**.

Test the pattern and then write it under *The Pattern* on the formal side of the chart.

Let's check and make sure we covered all of the sentences. *I work quickly.* Do we have *I*, *you*, *we*, or *they* paired with a bare verb?

STUDENTS: **Yes!**

How does *You work quickly* fit this pattern?

TEHJIA: **Umm, *you* is the subject and *work* is a bare verb.**

You're awesome! (I lead the students to check the remaining sentences to verify the pattern.) So let me write our second pattern for the formal side: ***I/you/we/ they* + bare verb**. (I write the pattern on the chart paper.)

Turn students' attention to the informal side of the chart. Describe how the subject–verb agreement pattern compares with the pattern on the formal side.

Now let's look at the informal sentences. Don't say anything yet! Just look for the subject–verb agreement pattern. (I give the students a minute or two to examine the data.) Okay, what's the pattern?

HEZEKIAH: **They're all the same!**

Let's focus on how we can write a pattern. On the formal side, we said that *he/ she/it* are used with a verb that has an *-s* on the end. What is the pattern for these subjects in the informal sentences?

DORIS: **They don't have an *-s* on the end.**

Well, we don't want to focus on what the verbs don't have. Let's just describe what the verb looks like. Remember that on the formal side, we called the dictionary form of the verb a *bare verb*, so we can also use *bare verb* to describe the verb on the informal side. What about the other subjects – *I*, *you*, *we*, and *they*? What does the verb look like with these subjects?

SEVERAL STUDENTS: **It's bare, too!**

Test the pattern description and write it under the *The Pattern* on the informal side of the chart.

So all of the subjects have a bare verb. Let's check this pattern and make sure all of the sentences have a subject plus a bare verb. (We check each sentence together. Once we verify the pattern, I write it on the chart paper.) So our rule for informal subject–verb agreement is **subject plus bare verb**.

ways of talking

While students may talk about what a vernacular sentence is "missing," we recast and redirect their attention to state the pattern in positive terms. We ask students to focus on what the verb looks like.

Guided Practice

Guide the students in writing practice sentences containing the subject–verb agreement pattern by choosing from a list of possible subjects and verbs.

Now we're going to practice writing some subject–verb agreement sentences. We are going to pretend that we are talking to a friend. On the chart paper here I have written a list of subjects and a list of verbs. We need to pick one subject and one verb and write a sentence. The sentence can be formal or informal.

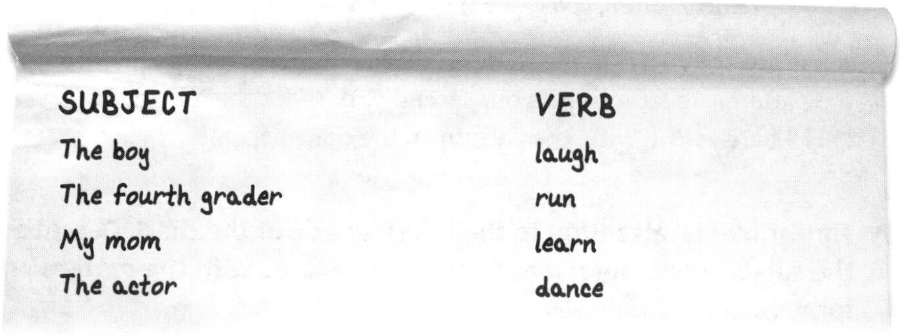

SUBJECT	VERB
The boy	laugh
The fourth grader	run
My mom	learn
The actor	dance

Let's write a sentence together. Should we write a formal sentence or an informal sentence? (The students voice their opinions.) I hear a lot of people saying formal, so let's write a formal sentence this time. Now which subject should we choose? (Several students call out different subjects.) Okay, I heard the words *My mom* first! Garrett, would you write *My mom* on the chart paper? Now let's choose a verb. I'm going to choose someone who has a quiet hand to pick the verb for us. Andrew?

ANDREW: **Learn.**

Okay, Andrew, please write the verb after the subject on the chart paper. (I point to a space after *My mom*.) We said we were going to write a formal sentence, so do you think Andrew should use a bare verb or a verb with an *-s* on the end?

SEVERAL STUDENTS: **A verb with an *-s* on the end!**

How do you know? Which formal pattern are you following?

I'ANA: ***She* plus a verb plus *-s*?**

Yes, the words *my mom* can be replaced with *she*, and our pattern is ***she* plus a verb plus *-s***. Now we want to write an interesting sentence, so we need to add some details about what my mom learns. What should she learn?

SAMUEL: **She can learn how to stand on her head!**

The sentence is *My mom learns how to stand on her head.* Samuel, would you finish the sentence for us?

My mom **learns** how to stand on her head.

Independent Practice

Have the students build their own sentences using the subjects and verbs on the chart.

Your job is to pretend you are talking to your friends and write two sentences. You have to use a different subject and verb for each sentence, and you need to have a detail in your sentence. Your sentence can be formal or informal. Does everyone understand what to do? (The students nod their heads.) Okay, you have five minutes to write your sentences. If you finish before time is up, see if you can write a bonus sentence. You can use any verb you'd like in your bonus sentence. (I walk around the room and help those who have difficulty with the assignment.)

Sharing for Understanding

Have students share their sentences in small groups.

Time's up! I'm going to give you a few minutes to share your favorite sentence with your group. While one person is sharing, it is the responsibility of the rest of the group to decide if the sentence is formal or informal. We'll use the thumbs-up for formal language and thumbs to the side for informal language. Once your group decides if the sentence is formal or informal, you will pick a member of your group to describe the pattern you used. For example, if I were using the sentence we wrote together, I would read *My mom learns how to stand on her head*. Then the group members use thumbs-up or thumbs to the side to show if they thought the sentence was formal or informal. Go ahead and show your thumbs. (The students put their thumbs up to show the sentence is formal.) Finally, I would ask my group, "How does my sentence follow the formal pattern?" (Several hands go up.)

DAWNNELLA: ***She* plus the verb plus *-s*.**

Does everyone agree?

STUDENTS: **Yes!**

And then the next person in the group would share. Does everyone understand what they are going to do?

STUDENTS: **Yes!**

(As students share their knowledge, I sit in on various groups to make sure the assignment is executed correctly.)

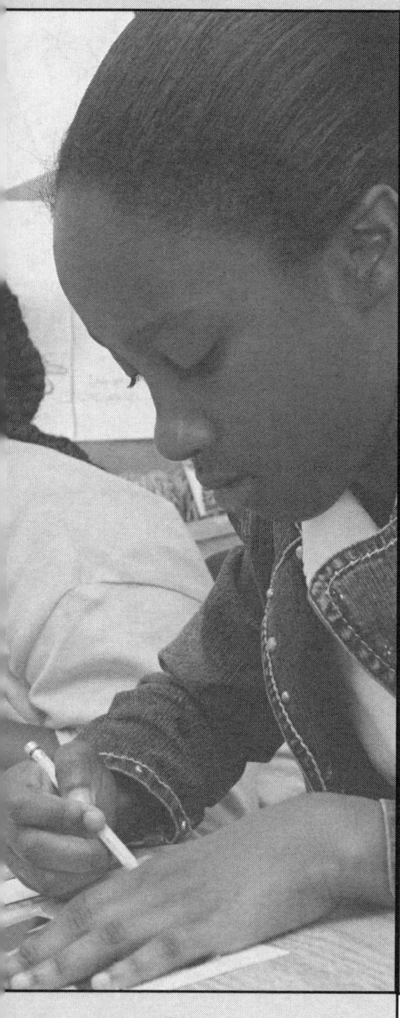

Assessing the Lesson

Throughout the lesson, I make mental notes regarding the students' understanding of the subject–verb agreement pattern. I listen closely to how students respond to their peers' sentences. Are they able to determine whether a sentence contains a formal or informal subject–verb agreement pattern? Are the students able to articulate the specific pattern displayed in a sentence?

During the lesson wrap-up, I check to see if students understood the purpose of the lesson. Acceptable responses include students saying that they learned how to determine how the formal and informal subject–verb agreement patterns are alike and how they're different, how to determine the formality of subject–verb agreement patterns, and how to write formal subject–verb agreement patterns. It would be unacceptable for students to say, for example, that the most important thing they learned about the lesson was that a subject is who or what the sentence is about. Since this was not the focus of the lesson, students should not find it a priority in the lesson.

Classifying Subject–Verb Agreement Patterns

Engagement

Have the students gather around the *Subject-Verb Agreement* chart they helped to complete in the first lesson. Review the terms *subject* and *action verb*.

Yesterday we discovered the formal and informal patterns for subject–verb agreement. Remember that the subject is who or what the sentence is about. Now let's review what makes an action verb. Who can help us out?

TAJANTA: **It shows something that is happening.**

Exactly. It shows an action. It shows something that someone or something does.

Ask students to compare and contrast the formal and informal subject–verb agreement patterns.

Let's take a look at the *Subject-Verb Agreement chart* and the patterns that we wrote down for informal and formal language. How are the patterns alike?

DAWNNELLA: **All of the informal patterns have a bare verb, and some of the formal patterns have a bare verb, too.**

Let's be a little more specific. Which informal and formal patterns are the same? With which subjects do both the informal and formal patterns use a bare verb?

QUINTIN: **With *I* and *you*.**

Any others?

TAJANTA: ***They* and *we*.**

So both the formal and informal patterns are the same for *I, you, they*, and *we* because these subjects all take a bare verb. How are the two patterns different?

QUATASIA: **On the informal side, they all have a bare verb.**

How is that different from the formal side?

QUATASIA: ***He, she*, and *it* take the *-s* on the end of the verb.**

The pattern for *he, she*, and *it* for formal language is ***he/she/it* + verb + *-s***. But in informal language, the verb is bare.

Lesson 2

materials

- *Subject-Verb Agreement* code-switching chart
- chart paper
- markers, pencils, paper

goals

- recognize subject–verb agreement patterns in formal and informal language.
- define subject–verb agreement patterns in formal and informal language.
- distinguish between formal and informal subject–verb agreement patterns.
- practice using the formal pattern on their own.

what if...

a student says that the formal and informal patterns are alike because some of the verbs don't have an *-s* on the end of them?

We make sure to always guide the students to describe patterns according to what they DO have. In this case, we might say, "Let's not talk about what the verbs don't have. Let's just describe the pattern. How did we describe these verbs?" Our students then usually recall the term *bare verbs*.

Direct Instruction

Introduce the purpose for the lesson.

It is very important that you learn how to write sentences using the formal subject–verb agreement pattern. You will need to be able to speak and write formally when you go to get a job or when you go to college. Also, when you're writing a story, you may want to use language to make the characters sound different from each other; some characters speak with formal English and some with informal. Today you are going to practice writing some formal sentences on your own. Yesterday I gave you some choices of subjects and verbs, and you used those to write your sentences. This time I am going to give you a choice of subjects for your sentences, but you will have to come up with your own verbs. Let's look at the subjects.

SUBJECTS

I

he

my mom

the principal

a bear

my friends and I

the three little pigs

the fourth-grade teachers

To write your sentences, you are going to choose a subject and then decide on a verb, or action word, you can use with that subject. The sentences can be fact or fiction. I'm going to tell you my thinking as I write a sentence. First, I need to pick a subject. I'm going to pick *my mom*. Something that my mom likes to do is shop, so I'm going to use *shop* as my verb. I want to make sure I am using the formal pattern, so let's see, what is another way to say *my mom*? Oh, I could say *she*, so I need to use the formal pattern for the subject *she*. That pattern is *she* plus a verb plus *-s*, so let me write this down. (I write "My mom shops" on the chart paper.) I want to make sure to write a good sentence with some juicy details, so I need to give a little more information in my sentence. I'm going to say that she shops for new clothes. So my sentence is *My mom shops for new clothes.*

My mom shops for new clothes.

Let me make sure I followed the formal pattern. My subject was *she* (I point to *My mom*) and I have a verb with an *-s* on the end (I point to *shops*), so I followed the pattern.

Remember, just like yesterday you'll have only one verb in your sentence and be sure you're talking about the present time. Choose a simple, familiar verb, but not *have* or *be*.

Guided Practice

Guide the students through writing a sentence or two together.

Now that you've had a chance to see how I write a sentence, let's try a couple together. Let's start by choosing a subject. (Several students suggest subjects.) Doris, which subject do you think we should use?

DORIS: **I want to do the fourth-grade teachers.**

Okay, Doris, go ahead and write "the fourth-grade teachers" on the chart paper. (As Doris writes the subject on the chart paper, I address the rest of the class.) Tell me something about the fourth-grade teachers. Make sure you use an action verb. Quintin?

QUINTIN: **Umm, they drive.**

Which form of the verb are we going to use? Are we going to use *drive* or *drives*?

SEVERAL STUDENTS: **Drive!**

Let's do thumbs-up if you think we should use *drive* and thumbs to the side if you think we should use *drives*. (I take a quick informal assessment of my students' understanding of the pattern. I then choose a student to explain his/her thinking.) Ontiana, why do you think we should use *drive*?

ONTIANA: **Because it says "fourth-grade teachers," and that is almost like *they*.**

You're right. *They* can take the place of *the fourth-grade teachers*, so which pattern are we following?

ONTIANA: ***They* plus bare verb.**

Exactly. Quintin, would you please add *drive* to our sentence. (Quintin adds *drive*.) *The fourth-grade teachers drive*. Now we need to add a detail. What can we add to this sentence?

I'ANA: **We can say they drive to school every day.**

The fourth-grade teachers drive to school every day. Excellent sentence! I'ana, go ahead and finish our sentence for us. (I'ana takes the marker and writes "to school every day" at the end of the sentence. The students help in writing another sentence before moving to the independent practice portion of the lesson.)

what if...

the students choose a verb such as *teach* or *cry*, in which the third-person singular requires more than just the addition of an *-s*?

If the majority of the students are unaware that an *-es* must be added to some verbs and for others the y must be changed to an *-i* before adding *-es*, you may need to teach an additional lesson to address these types of verbs. However, for the purpose of this lesson, simply explain how to change the verb they are using. For example, suppose a student is using the verb *teach* in a sentence, and writes *teachs*. You might say, "You have a great sentence here, but *teaches* is spelled with an *-es* on the end, not just an *-s*. There are actually several verbs that are spelled with an *-es*. We haven't talked about those types of verbs yet, so you'll be ahead of the class when we do!"

Independent Practice

Explain the guidelines for writing sentences independently.

You did an awesome job writing these two sentences! Now it's time for you to write your own sentences. You are going to write six sentences on your own. You can choose any of the subjects on the board, but you can only use them in one sentence. If you use *Bobby* in your first sentence, you can't use *Bobby* as the subject in any of the other sentences. You must choose from the subjects on the board for your first five sentences, but for the last sentence, you may either choose one of the subjects on the board or write your own subject. Make sure you are following the formal subject–verb agreement pattern. Any questions? Okay, let's write some really juicy sentences! (The students return to their seats and begin writing their sentences. I walk around and help students on an individual basis.)

Share student success stories as they occur.

I see some great formal sentences as I'm walking around. Tyreek used the formal pattern in his sentence *A bear sleeps in a cave.* Dawnnella remembered to use the formal pattern and wrote *The principal wears silver glasses when she reads.* (I share several sentences in this way.)

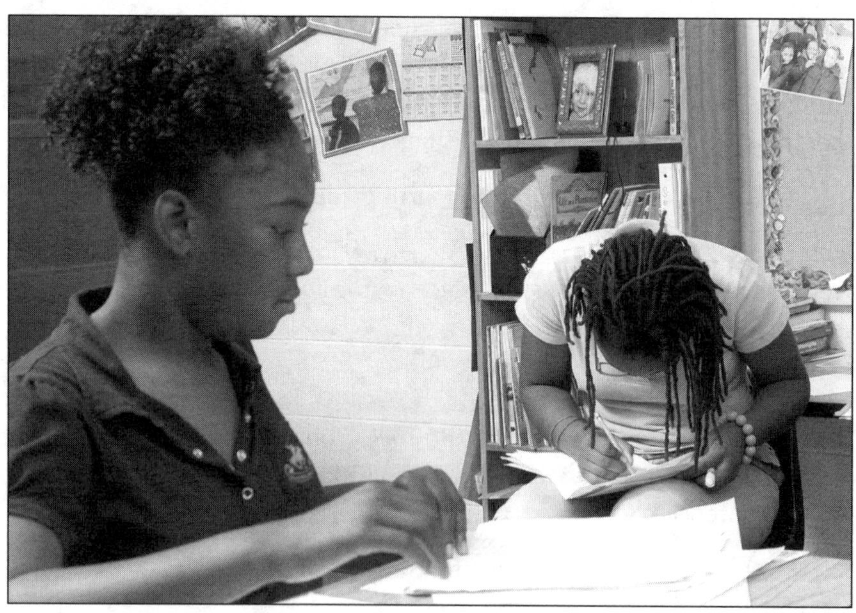

Sharing for Understanding

Allow students to share their favorite sentences with the class.

There were so many great sentences that this next part might be hard to do! I want you to choose one sentence to share with the class. Once you've selected a sentence, put your eyes on me so that I know you're ready to share. As you listen to your classmates' sentences, your job will be to decide if the sentence is formal. If you agree that the sentence is formal, give the thumbs-up sign. If you disagree and think the sentence is informal, give a thumbs to the side. Destiny, you can share first.

DESTINY: **I wrote *My brother gets on my nerves!***

Thumbs-up or thumbs to the side? Samuel, what made you agree that the sentence was formal? What pattern did she follow?

SAMUEL: **Her *brother* is the same as *he*, and she has a verb with an *-s* on the end.**

Nice job! Garrett, let's hear your sentence. (Time permitting, I allow each student to share his/her sentence in this manner. If we run out of time, the students who did not share take their turns during writing time the next day.)

Conclude the lesson with a quick wrap-up.

Wow, we heard some really terrific sentences today. I want you to think about today's lesson. We compared and contrasted the formal and informal subject–verb agreement patterns, we wrote sentences using the formal subject–verb agreement, and we shared some of those sentences with the class. What do you think was the most important thing we did today, and why was it important?

ANDREW: **We wrote formal sentences.**

It is important to be able to write formal sentences. Why is it important?

I'ANA: **So we can get good grades.**

GARRETT: **We need it for when we hang our work in the hallway.**

BOBBY: **And when our parents come to see what we did.**

Sure, knowing how to use formal language can help you get good grades. It's also important to use formal language when we publish our work for other students, other teachers, and our families to see. Those are excellent reasons.

what if...

you have a student who writes something like "She will walks to school tomorrow"?

Focus on the student's ability to follow the pattern of subject + verb + *-s*. The example sentence does not follow our pattern. Help the student to follow the pattern and change the sentence to "She walks to school." Let your student know that the subject–verb agreement pattern you're exploring happens only when there's one verb in the sentence, not when there's a helping verb.

Assessing the Lesson

During the Sharing for Understanding portion of the lesson, I do some informal assessing of both the students sharing and the students evaluating the sentences. I specifically note which students are able to quickly determine the formality of a sentence and which students seem a little unsure. I always collect the work the students complete and use it to evaluate the students' abilities to write sentences using the formal subject–verb agreement pattern. Although I notice punctuation and capitalization, I'm specifically looking for their ability to follow the formal patterns. I also make a note, on the paper, if the student used an informal pattern that we have already discussed. For example, if the student includes an informal plural in the sentence, I write a note for the student to use formal plurals. I also make notes if a student uses a formal pattern that we have already practiced. I might simply write, "formal plural pattern!" on the paper. When I have students who struggle with the concept, I work with them one-on-one or in a small-group setting. During this time, the students receive guided practice on writing sentences using the formal subject–verb agreement pattern.

Practicing Subject–Verb Agreement Patterns

Engagement

Display the *Subject-Verb Agreement* code-switching chart you created in Lesson 1 along with a piece of flip-chart paper containing a couple of subjects and a verb. Review when *-s* should be added in the formal pattern.

We have been working on writing sentences using the formal subject–verb agreement patterns. Let's take a minute to review how we use these formal patterns. I have two subjects on the chart paper along with the verb *dance*.

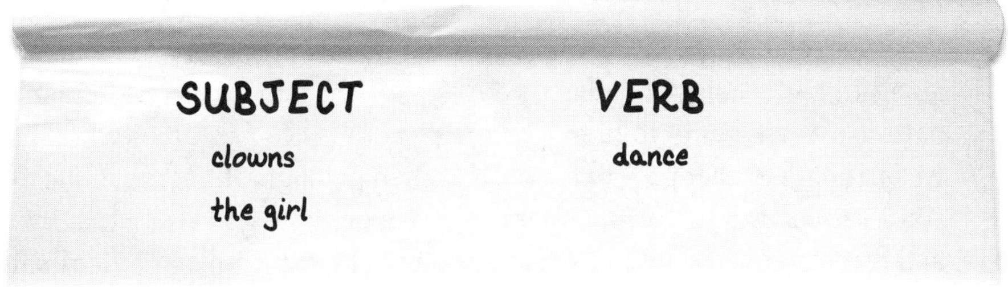

I'm just going to call on a few people to share a sentence using these subjects and the verb *dance*. You'll need to decide if you need to add an *-s* to the end of *dance* to make it formal in your sentence. Let's start by using *clowns* as our subject. Who has a sentence using *clowns* and *dance*?

NIJE: **Clowns dance at the circus.**

Clowns dance at the circus – thumbs-up if this sentence is formal, and thumbs to the side if it is informal. Good, it is formal. Here's a trickier question: How do you know it's formal? What pattern did Nije follow?

DORIS: ***They* plus a bare verb.**

Which other subjects use a bare verb for formal language?

QUINTIN: ***I* and *we* and *you*.**

Yes, *I, we, you*, and *they* all take a bare verb when we use formal language. Let's try creating a formal sentence using *the girl* with *dance*.

ONTIANA: **The girl dances to the music.**

Thumbs-up if this sentence is formal, and thumbs to the side if it is informal. It is formal. Which pattern did Ontiana follow?

DESTINY: ***She* plus a verb plus an *-s*.**

The girl is a *she*, so you're right. What other subjects follow the pattern of verb plus *-s*?

HEZEKIAH: ***He* and *it*.**

Yes, *he, she*, and *it* all follow the same pattern.

Lesson 3

materials

- *Subject–Verb Agreement* code-switching chart
- chart paper with "My Dad" paragraph written on it
- chart paper with a writing sample for subject–verb agreement editing practice (one for each small group)
- markers, highlighters

goals

- recognize subject–verb agreement patterns in formal and informal language.
- define subject–verb agreement patterns in formal and informal language.
- distinguish between formal and informal subject–verb agreement patterns.
- practice using the formal subject–verb agreement patterns.
- edit a paragraph, changing informal subject–verb agreement patterns to formal patterns.

Direct Instruction

Set the purpose of the lesson.

We've been writing sentences using the formal subject–verb agreement pattern, and now we're going to edit for the formal subject–verb agreement pattern. Since most of your school writing is formal, this will be an important part of your editing process.

Show the paragraph "My Dad" written on chart paper. Model the process of editing a paragraph for subject–verb agreement.

I have a paragraph written by a student a few years ago. Let's read the paragraph together; then we can make sure all of the subject–verb agreement patterns are formal. (We read the paragraph together.)

When we edit, we want to make sure we have a purpose. As we edit, we are going to be looking for subject–verb agreement patterns. If we find a formal pattern, we are going to highlight the pattern. If we find an informal pattern, we are going to change it to formal and then highlight it. Let me model this for you. I've already read the paragraph; now I'm going to go back to the beginning and read carefully. My purpose is to find the subject–verb agreement patterns.

My Dad

My dad work at the shipyard. He help other men and women fix ships that are broken. Sometimes he paint old ships so that they look new. Many of my dad's friends work at the shipyard. His friend Dan use a computer for his job. He order parts for the ship and other people fix them. My dad's friend Bill work at the shipyard too. I think he work on the ships like my dad. My dad and his friends work hard everyday.

note

A customizable version of the paragraph "My Dad" is available on the CD-ROM.

My dad work at the shipyard. Hmm, it starts out *My dad work. My dad* is the subject. That's the same as *he*, and *work* is the verb, so substituting in a pronoun gives *He work*. I know that the formal pattern is ***he* + verb + *-s***, so this sentence is informal. I need to change it to formal by adding an *-s* to the end of *work*. (I add the *-s* to *work* on the chart.) Now I have *My dad works at the shipyard,* and that fits our formal pattern, so I can highlight *My dad works*. Do you see how I looked for a subject and verb pattern first and then I decided if it was formal or informal? Once I decided that it was informal, I changed the pattern to formal. Finally, I highlighted the formal pattern. Are there any questions about how the editing process works?

Guided Practice

Guide students through the process of editing the rest of the paragraph.

Let's finish editing this paragraph together. Remember that we set a purpose for editing, and that purpose is to make sure that all subject–verb agreement patterns are formal. Let's read the next sentence together: "He help other men and women fix ships that are broken." Do we have any subject–verb agreement patterns in this sentence?

SAMUEL: **It should be *he helps*.**

Let's focus on the pattern. Is *He help* formal or informal? Thumbs-up for formal, thumbs to the side for informal.

SAMUEL: **Informal.**

So what do we need to do to make it formal?

SAMUEL: **Make it *helps*.**

So we're going to add an *-s* to help to make it formal. Now we have *He helps*. Thumbs-up if that's formal, and thumbs to the side if it's informal. Okay, Samuel, go ahead and change it to formal on the chart. (Samuel adds the *-s* to *help*.) And now that it's formal, you can go ahead and highlight it. (Samuel highlights *He helps*.) Are there any other subject–verb agreement patterns in the sentence *He helps other men and women fix ships that are broken?*

TYREEK: **Men and women fix.**

Thumbs-up if it's formal, and thumbs to the side if it's informal. Garrett?

GARRETT: **It's already formal. Can I highlight it?**

Yes, since it is already formal, all we have to do is highlight it. (Garrett highlights the pattern. We continue to edit the remainder of the paragraph together.)

what if...

a student says what the verb "should be" or that the verb is missing an ending?

Just redirect the student's attention back to what they actually see inside the sentence. We're trying to *describe* the language that's there.

tip

Build on students' answers to anchor in and restate the grammar patterns they've discovered. This helps solidify their learning.

Independent Practice

Break students into groups of three. Give each group a piece of chart paper with a practice writing sample.

I have several different pieces of writing from different students in our class. I wrote portions, or parts, of some of your writing on chart paper. To help us focus on the subject–verb agreement patterns, I did change other informal patterns in your papers to make them formal. Today we are going to practice peer editing this writing in small groups. You will work in groups of three, and each group will have a different piece of writing to edit. I'll give one person in the group a marker; the person with the marker is responsible for making the editing changes on the paragraph. I will give another group member a highlighter. Your job, if you get the highlighter, is to highlight the formal subject–verb agreement patterns. The last member of the group is the pattern checker. Your job is to check the chart and make sure each subject–verb pattern is formal. (I hand out the markers, the highlighters, and the paragraphs written on chart paper.) Are there any questions about what you are going to do?

Allow groups time to complete editing their writing samples for subject–verb agreement.

(I walk around helping the groups as they edit the work. As the students finish, I hang the chart papers on the wall.)

Sharing for Understanding

Have students share their thoughts about the ways the assignment was easy and the ways it was difficult.

As you finished editing, I hung the papers on the wall to show the editing. Let's take a few minutes to discuss how you felt about this assignment. In what ways was this assignment easy?

DAR'ASIA: **It was easy to me because everybody had a job, and we worked together.**

Did anyone else find it easier to work as a team? (Several hands go up.) Does anyone have something else they found easy about the assignment? (A few students share their thoughts.) What did you find difficult about the assignment?

DAWNNELLA: **It was hard to find all the patterns.**

You really had to read carefully, didn't you? Any other difficulties with the assignment? (I allow several students to share.)

Let's reflect on what we did today. How will what we did today help you with your writing in the future?

> TYREEK: **We can edit the subject–verb agreement pattern so we have formal patterns.**

You thought today's lesson was helpful because you were able to edit a paper and use the formal subject–verb agreement pattern. Who else found that helpful? (Several students raise their hands.) Did anyone have a different response? (Several students share their reactions to the assignment.)

Assessing the Lesson

The success of this lesson is best determined during the Sharing for Understanding time. The difficulties students had with the lesson help to guide the next lesson. For example, if the majority of the class found it difficult to locate the subject–verb agreement patterns, I will spend more time focusing on the Guided Practice portion of the next lesson. If only a few students found the editing difficult, I will pull a small group during the Independent Practice portion of the next lesson.

Lesson 4

Editing for Formal Subject–Verb Agreement Patterns

Engagement

Have the students gather around the *Subject–Verb Agreement* code-switching chart. Review the informal and formal subject–verb agreement patterns.

We have now spent several days working with the subject–verb agreement patterns. We are working toward our goal of being able to use formal language when we speak and write for formal occasions. So let's take a minute to review the formal and informal subject–verb agreement patterns. Using *he* as the subject, who thinks they have an example of a sentence with an informal subject–verb pattern?

GARRETT: **He ride his bike.**

How does *He ride his bike* follow the informal subject–verb agreement pattern?

QUATASIA: **Any subject plus a bare verb.**

That's exactly right! Let's change Garrett's sentence to make the subject–verb agreement pattern formal. Ontiana?

ONTIANA: **He rides his bike.**

How does *He rides his bike* follow the formal subject–verb agreement pattern?

NIJE: ***He* plus a verb plus *-s*.**

What other subjects follow the formal pattern of verb plus *-s*?

I'ANA: ***He, she,* and *it*.**

The formal pattern is *he, she*, or *it* plus a verb plus *-s*.

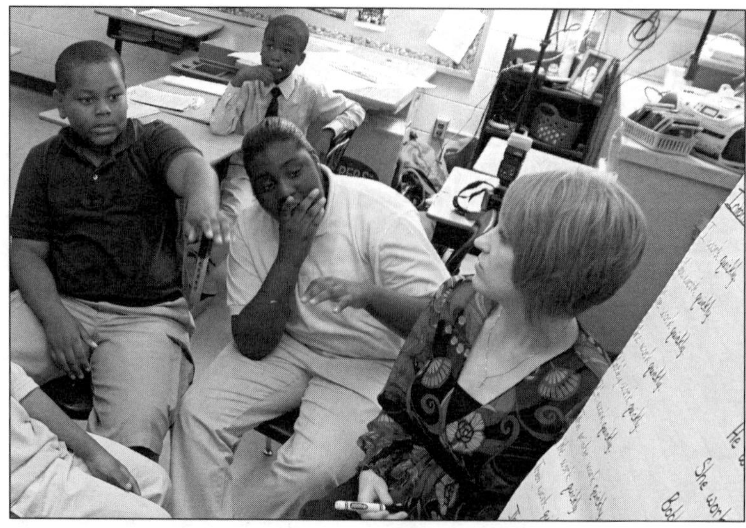

materials

- *Subject–Verb Agreement* code-switching chart
- chart paper with "The Zoo" writing sample
- current or previous formal writing assignments
- chart paper
- markers, pencils, highlighters

goals

- recognize subject–verb agreement patterns in formal and informal language.
- define subject–verb agreement patterns in formal and informal language.
- edit their own work to include formal subject–verb agreement patterns.

Direct Instruction

Explain the purpose of the lesson. Show students the chart paper with "The Zoo" sample paragraph to be edited.

We have spent time working in groups to edit for the formal subject–verb agreement pattern. Today you are going to use the piece of writing you've been working on, and you are going to edit your own writing. Before you begin editing your own writing, we are going to edit a paragraph written by a student last year. Let's read through the paragraph together. (We read through the paragraph.)

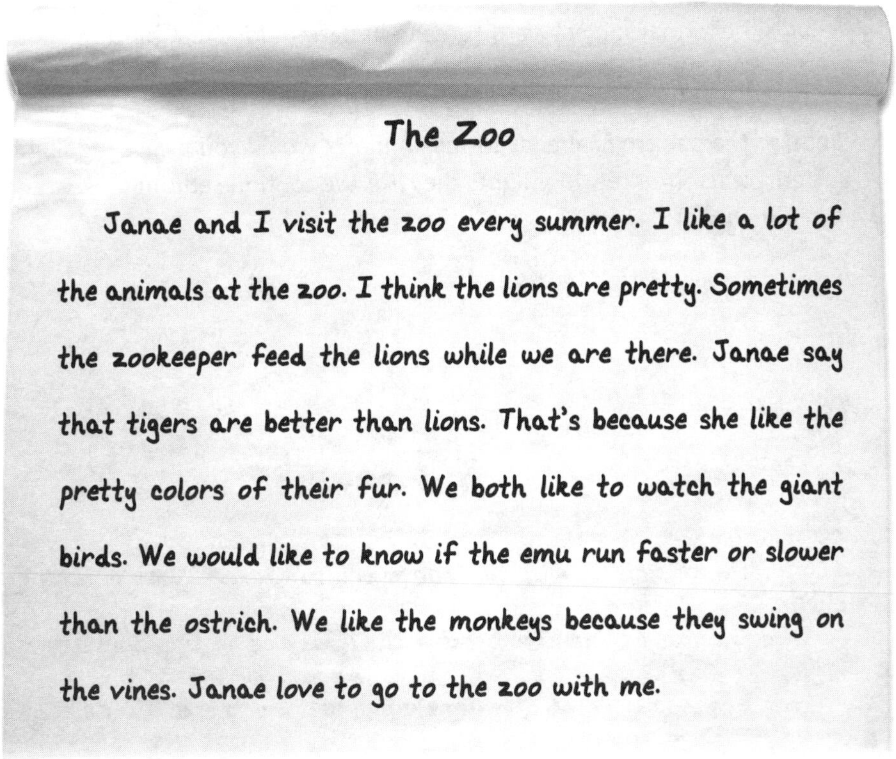

The Zoo

Janae and I visit the zoo every summer. I like a lot of the animals at the zoo. I think the lions are pretty. Sometimes the zookeeper feed the lions while we are there. Janae say that tigers are better than lions. That's because she like the pretty colors of their fur. We both like to watch the giant birds. We would like to know if the emu run faster or slower than the ostrich. We like the monkeys because they swing on the vines. Janae love to go to the zoo with me.

note

A customizable version of the paragraph "The Zoo" is available on the CD-ROM.

Review the process of editing for subject–verb agreement.

As we edit the paragraph, we are going to read each sentence carefully so we can look for the subject–verb agreement pattern. If we find a formal subject–verb agreement pattern, we are going to highlight it. If we find an informal subject–verb agreement pattern, we are going to change it to the formal pattern; then we are going to highlight it. Let's look at the first sentence: *Janae and I visit the zoo every summer.* The subject in this sentence is *Janae and I.* I know that I can use *we* to replace *Janae and I.* The formal pattern for *we* is *we* plus a bare verb. Since *visit* is already a bare verb, *Janae and I visit* follows the formal subject–verb agreement pattern, so all I have to do is highlight the pattern. (I highlight *Janae and I visit.*) Let's finish editing this paragraph together.

Guided Practice

Finish editing the sample paragraph as a group.

I like a lot of the animals at the zoo. Do we have a subject–verb agreement pattern in this sentence?

> **ANDREW: I like.**

What is the subject?

> **ANDREW: I.**

What is the formal subject–verb agreement pattern for the subject *I*?

> **ANDREW: *I* plus the bare verb.**

Right, so the pattern is already formal. Andrew, would you please highlight the pattern for us? (Andrew highlights the *I like*. We continue editing the paragraph in this manner.)

The Zoo

Janae and I visit the zoo every summer. I like a lot of the animals at the zoo. I think the lions are pretty. Sometimes the zookeeper feedS the lions while we are there. Janae sayS that tigers are better than lions. That's because she likeS the pretty colors of their fur. We both like to watch the giant birds. We would like to know if the emu runS faster or slower than the ostrich. We like the monkeys because they swing on the vines. Janae loveS to go to the zoo with me.

Independent Practice

Have the students retrieve a current draft of their writing in progress. Remind them of the steps to edit for subject–verb agreement. Allow students to work individually editing their own writing.

Now you are going to edit the piece of writing you have been working on for the past several days. You are going to use the same process we used while editing "The Zoo" paragraph. Read through your work carefully. When you find a subject–verb agreement pattern, decide if it is formal or informal. If you used the formal pattern, simply highlight it. If you find an informal subject–verb agreement pattern, change the pattern to formal and then highlight it. (I give the students approximately ten minutes to edit their work. During this time, I walk around the room, helping students on an individual basis.)

Sharing for Understanding

Have the students gather in a circle on the carpet to share some examples of subject–verb agreement patterns they found in their writing.

I saw a lot of highlighting as you edited your work today. Now it's time for you to share some of the patterns you found. Choose one pattern you highlighted to share with the class. Since we have just finished editing, all of the patterns we share should be formal. If you would rather not share with the class, simply say "Pass." Okay, Bobby, would you like to get us started?

BOBBY: **I picked *My mom works at Walmart.***

Which part did you highlight?

BOBBY: ***My mom works.***

How does *My mom works* fit the formal subject–verb agreement pattern?

DORIS: ***She* plus a verb with an *-s* on the end.**

Excellent. I'ana, what is your sentence? (I continue around the circle until everyone has had a turn or until we run out of time. I occasionally ask students how a sentence fits the formal pattern.)

Let's take a moment to reflect on what we learned today. How do you think what you did today will help you with your writing?

HEZEKIAH: **We can make sure we have formal patterns when we edit.**

You're absolutely right. That is certainly useful practice for when you edit your work.

ONTIANA: **Now we already edited for the formal subject–verb agreement pattern on this. (She holds up her writing.)**

Yes, now we've already edited the piece you've been working on – at least for the formal subject–verb agreement patterns!

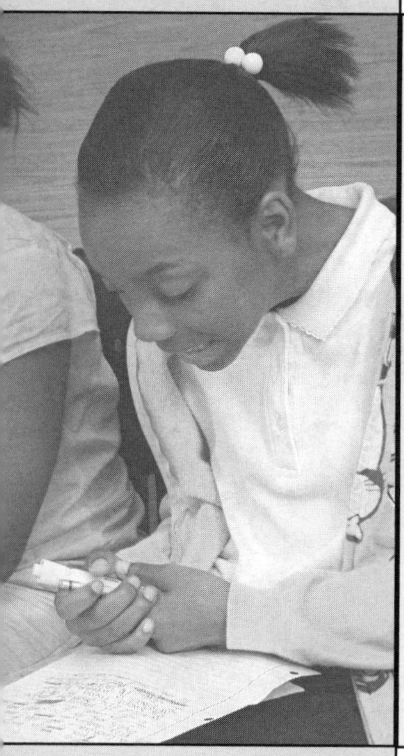

Assessing the Lesson

As students edit their own work, I keep in mind that they are still practicing using the formal pattern. Therefore, it is not unusual to see some students leaving informal patterns in their work. When this happens, I simply help them edit their work one sentence at a time. By focusing their attention on a small portion of the writing, the students are less likely to be distracted or overwhelmed by the length of the paper they are reading. To assess the success of this lesson, I listen to the student responses as to how the lesson was helpful to them. Students should be able to articulate the purpose of the lesson, which is to edit their own writing to make sure it includes the formal subject–verb agreement pattern.

7

Was/Were

Lessons

THIS UNIT INCLUDES THE FOLLOWING LESSONS:

1. Defining Informal and Formal *Was/Were* Patterns
2. Classifying *Was/Were* Patterns
3. Practicing Formal *Was/Were* Patterns
4. Editing for Formal *Was/Were* Patterns

This unit addresses the vernacular use of *was/were*, both as auxiliary and as main verb in examples such as *We was going to the store, You was doing good,* or *They was the best ever.*

While this unit explores the past tense patterns of the verb *be*, we can't just call the unit "past time." For one thing, we already have a unit of that name. The unit on "Showing Past Time" explores the past of regular verbs, that is, verbs that take *-ed* to form the past in Standard English (*walk, talk, bake, look*, etc.). Though *was/were* is past tense, it is past tense of a highly irregular verb – *be* – and it follows a different pattern. The verb *be* doesn't use *-ed* to signal past time. Because each code-switching unit explores a particular pattern, we need to address the particularities of *be* in past tense separately. Similarly, the present tense of *be* has its own patterns (*am/is/are)*, so we'll be looking at those in the next unit.

Was/Were

The Pattern

We frequently find that our students follow the vernacular pattern for showing past time: *We was going to the store, You was doing good, We was doing good,* or *They was the best ever.* We also want students to have command of the Standard English equivalents: *We were going to the store, You were doing good, We were doing good,* or *They were the best ever.* Of course it's more complex than telling students "not to use *was*" because sometimes Standard English *does* use the word *was*: *I was happy,* or *I was going.* Instead, we'll have to draw the distinction a bit more finely.
Here are the patterns for informal and formal English:

Vernacular pattern:
any subject + *was*

Standard English pattern:
I, he/she/it* subjects + *was
other subjects + *were*

The Code-Switching Chart

Identifying vernacular *was/were* patterns in kids' work

Identifying vernacular instances of *was/were* in students' work is straightforward – we simply attend to any instance where students use the verb *was* in cases where Standard English would use the form *were.*

This student has used the informal pattern for subject–verb agreement: **any subject plus *was*.**

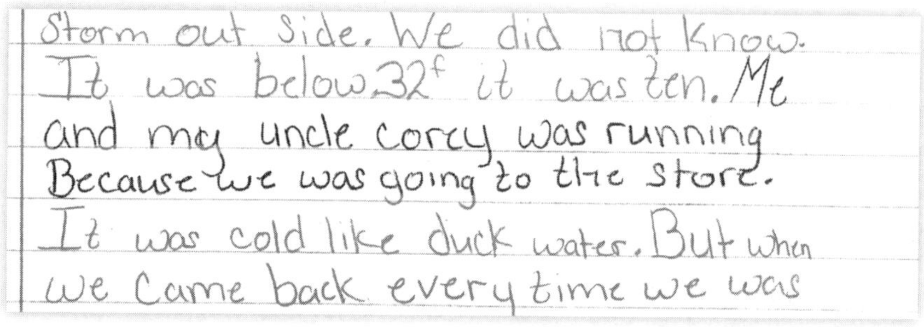
Storm out Side. We did not Know.
It was below 32^f it was ten. Me
and my uncle corey was running
Because we was going to the store.
It was cold like duck water. But when
we Came back every time we was

Me and my uncle Corey was running because we was going to the store.

Choosing/creating the examples

In choosing examples for verb charts, we'll always use more sentences than the noun-based code-switching charts. We're on the lookout for examples from each of the persons and numbers of subjects – *I, you, he/she/it, we, you, they* – so students will look for the relationships between all the different possible subjects and their corresponding verbs.

Unlike listing subject–verb agreement or showing past time, collecting examples for the *was/were* pattern is easy. All we do is look for sentences following the vernacular pattern (any subject plus *was*). We choose examples showing *was* both as an auxiliary and as a main verb.

Creating the code-switching chart

We title our chart "Was/Were Patterns" because "Subject–Verb Agreement and "Past Time" have already been used. As always, we list informal sentences from student writing on the left, writing their formal translations next to them on the right.

We order the sentences by person and number of subject (*I, he/she/it, we, you, they*) in order to provide a consistent structure for student learning. To help our students see the pattern more easily, we simplify the chart visually. Since any instance of *you* (singular or plural) takes *were*, the form that goes with plural subjects, we omit sentences for singular *you*. That helps our students see the verb groupings inside formal English. All instances of *was* occur in the top half of the chart, and all instances of *were* occur in the bottom half of the chart. The trick here is that both forms of *you* (singular and plural) take *were.*

We continue to underline the subject and verb in order to focus the students' attention on the relevant portion of the sentences. Finally, we write *The Pattern* under each column of the chart, leaving space to write the pattern during the lesson.
Now we're ready for the lesson!

WAS/WERE PATTERNS

INFORMAL	**FORMAL**
I was working.	I was working.
The clock was working.	The clock was working.
She was working.	She was working.
My Dad was working.	My Dad was working.
We was working.	We were working.
You was working.	You were working.
They was working.	They were working.
THE PATTERN	**THE PATTERN**
any subject + *was*	***I, he/she/it* subject + *was*** **any other subject + *were***

Lesson 1

Defining Informal and Formal *Was/Were* Patterns

Engagement

▶ **Have the students gather around the easel. Review the terms *subject* and *verb*. As a group, identify the subject and verb in some sample sentences.**

We have just finished discussing how to show subject–verb agreement in formal and informal language. Who would like to explain what I mean when I talk about the subject of a sentence?

TEHJIA: **It's the person or the thing that the sentence talks about.**

The subject refers to who or what the sentence is about, exactly.

I have three sentences written down (I reveal some sample sentences):

The children walked to the bus stop.
The hallway is very crowded.
Mom and I painted my room last week.

Let's see who can rise to the challenge here. Read the sentences to yourself. Don't say anything yet! How many of you think you can find the subject in all three sentences? (Most of the students raise their hands.) As I call on someone to identify the subject in each sentence, give a thumbs-up or thumbs-down to show if you agree or disagree. Hezekiah, what's the subject in the first sentence?

HEZEKIAH: ***The children.***

Thumbs-up or thumbs-down? Yes, Hezekiah is correct. Let's look at the next sentence. (We go through each sentence in the same manner.)

Direct Instruction

▶ **Introduce the topic for today's lesson.**

I'm so glad that everyone was able to find the subjects in each sentence because today we are going to use our understanding of sentence subjects to define patterns for when to use the words *was* and *were*. We're going to look at how *was* and *were* are used with different subjects.

materials

- chart paper with sample sentences for reviewing subject–verb agreement
- *Was/Were Patterns* code-switching chart
- flip-chart paper
- three sentence strips for each small group
- markers, pencils, paper

goals

STUDENTS WILL:

- recognize *was/were* patterns inside formal and informal language.
- define *was/were* patterns inside formal and informal language.
- distinguish between formal and informal *was/were* patterns.

Show the students the *Was/Were Patterns* code-switching chart. Ask them to study the chart and look for patterns.

I have a chart with some sentences from your writing to help us focus on the patterns. Let's take a look at the chart. (I reveal the chart.)

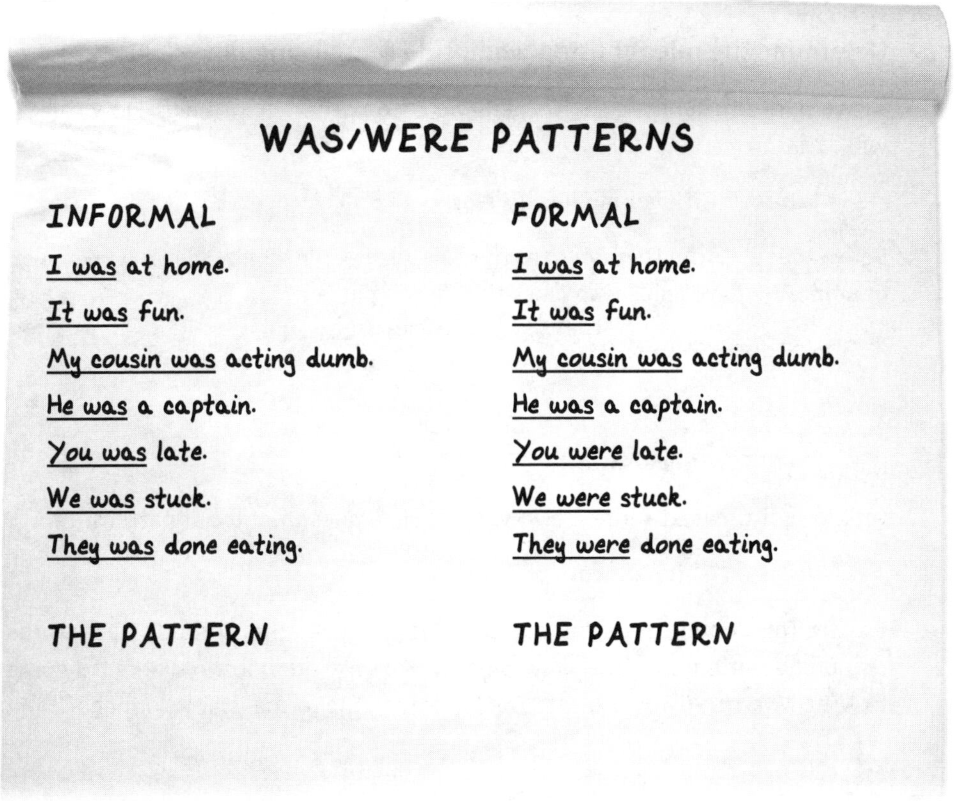

WAS/WERE PATTERNS

INFORMAL	FORMAL
I was at home.	I was at home.
It was fun.	It was fun.
My cousin was acting dumb.	My cousin was acting dumb.
He was a captain.	He was a captain.
You was late.	You were late.
We was stuck.	We were stuck.
They was done eating.	They were done eating.
THE PATTERN	THE PATTERN

Take a minute to look at the chart and read through the sentences. See if you can find the differences between the informal pattern and the formal pattern. Don't give away your answers! Just look quietly for a few minutes.

Identify the differences between the formal and informal patterns.

What do you notice? Does anyone have any observations about the patterns? (Several hands shoot up.)

TYREEK: **The formal side has *was* and *were*, and the informal side only has *was*.**

Okay, let's start with the formal side. Which subjects are used with *was*?

ONTIANA: ***I, it, my cousin*, and *he*.**

Who can think of a word that we can use to take the place of *my cousin*? What is another word we can use instead of *my cousin*?

QUINTIN: ***He*?**

ways of talking

Note that the teacher's questions are less specific and leading than in previous lessons. The students are prompted only to look for patterns rather than being led to notice specific patterns. In this way, we begin to give students more responsibility in recognizing and describing formal and informal patterns in language.

You got it! We can say *He was acting dumb* instead of *My cousin was acting dumb.* What if the cousin is a girl? What word could we use to take the place of *my cousin* if the cousin is a girl?

TEHJIA: **She.**

We could say *She was acting dumb.*

Determine the rule for using *was* inside formal language.

So we have the subjects *I, it, she*, and *he* used with the word *was*. How can we write that?

I'ANA: ***I, it, she*, and *he* plus *was*.**

Before we can write that down as our rule, we need to check that it works. *I was at home.* We have *I* plus *was*. Does that fit the pattern?

STUDENTS: **Yes!**

How?

ANDREW: ***I* plus *was*.**

Let's look at the next sentence: *It was fun.* How does that fit our pattern?

GARRETT: ***It* plus *was*.**

Exactly. This sentence fits the pattern of *it* plus *was*. (I go through each of the remaining sentences in this way.) Since it looks like our pattern works, I'm going to write ***I/he/she/it* + was** under *The Pattern* on the formal side of our chart.

Guided Practice

Allow students to take on the role of teacher to determine the rule for using *were* inside formal language.

Now that we've described the pattern for using *was*, we need to write a rule for describing the pattern using *were*. This time I'm going to ask some of you to take on the teacher role. Let's take a look at which subjects are paired with *were*. Who thinks they have a rule to describe which subjects go with *were*?

QUINTIN: ***You, we*, and *they* plus *were*.**

Who would like to take the teacher role and lead us through checking this pattern? Samuel?

SAMUEL: ***You were late*. How does that fit the pattern?**

TEHJIA: ***You* plus *were*.**

ways of talking

Note that the students have been given the responsibility of describing the pattern. In previous lessons, the teacher paraphrased student responses to create a rule. Now the students are prompted to determine the rule in their own language.

SAMUEL: **Yep. The next sentence with *were* is *We were stuck.* Does that fit the pattern?**

STUDENTS: **Yes.**

(Samuel leads the students through the remaining sentence.) It looks like our pattern works. Samuel, would you please write the pattern for using *were* under the formal side of our chart? (Samuel writes ***you/we/they + were*** on the chart.)

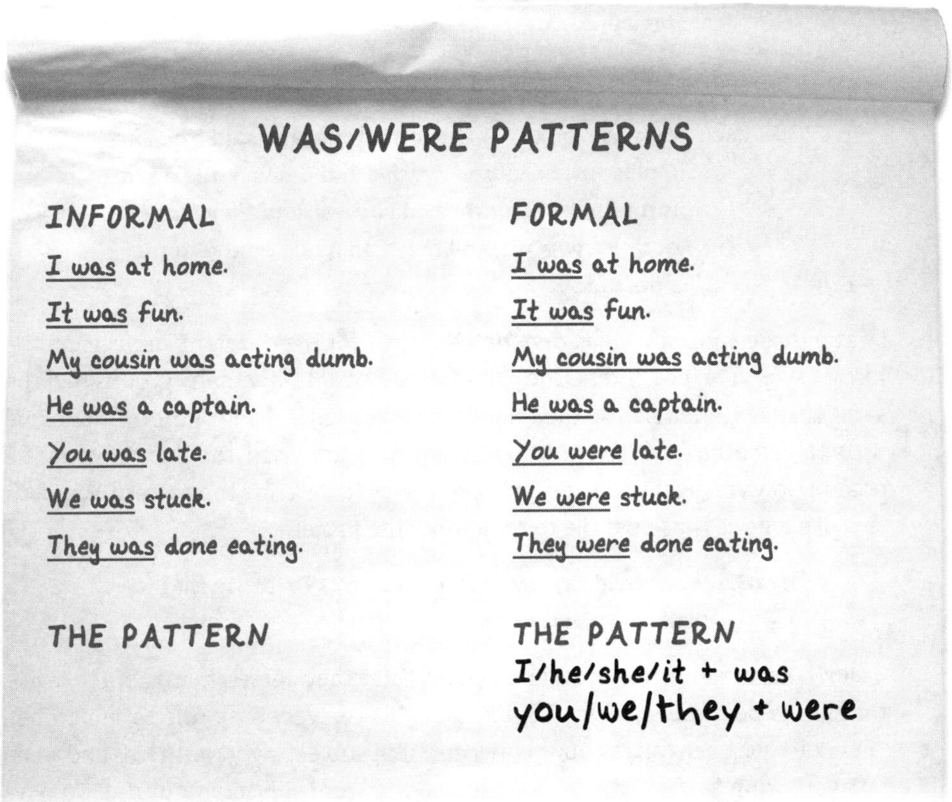

WAS/WERE PATTERNS

INFORMAL	FORMAL
I was at home.	I was at home.
It was fun.	It was fun.
My cousin was acting dumb.	My cousin was acting dumb.
He was a captain.	He was a captain.
You was late.	You were late.
We was stuck.	We were stuck.
They was done eating.	They were done eating.
THE PATTERN	THE PATTERN I/he/she/it + was you/we/they + were

Independent Practice

Have the students work in groups to determine the informal *was/were* rule(s).

So we have two patterns for the formal *was/were*, and now we're going to take a look at the informal side. You are going to work with your group to decide how to describe the pattern. Then I want you to check your pattern, just like we did with the formal side of our chart. If your pattern works, go ahead and write it on your sentence strip. I am giving each group three sentence strips in case you have more than one pattern. Does everyone understand what to do? (The students nod.) Okay, you may go back to your groups and get started! (I circulate around the room to facilitate discussions and prompt group members who are having difficulty getting started.)

what if...

your students describe the pattern as "everything else plus *were*"?

It is perfectly acceptable and accurate to describe the pattern in this way. If students determine that the pattern is "everything else plus *were*," they will need to check each sentence that contains *were* to make sure the subject is something other than *I, he, she,* or *it.* The pattern can then be written as "all other subjects plus *were*."

Sharing for Understanding

▶ **Have the students gather around the partially completed *Was/Were Patterns* chart with their sentence strips.**

Let's look at how you described the informal *was/were* patterns in your groups. Who would like to go first? Ontiana, what did your group decide?

> ONTIANA: **We had two rules. *I, he, she, it* plus *was* and *you, we, they* plus *was*.**

How did your group decide on these two rules? Andrew?

> ANDREW: **First, we looked at the formal side and said *I, he, she, it* plus *was* because *I, he, she,* and *it* had a rule on the formal side. Then we said *you, we,* and *they* plus *was* because *you, we,* and *they* had a rule on the formal side, too.**

So you made sure your rules matched the rules for the different subjects on the formal side. Very nice. (I tape the rules to the board.) How many groups had the same rules? (Students raise their hands in response.) Did any of the groups come up with something different? (All different rules are discussed and hung on the board.) Now we need to decide on the best way to describe the pattern. We want to make it as easy as possible to remember the pattern.

> DORIS: **We should say "everything plus *was*" because that is really easy to remember.**

(I allow the students to discuss this option. Once they agree, I help them to revise the rule to be more specific.) I agree that this is a very easy rule to remember. Since we have been talking about how different subjects work with *was* and *were*, I was thinking that maybe we should use the word *subject* in our rule, so how could we change the word *everything* to say something about the subjects?

> TEHJIA: **We could say *every subject*.**

Oh, that's good. Let's say **every subject + *was***. Would you please write that on the chart for us, Tehjia? (Tehjia writes **every subject + *was*** under the informal side of the chart.)

▶ **Conclude the lesson by prompting students to share what they liked about the lesson.**

Now that we have written the patterns for the formal and informal *was/were* patterns, I want you to think about everything we did during this lesson. What is something that you really liked about this lesson, and how did it – the thing you really liked about the lesson – help you?

> CHA'ZON: **I liked that we worked together to come up with the patterns.**

WAS/WERE PATTERNS

INFORMAL	FORMAL
I was at home.	I was at home.
It was fun.	It was fun.
My cousin was acting dumb.	My cousin was acting dumb.
He was a captain.	He was a captain.
You was late.	You were late.
We was stuck.	We were stuck.
They was done eating.	They were done eating.
THE PATTERN	**THE PATTERN**
every subject + was	I/he/she/it + was you/we/they + were

How did that help you?

CHA'ZON: **It would be hard to find the patterns by myself.**

So you found it helpful to work in a group situation because you were able to learn from your classmates. Anyone have something different that they liked?

SAMUEL: **I liked being the teacher!**

How did that help you?

SAMUEL: **Because I got to think about how to ask questions. Plus if I decide to be a teacher, I'll know what to do.**

Oh, you'd make an excellent teacher! Anyone else want to share? (I allow several students to share.) Why do you think I taught this lesson in this way? Why do you think I had Samuel take the teacher role? Why did I have you write the patterns?

ONTIANA: **You wanted us to think for ourselves.**

TYREEK: **Maybe you wanted us to work together.**

I did want you to work together, but I really wanted you to think through the example sentences and determine the patterns for yourselves. It's important for you to be able to problem-solve on your own. That is a skill you will use for the rest of your lives, and I think you really rose to the challenge today!

Assessing the Lesson

To assess the success of this lesson, I rely on my observations of students during Guided Practice and Independent Practice. During the Guided Practice portion, I watch for students who seem confused or lack participation. These are the students I focus on during the Independent Practice.

As I circulate around the room during the Independent Practice portion of the lesson, I make sure the students who struggled during the Guided Practice are participating rather than relying on their group members to do the work. I ask specific questions of them, such as "What do you think would be a good rule to describe when to use *was*? How did that sentence fit the pattern your group described? Is there a better way to describe this pattern?" The goal of these questions is to make sure all group members are actively participating in the writing of the rule.

Typically, students come up with a range of acceptable patterns for describing the *was/were* pattern. Some groups want to create rules that reflect equality, in both the number and wording of the rules, to the formal patterns. For example, these groups may determine that there are two rules for the informal pattern: *I/he/she/it* plus *was* and *you/we/they* plus *was*. Other students might come up with a different rule: all subjects plus *was* or *I/you/he/she/it/we/they* plus *was*. Any of these examples is acceptable and correct. I am primarily evaluating the accuracy of the rule(s) and the process the students use to create the rule(s).

Classifying *Was/Were* Patterns

Engagement

Have the students gather around the *Was/Were Patterns* chart. Lead the students to compare and contrast the formal and informal patterns for using *was/were*.

You guys did an amazing job writing the patterns using *was* and *were* yesterday. Let's take just a few minutes to review those patterns before we start today's lesson. Remember that our goal yesterday was to describe how *was* and *were* are used with different subjects. How did we describe the informal pattern?

> BOBBY: **Every subject plus *was*.**

Every subject is paired with *was*. How is that different from the formal pattern?

> ONTIANA: **Only *I, he, she*, and *it* used *was* on the formal side.**

I, he, she, and *it* were paired with *was* on the formal side. What about the other subjects?

> BOBBY: **The other subjects used *were*.**

The other subjects, *you, we*, and *they*, used the word *were*.

Lesson 2

materials

- *Was/Were Patterns* code-switching chart
- chart paper with a list of subjects plus *was/were*
- paper, markers, pencils

goals

STUDENTS WILL:

- recognize *was/were* patterns inside formal and informal language.
- define *was/were* patterns inside formal and informal language.
- distinguish between formal and informal *was/were* patterns.
- write sentences using formal and informal *was/were* patterns.

Direct Instruction

Introduce the focus of the lesson.

Today we are going to use our understanding of *was/were* patterns to write formal sentences. We are focusing on the formal patterns because we need to practice the type of language we will use when we write formal papers for school. On the chart paper, I have written several subjects. You will be using these subjects to write sentences using *was* and *were*.

Reveal a sheet of chart paper with a list of subjects and the verbs *was/were*. Model writing a formal sentence using one of the subjects and the form of *was/were* following the formal pattern.

First, I will model writing a formal sentence using one of these subjects; then we'll try one together before you write some on your own.

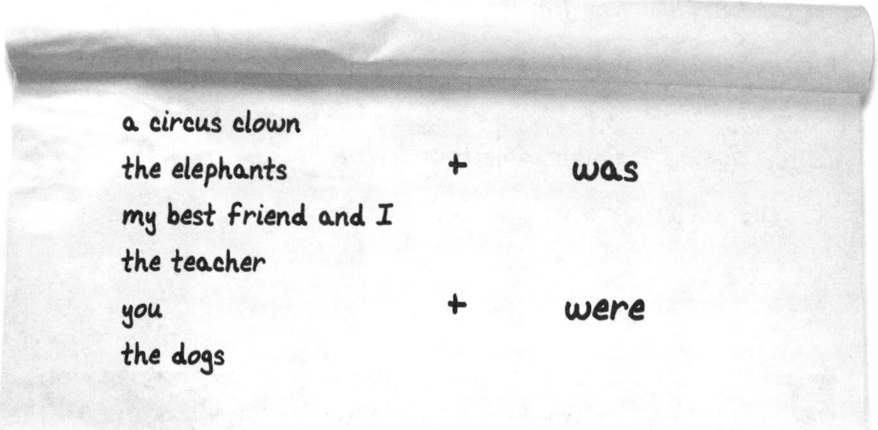

Let me see. I think I'm going to write a sentence using *the dogs* as my subject. *The dogs* can be replaced with *they*, and the formal rule is ***they* + *were***, so my sentence is going to start with *the dogs were*. I have to make sure I start with a capital here. (I write, *The dogs were* on the chart paper.) Dogs like to run, so I'm going to write *The dogs were running*. (I add *running* to *The dogs were*.) Of course I want my sentence to be nice and juicy, so I will need to add more details to it. Dogs like to chase things, so I'm going to write *The dogs were running after a squirrel*.

The dogs were running after a squirrel.

So I have *the dogs*, which can be replaced with *they*, plus *were*. That fits the formal pattern!

Guided Practice

Lead the group in writing another formal sentence using one of the subjects listed on the chart paper.

Let's try one together now. Which subject should we choose? (Several hands go up.) Doris?

DORIS: **"My best friend and I."**

Okay, our subject is *my best friend and I.* While Doris writes that on our chart paper, let's decide if we're going to use *was* or *were* with *my best friend and I.* (Doris begins writing the sentence on the chart paper.) Which pattern does *my best friend and I* fit?

QUATASIA: **Were.**

Why?

QUATASIA: **It's the same as *we* so we use *were*.**

My best friend and I can be replaced with *we*, and our pattern is ***we + were***. Quatasia, would you please add *were* to our sentence? (Quatasia writes *were* after *my best friend and I.*) My best friend and I were doing what?

NIJE: **Laughing.**

My best friend and I were laughing. While Nije adds the word *laughing* to our sentence, let's think of a detail we could add to make the sentence more interesting.

TYREEK: **We were laughing at a funny joke someone told us.**

My best friend and I were laughing at a funny joke someone told us – excellent sentence! Tyreek, you can finish writing the sentence for us.

My best friend and I were laughing
at a funny joke someone told us.

How do we know we followed the formal pattern?

ONTIANA: ***We* plus *were*.**

Our subject was *we*, and the pattern is *we* plus *were*, so our sentence is formal.

Independent Practice

Have the students write three more formal sentences using the subjects listed on the chart paper.

I've modeled a sentence. We wrote a sentence together. Now it's time for you to write your own sentences. I want you to choose three different subjects and use them to write three juicy sentences using the formal *was/were* pattern. If you finish early, see if you can write a bonus sentence using a subject that is *not* on the board. Let's get started! (The students return to their seats to work, and I help students who are having difficulties. I give the students about ten minutes to complete the task. After about five minutes, I begin announcing student successes as they occur.) Nije wrote a fantastic sentence. He wrote "The dogs were scared of the thunder." Oh, here's a juicy one from Ontiana: "The elephants were marching in the parade to announce the circus was coming." Wow, Ontiana, I'm impressed! (I continue to announce successes until the students have exhausted their ten minutes of writing time.)

Sharing for Understanding

Have students share the most important thing they did during the lesson.

Let's take a few minutes to share our thoughts about the lesson. We compared and contrasted the formal and informal *was/were* patterns, and we wrote formal sentences using the *was/were* patterns. What do you think was the most important thing we did today, and why was it so important?

DESTINY: **When we looked at how formal is different from informal.**

Why was that important to you?

DESTINY: **Cuz we have to know if it's formal or informal!**

We do need to be able to distinguish, or tell apart, the formal and informal patterns. We're going to work on editing next time, and we can't edit a lesson if we don't know if our words are formal or informal. Who can talk about another important thing we did during this lesson?

GARRETT: **We practiced writing our own sentences.**

Why was that important?

GARRETT: **Because if you don't practice it, you might always just use informal. Then you might not ever get a good job.**

Empower the students to evaluate the lesson.

Let's quickly show how much we learned today. Thumbs-up if you feel like you learned a lot from this lesson, thumbs-down if you didn't learn anything, and thumbs to the side if you learned a little. (The students show their hand gestures.)

Assessing the Lesson

I collect the sentences written by the students so that I can evaluate their ability to use the formal *was/were* patterns on their own. Generally speaking, students typically do not have difficulties with patterns involving *I, he, she,* or *it*. This is most likely because the informal and formal patterns are the same in regards to these subjects. For this reason, I give students only a couple of options for writing sentences with *I, he, she,* or *it*. My main focus, then, becomes sentences with the *you/they/we* subjects. As I look at the students' papers, I look for accuracy in using the patterns as well as indications of uncertainty. For example, I might find sentences that have been marked out or an erasure mark where the student has used *was* or *were* in the sentence and then changed his/her mind. These indicate that student might lack confidence in his/her ability to use the formal *was/were* patterns. Since the students have just started learning about these patterns, it is understandable that they may just need more practice; however, I will monitor these students more closely than those who seem to have little or no difficulty code-switching.

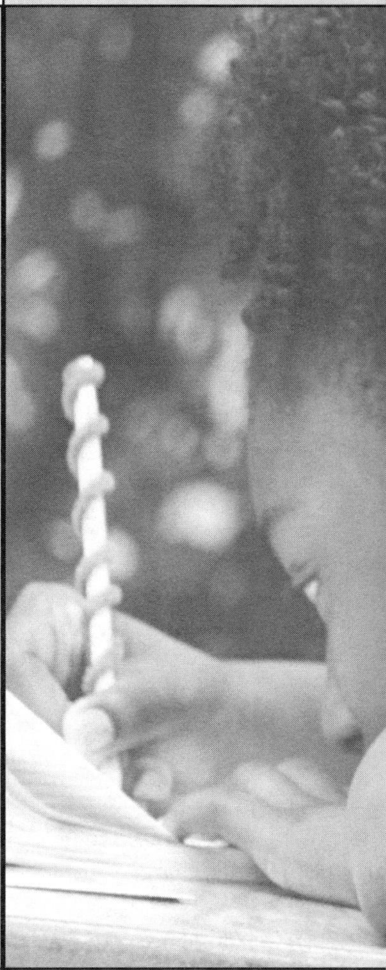

Lesson 3

Practicing Formal *Was/Were* Patterns

Engagement

Have the students gather around the *Was/Were Patterns* chart. Briefly review the formal *was/were* patterns.

We have been working on *was/were* patterns. Let's take a few minutes to review writing sentences using formal *was/were* patterns. I have two subjects here (I point to the board where I have written "my little sisters" and "my best friend.")

my little sisters
my best friend

Let's start with *my little sisters*. Are we going to use *was* or *were* with *my little sisters*?

SEVERAL STUDENTS: **Were.**

How do you know? What is the pattern we're following?

I'ANA: ***They* plus *were*.**

We can replace *my little sisters* with *they*, so I'ana is right; we need to follow the formal pattern of *they* plus *were*. Who has a formal sentence using *my little sisters* as the subject?

DAR'ASIA: **My little sisters were driving me crazy!**

They can do that! Let's get two more sentences with *my little sisters* and the formal *was/were* pattern. (I allow two more students to share their sentences.) Now let's try some sentences with *my best friend* and the formal *was/were* pattern. Are we going to use *was* or *were*?

STUDENTS: **Was.**

Which pattern are we following?

DAWNNELLA: ***She* plus *was*.**

HEZEKIAH: **Or *he* plus *was*.**

You're right. Your best friend could be a *he* or a *she*, but we'll be using *was* either way. Who has a sentence using *my best friend* and the formal *was/were* pattern? (I allow two or three students to share their sentences.)

materials

- *Was/Were Patterns* code-switching chart
- chart paper with "Last Weekend" paragraph written on it
- chart paper with a writing sample for subject–verb agreement editing (one for each small group)
- markers, highlighters

goals

STUDENTS WILL:

- recognize *was/were* patterns inside formal and informal language.
- define *was/were* patterns inside formal and informal language.
- distinguish between formal and informal *was/were* patterns.
- edit pieces of writing for the formal *was/were* patterns.

Direct Instruction

Introduce the focus of the lesson.

Today we are going to work on editing to make sure we are using the formal *was/were* patterns in our school writing. I have a paragraph written by a student a few years ago. We're going to work together to edit this paragraph so that it only contains the formal *was/were* patterns.

Show students the chart paper with the paragraph "Last Weekend." Model the process of editing for formal use of *was/were*.

Let's take a look at a paragraph written by a student a few years ago. I rewrote the paragraph on chart paper so we can all see it easily. (I reveal the paragraph.)

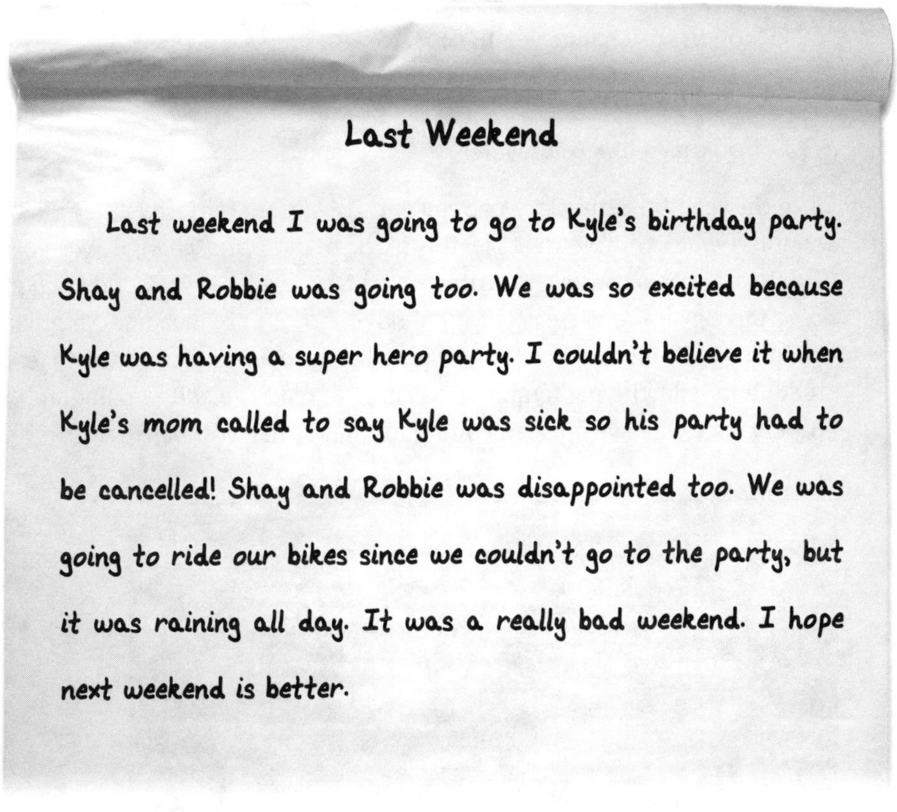

Last Weekend

Last weekend I was going to go to Kyle's birthday party. Shay and Robbie was going too. We was so excited because Kyle was having a super hero party. I couldn't believe it when Kyle's mom called to say Kyle was sick so his party had to be cancelled! Shay and Robbie was disappointed too. We was going to ride our bikes since we couldn't go to the party, but it was raining all day. It was a really bad weekend. I hope next weekend is better.

The first thing I am going to do when I prepare to edit a piece of writing is read the entire piece of writing all the way through. (I read the paragraph, including the title, aloud to the students.) I'm going to model how to edit for the formal *was/were* patterns; then we'll practice together. Let me start at the beginning. *Last weekend I was going to go to Kyle's birthday party. I was* – does that follow the formal pattern? Let me check our chart: ***I/he/she/it + was***. Yep, it follows the *I* plus *was* pattern. Since it is already formal, I don't need to change anything. I just need to highlight the pattern to show that it is formal. (I highlight *I was*.) Now that you've watched me edit the first sentence, we'll do some editing together.

note

A customizable version of the paragraph "Last Weekend" is available on the CD-ROM.

Guided Practice

Lead the students in editing the remainder of the paragraph together.

Let's read the next sentence together: *Shay and Robbie was going too.* Do we have a *was/were* pattern in this sentence?

> **STUDENTS: Yes!**

What is the *was/were* pattern?

> **TEHJIA: *Shay and Robbie was.***

Is *Shay and Robbie was* a formal or an informal pattern? Thumbs-up if you think it is formal, and thumbs to the side if you think it is informal. (Most or all of the students show a thumbs to the side.) So what do we need to do to make it formal?

> **QUINTIN: Change *was* to *were*.**

What is the formal pattern you're following?

> **QUINTIN: *They* plus *were*.**

Since *they* can take the place of *Shay and Robbie,* our pattern is *they* plus *were*. Quintin, would you please take the black marker and change *was* to *were*. (Quintin crosses out *was* and writes *were*.) Now we have *Shay and Robbie were going too*. Since the pattern is formal now, you can go ahead and highlight it. (Quintin highlights *Shay and Robbie were going too*. Then I continue to lead the students to edit the paragraph as a class. We read the edited paragraph in its entirety once we have finished editing for the formal *was/were* patterns.)

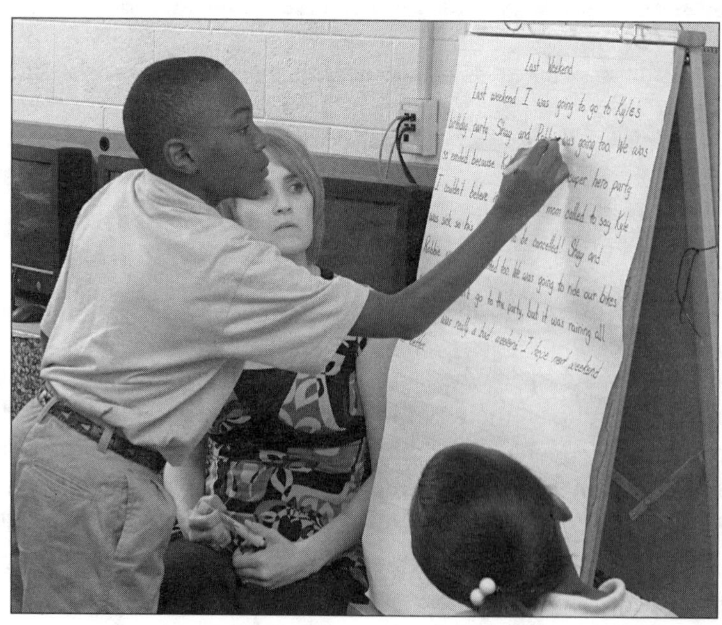

ways of talking

Positive ways of talking about language patterns are a mainstay of our work. We don't talk about correcting student grammar. Instead, we ask, "What do we need to do to make it formal?"

what if...

your students are unable to determine which pattern you are following because they do not know which pronoun to use?

If this happens, ask questions to guide the students' thinking. Start by referring to the *Was/Were Patterns* chart. You might say, "well since *Shay and Robbie* are not listed as subjects under the patterns we discovered, we are going to have to find another word that can take the place of *Shay and Robbie*. Let's look at our choices and see which one fits the best." Once directed to the chart, the students should determine that *they* is the only option that makes sense.

Independent Practice

Have the students work in groups to edit authentic paragraphs written by members of the class.

Now that we have a formal paragraph, you are going to work in groups to practice some peer editing. I have several paragraphs that I took from writings some of you created. I took these pieces of writing and put them on chart paper to make it easier to edit them as a group. As you work in your group, you are going to do exactly the same thing we did as a class. First, you will need to read through the paragraph. One person in the group will have the responsibility of making the editing changes on the paragraph; I'll give that person in the group a marker, but every group member is responsible for deciding on what editing changes need to be made. I will give one group member a highlighter, and that person will be responsible for highlighting the formal *was/were* patterns. The third member of the group will be responsible for checking the chart and making sure that each *was/were* pattern is formal. (I hand out the markers, the highlighters, and the paragraphs written on chart paper.) Does anyone have any questions about the assignment? (I answer any questions the students have before dismissing them to work in their groups. I work with each group to monitor the peer editing session.)

note

It is important to assign specific tasks to each member of the group. This increases the likelihood that all of the students will be actively engaged in the editing process.

Sharing for Understanding

Have students share the edited paragraphs.

I saw a lot of thinking going on just now! Let's take a few minutes to share your work with the class. When your group is called, I would like the person who was in charge of checking the chart to make sure the patterns were formal to read the edited paragraph out loud. As you listen to each group read their paragraphs, it will be your job to make sure they did not miss any of the patterns. Dar'Asia, Tyreek, and I'ana, would you get us started? (I tape the group's edited paragraph on the board, and Tyreek reads it aloud.) Are there any patterns this group missed?

STUDENTS: **No!**

I agree. They did an excellent job editing. Let's hear from the next group. (Each group shares their paragraphs in the same manner.)

Have students assess their comfort levels in regards to editing for the *was/were* patterns.

You did a great job working together to edit paragraphs today. Tomorrow you are going to be doing some editing on your own. How comfortable are you with editing for the *was/were* patterns? Thumbs-up if you're very comfortable – you don't think you'll have any difficulties. Thumbs-down if you're very uncomfortable – you think it will be very difficult to edit on your own. Thumbs to the side if you're a little uncomfortable – you think it will be difficult, but you think you'll be able to handle it with a little help. (The students show the thumbs-up, thumbs-down, or thumbs to the side to describe their feelings about editing for the *was/were* patterns.)

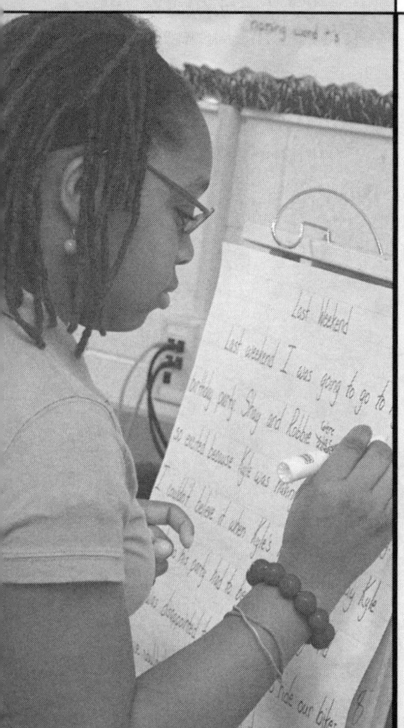

Assessing the Lesson

I rely primarily on teacher observation during the Independent Practice portion of the lesson to assess the students' understanding of using the formal *was/were* patterns. As I walk from group to group, I look to see that each member of the group is contributing to the editing process. I ask the students questions such as "Why did you highlight this pattern?" and "Why did you decide to use *were* here?" In addition to the observations I make during Independent Practice, I take note of the students who, during their self-assessment, indicated they were uncomfortable with editing the *was/were* patterns. These are the students I will check with first during the fourth lesson; I will also focus on these students during the Guided Practice of the next lesson.

Editing for Formal *Was/Were* Patterns

Engagement

Have the students gather around a chart paper with several sentences using the formal and informal *was/were* patterns written on it.

Yesterday we worked in groups to edit some paragraphs that contained formal and informal *was/were* patterns. We looked to make sure only the formal *was/were* patterns were used. Let's take a few minutes to edit some sentences I found in some of your work.

My mom and dad was proud.
My summer was great.
My mom and auntie was the only two adults there.

In the sentence *My mom and dad was proud*, who or what is the subject?

TYREEK: **Mom and dad.**

Not just any mom and dad but *My mom and dad*. So we have *My mom and dad* plus *was*. Is that formal or informal?

SEVERAL STUDENTS: **Informal.**

What do we need to do to change it to formal?

DORIS: **Change *was* to *were*.**

What pattern will we be following then?

DORIS: ***They* plus *were*.**

Doris, would you please change *was* to *were* and then go ahead and highlight the formal pattern. (We finish editing the last two sentences in the same manner.)

My mom and dad ~~was~~ were proud.
My summer was great.
My mom and auntie ~~was~~ were the only two adults there.

Lesson 4

materials

- chart paper with sample sentences using informal and formal *was/were* patterns
- *Was/Were Patterns* code-switching chart
- chart paper with writing sample
- current or previous formal writing assignments
- paper, markers, pencils, highlighters

goals

STUDENTS WILL:

- recognize *was/were* patterns in formal and informal language.
- define *was/were* patterns in formal and informal language.
- edit their work for formal *was/were* patterns.

Direct Instruction

Explain the purpose for the lesson. Show students the chart paper with the writing sample to be edited.

Yesterday we worked on peer editing. Today you are going to work on editing your own writing. Before I send you to your seats to edit your own work, let's take a few minutes to edit a portion of a piece of writing written by a student a few years ago. This student used both formal and informal *was/were* patterns in the writing. Let's read it together (I run my finger under the words as we read aloud together.) We are going to go sentence by sentence as we edit this piece of writing.

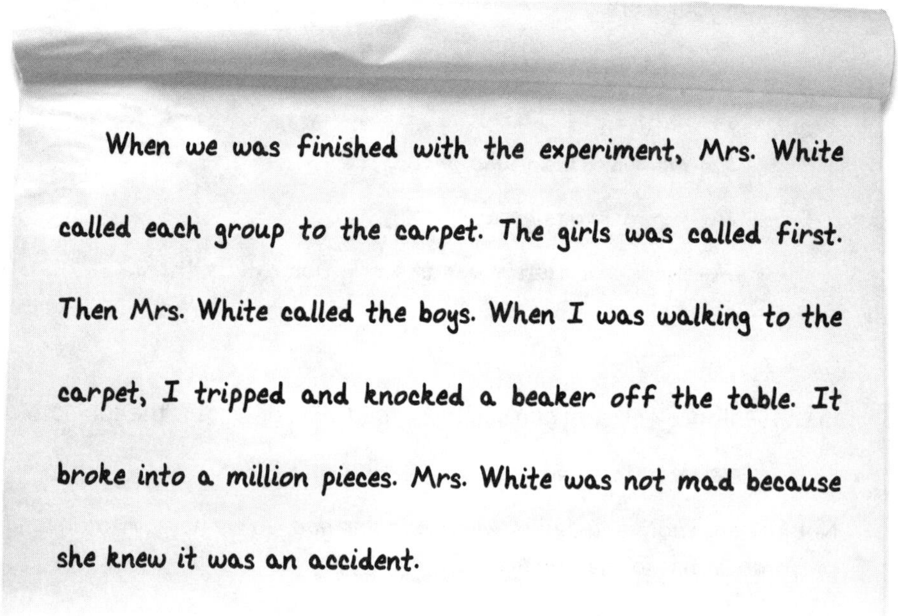

When we was finished with the experiment, Mrs. White called each group to the carpet. The girls was called first. Then Mrs. White called the boys. When I was walking to the carpet, I tripped and knocked a beaker off the table. It broke into a million pieces. Mrs. White was not mad because she knew it was an accident.

Model editing the first sentence for *was/were* patterns.

I want you to listen closely as I describe my thinking because when I'm finished, I'm going to ask one of you to model your thinking with one of the sentences. When I read this paragraph, I see a lot of *was/were* patterns. The first sentence says *When we was finished with the experiment, Mrs. White called each group to the carpet.* Hmm... *we was*. The formal pattern is *we* plus *were*, so this sentence does not follow the formal *was/were* patterns. I'm going to edit this sentence by putting a line through *was* and writing *were* above it. *When we were finished.* Now I have the formal pattern. Let me highlight *we were* because I have edited the pattern and made it formal. (I highlight *we were*.)

ways of talking

We was finished isn't wrong – it successfully follows the vernacular pattern. It simply does not follow the formal, academic English pattern, so we'll prompt our students to code-switch to formal English.

Guided Practice

▶ **Have the students take the teacher role as they finish editing the piece of writing.**

Now it's your turn. Who thinks they can take over the teacher role and explain their thinking with the next *was/were* pattern in the writing? Tyreek?

> TYREEK: **Okay. The next sentence is *The girls was called first*. The pattern is *girls was*. I know it is informal because *girls* is like *they*, and the formal pattern is *they* plus *were*. (Tyreek changes the word *was* to *were* and highlights *girls were*.) That's it.**

Why did you highlight *girls were*?

> TYREEK: **Because it's formal.**

Excellent job! Who would like to share their thinking for the next *was/were* sentences? (We continue to edit the paragraph in this manner. The students read the entire edited paragraph aloud for the class.)

Independent Practice

▶ **Have the students individually edit their own formal writing.**

Now that we have edited a paragraph together, it's your turn to show how brilliant you are by editing some of your own writing. As you read through your own work, take your time. If you find a formal *was/were* pattern, highlight it. If you find an informal pattern, change it to formal and then highlight it. Does anyone have any questions about what you are going to do? (The students shake their heads.) Okay, you can get to work. You'll have ten minutes to work on editing your papers. (I circulate around the room to help individual students as they complete their independent work.)

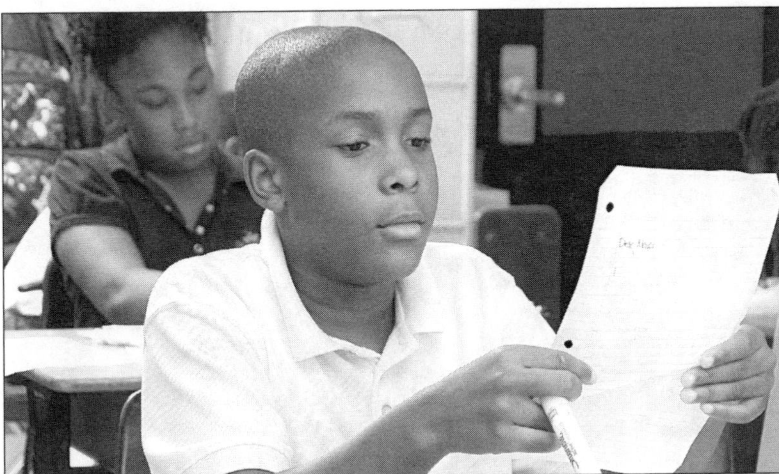

what if...

your students have difficulty with reciprocal teaching?

If your students struggle to adopt this metacognitive approach, use questioning techniques to help them clarify their thoughts. For example, you might ask, "how were you able to find a *was/were* pattern in this sentence? What was your thinking when you decided that? Why did you make that decision?" These types of questions will help focus students so they can better explain their thought process.

Sharing for Understanding

Have students share their work with the class.

Now that you have had a chance to edit your own work, let's take a few minutes to share what you found. I want you to take a moment to pick one of the patterns you highlighted to share with the class. Since all of your highlighted patterns are formal, everyone will be sharing a formal pattern. After you share your pattern with the class, you may write it on the board under *was* or *were*, depending on which one you used. (As I speak, I write *was* and *were* on the board.) If you would rather not share, just say "Pass," and we'll keep going. Let's see. I'ana, would you like to start us out?

> I'ANA: **My baby sister was crying so loud she woke me up.**

What did you highlight?

> I'ANA: ***My baby sister was.***

What formal pattern did I'ana follow?

> BOBBY: ***She* plus *was.***

Exactly. I'ana, you can write *My baby sister was* under *was* on the board. (While I'ana writes the pattern on the board, the next student shares his or her sentence. We continue sharing until everyone has had a chance to share.)

Close the lesson by polling the students on the difficulty of the lesson.

Thumbs-up if you thought editing your work was easy, thumbs-down if it was difficult, thumbs to the side if it was a little difficult. Anyone want to share why they chose to show thumbs-up, thumbs-down, or thumbs to the side?

> QUATASIA *(who shows a thumb to the side):* **It was easy to find a pattern because I just looked for *was*, but it was kinda hard to decide if I should leave it *was* or change it to *were*.**

Did anyone else find that to be true? (I allow several students to share.)

As you edit your own work in the future, I think you'll find that it will become easier and easier to use the formal *was/were* patterns.

what if...

you do not have time to allow everyone to share?

If time is a concern, simply have the students write a pattern of their choice on the board. Then give the class a few minutes to read the patterns on the board before closing the lesson.

Assessing the Lesson

I assess the success of this lesson in two ways. First, I use the students' abilities to edit their own work. I look to see that students are locating *was/were* patterns and are then accurately using the formal *was/were* patterns. I often notice that one or two students will fail to locate several *was/were* patterns in their writing. Generally, this occurs when students do not check each individual sentence as they read through their work. This can be corrected simply by having students do peer editing. During peer editing, each student should read his/her own work aloud. As *was/were* patterns are read, the student should pause to highlight formal patterns and edit informal patterns. The partner's job is to help locate these patterns by listening carefully to each sentence. This strategy usually solves the problem of rushing.

I also determine the success of the lesson based on the students' evaluations of the level of difficulty. Students who find the lesson difficult will most likely struggle with locating and editing *was/were* patterns in subsequent editing sessions. I simply make a note of these students so that I can offer additional support as needed. This might come in the form of small-group editing lessons, one-on-one editing sessions, or assigned peer editing (where I assign the editing partner based on his/her strength in editing for the *was/were* patterns). Ultimately, the success of the lesson will be determined by the students' abilities to independently use the formal *was/were* patterns.

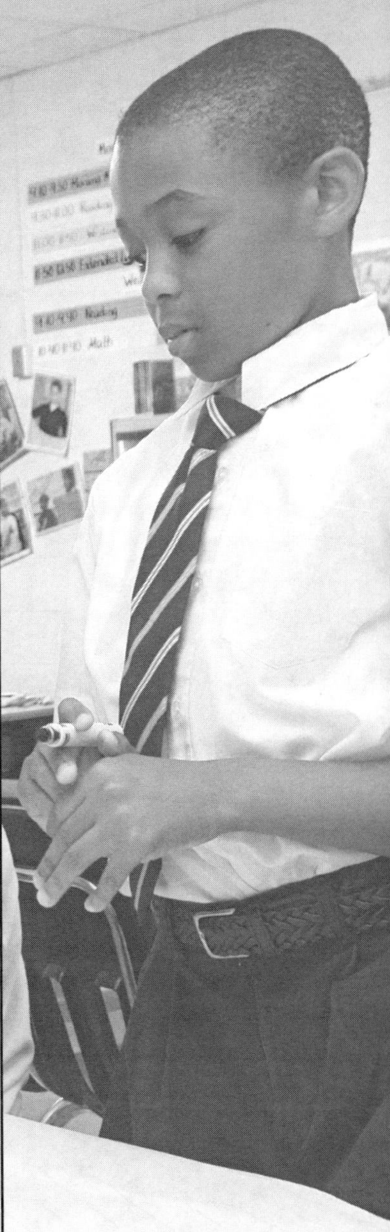

Am/Is/Are

8

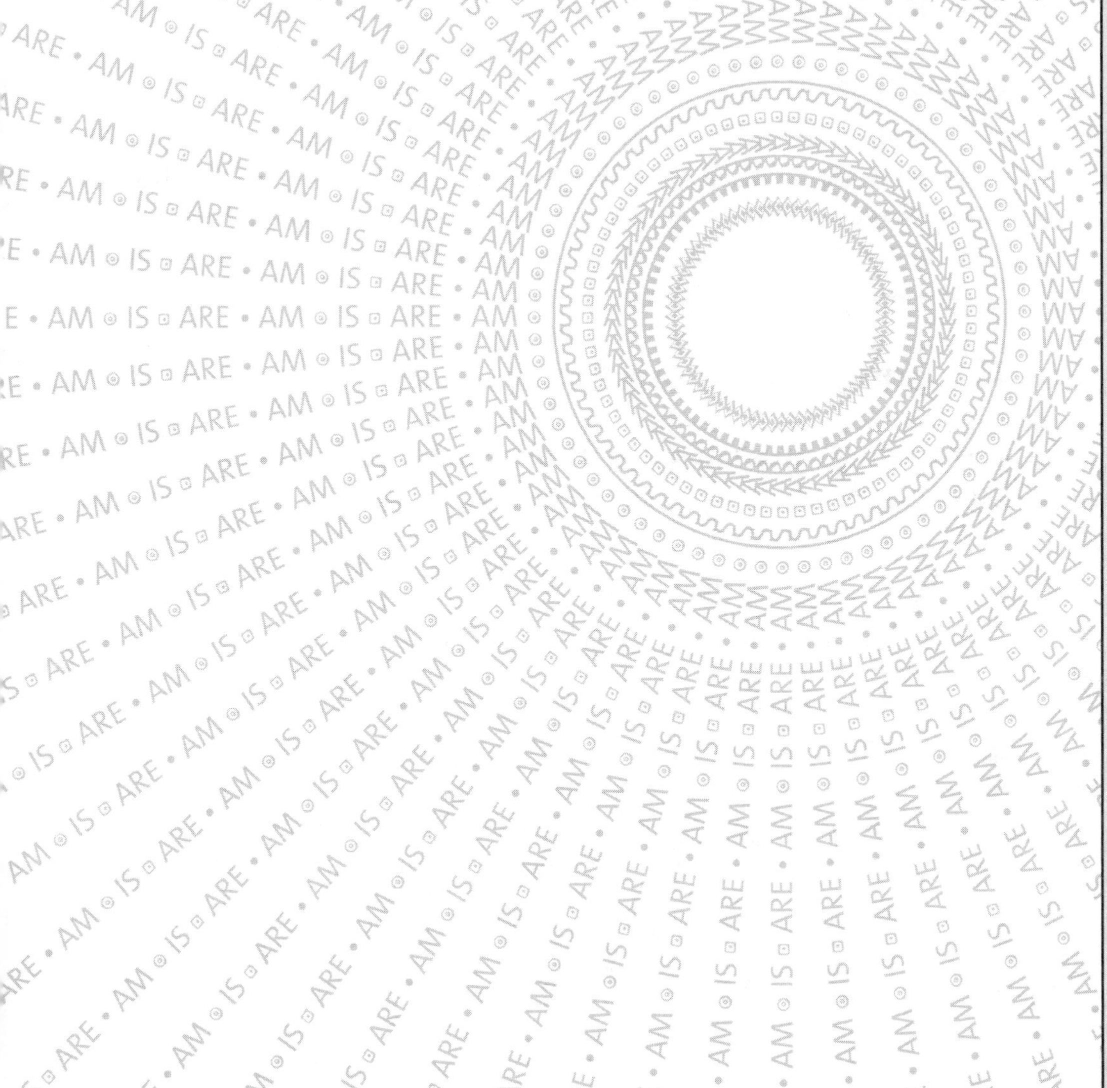

Lessons

THIS UNIT INCLUDES THE FOLLOWING LESSONS:

1. Defining Informal and Formal *Am/Is/Are* Patterns
2. Classifying *Am/Is/Are* Patterns
3. Practicing Formal *Am/Is/Are* Patterns
4. Editing for Formal *Am/Is/Are* Patterns

We have looked at subject–verb agreement with the irregular verb *be* in past tense (*I was going to the store, You were doing good, It was the best ever*). This unit looks at patterns with the verb *be* in present tense (*I am going to the store, You are doing good, It is the best ever*).

In our students' writing, we often see examples like *We is working* or *They is working*. In this unit, we show how to add the Standard English pattern to our students' repertoire: *We are working, They are working*. This unit comes after the past tense *was/were* unit due to the added complexity of a third form of the verb.

Am/Is/Are Patterns

The Pattern

The patterns for vernacular and Standard English *am/is/are* have a lot in common:

Vernacular pattern:
I + am
any other subject + *is*

Standard English pattern:
I + am
he/she/it + is
any other subject + *are*

Both vernacular and Standard English use *am* with first-person singular, *I*. Both use *is* with *he/she/it* subjects. The place that vernacular and Standard English differ lies in the verbs used for *you, we*, and *they*. Vernacular continues with *is*, whereas Standard English uses *are* with these subjects.

The Code-Switching Chart

Identifying vernacular *am/is/are* patterns in kids' work

Identifying *am/is/are* examples in your students' writing is easy – you'll notice that students use *is* with the subjects *we, you*, and *they* as well as with full noun phrase subjects corresponding to these pronouns (*Janae and me is going to the movies, My cousins is coming to visit*).

Here the student used the vernacular pattern for *am/is/are*:

got in a arguement because harry said
he wear's the best clothes.
So this Dognamed Shallow said what
is you two Fussing about. peter said
because harry said that he wears the
best clothes. The first thing is to go back
in the time machine and compare who has

So this dog named Shallow said what is you two fussing about?

Choosing/creating the examples

In our code-switching chart, for each of the places that vernacular differs from Standard English (*we, you, they*), we'll want to have at least one example with a full noun phrase subject and one example with a pronoun subject. This means that we will look for student examples with a full noun phrase subject like *My sister and I is going* (*we*); *All those students is going* (*they*). If we don't naturally find examples of subjects using the pronouns *we, you*, and *they*, we can take sentences with full noun phrase subjects and substitute the appropriate pronoun. We need a good mixture of full noun phrase subjects and pronoun subjects for two reasons: First, students will need to command the subject–verb agreement for both full noun phrase subjects and pronoun subjects; second, the interrelation between full noun phrase subjects and pronoun subjects will play a key role in students discovering the grammar rule, so we want to be sure students have plenty of data for their grammar exploration.

Creating the code-switching chart

While we might initially think of calling this the *Subject–Verb Agreement* chart, that name is taken already in our chart for present-tense regular third-person singular agreement (*She walk* vs. *She walks*), so we'll name this chart *Am/Is/Are Patterns*.

As always, the chart shows the informal and formal equivalents, with informal on the left and formal on the right. As we do with all other verbs, we'll include sentences for each person and number of subject: *I, he/she/it, we, you, they*. We include *you* examples only with the plural subjects on the chart. Whether singular or plural, *you* in Standard English requires *are*. We noticed that if we only write *you* under the plural part on the bottom half of the chart (*we, you, they*), it helps students discover the patterns more easily, because it groups all the instances of *are* together.

We continue to underline the subject and verb to focus the students' attention on the relevant portion of the sentences. Finally, we write *The Pattern* under each column of the chart, leaving space to write the pattern during the lesson.

AM/IS/ARE PATTERNS

INFORMAL	**FORMAL**
I am working.	I am working.
The car is working.	The car is working.
Marquis is working.	Marquis is working.
Kate is working.	Kate is working.
My sister and I is working.	My sister and I are working.
We is working.	We are working.
You is working.	You are working.
All those students is working.	All those students are working.
They is working.	They are working.
THE PATTERN	**THE PATTERN**
I + am	***I + am***
any other subject + *is*	***he/she/it* subject + *is***
	any other subject + *are*

Now it's lesson time!

Lesson 1

Defining Informal and Formal *Am/Is/Are* Patterns

materials

- chart paper with sample sentences using informal and formal *was/were* patterns
- *Am/Is/Are Patterns* code-switching chart
- flip-chart paper
- five sentence strips for each small group
- markers, pencils, paper

goals

STUDENTS WILL:

- Recognize *am/is/are* patterns inside formal and informal language.
- Define *am/is/are* patterns inside formal and informal language.
- Distinguish between formal and informal *am/is/are* patterns.

Engagement

Have the students gather around the easel. As a group, review finding the subject and determining the *was/were* pattern in some sample sentences.

Last week we spent several days working on *was/were* patterns. Let's take a few minutes to review the *was/were* patterns. I have three sentences I want you to look at. First, we are going to decide what the subject is in each sentence; then I want you to give the formal *was/were* pattern the sentence is following.

The dog was barking all night.

Chelsea and Devante were playing soccer.

Keisha and I were planning a trip to the mall.

In the first sentence, *The dog was barking all night,* what is the subject?

> TYREEK: ***The dog.* (I underline *The dog.*)**

And what formal pattern is the sentence following?

> ONTIANA: ***He* plus *was.***

Since *The dog* could be replaced by *he* or *she*, the sentence is following the formal pattern of *he/she/it* plus *was*. Let's look at the next sentence: *Chelsea and Devante were playing soccer.* What is the subject? (I lead the students through each sentence in the same way.)

Direct Instruction

Introduce the topic for today's lesson.

You all have become experts at finding the subjects in sentences. That is really going to make today's lesson easier for you. Today we're going to discover the patterns for using *am, is,* and *are* in sentences. Let's start by looking at the chart together. You'll notice that the chart contains rather simple sentences. This will help us focus on the patterns.

Show students the *Am/Is/Are Patterns* code-switching chart. Give students a minute to discover patterns on their own.

Let's take a look at the sentences, or data, we have for the *am/is/are* patterns. (I reveal the chart.)

Read the sentences to yourself, but don't say anything! You don't want anyone stealing your answers! (I give the students a few minutes to study the chart.)

AM/IS/ARE PATTERNS

INFORMAL	FORMAL
I am leaving.	I am leaving.
It is wonderful.	It is wonderful.
Marquis is working.	Marquis is working.
She is small.	She is small.
You is fussing a lot.	You are fussing a lot.
We is at home.	We are at home.
The rules is important.	The rules are important.
THE PATTERN	THE PATTERN

Start with the informal side. Lead students to name the informal pattern for *am*.

Let's start with the informal side today. What do you notice?

> HEZEKIAH: ***Am* is used one time; then everything else has *is*.**

Okay, let's start with *am*. What subject or subjects do we have with *am*?

> BOBBY: ***I*.**

How can we write a pattern to describe which subject is used with *am*?

> BOBBY: ***I* plus *am*.**

Let's check that. *I am leaving*. We have ***I* plus *am***, so that fits our pattern! (I write **I + *am*** on the informal side of the chart.)

Guided Practice

Allow students to take on the role of teacher to determine the rule for using *is* in informal language.

As Hezekiah pointed out, both *am* and *is* are used in informal language. We already determined the pattern for using *am*, so now we need to write a pattern for using *is*. Raise a quiet hand when you think you have a rule that describes which subjects are paired with *is*. Remember that we want our rules to be as simple as possible so they'll be easier to remember.

QUATASIA: **Everything plus *is*, except *I*.**

Thumbs-up if you think that pattern works; thumbs-down if you don't think it works. It looks like most people agree, but we'll have to check it before we write it down. Another way to write the pattern might be to say otherwise, any subject plus *is*. Do you think that might be easier to remember? (The students nod their heads.) Quatasia, I'm going to have you take over the teacher role and lead us through the process of checking your pattern to see if it really works. I'll get you started. *You is fussing a lot*. What is our subject in this sentence?

I'ANA: ***You.***

So how does this sentence fit our pattern?

I'ANA: **Any subject plus *is*.**

I is the only subject that we do not pair with *is*. So, *you is* fits our pattern of any subject plus *is*. Okay, Quatasia, take it from here!

QUATASIA: **How does this sentence fit the pattern? (She points to the sentence.) *Marquis is working*.**

ANDREW: **Any subject, except *I*, plus *is*.**

QUATASIA: **Okay. (She leads the students through the rest of the sentences.)**

So our pattern works! I'ana, would you please write our pattern, **any other subject + *is*** on the informal side of the chart. (I'ana writes the pattern on the chart.)

what if...

the students have a difficult time understanding or using the "any other subject plus *is*" pattern?

The patterns should be easily understood by the students. If the students find it easier to use a pattern such as "*you/he/she/it/we/they* plus *is*," then that is the pattern I use.

Independent Practice

Break students into small groups, and hand out sentence strips. Ask the groups to determine the formal *am/is/are* rules and write each one on a sentence strip.

Now that we have written the rules to describe the informal *am/is/are* patterns, you are going to work with your group to describe which subjects are paired with *am*, *is*, and *are* inside formal language. In your group, I want you to decide how to describe a pattern. Then you are going to check that pattern just like we did on the informal side. If the pattern works, go ahead and write it on a sentence strip. You will have to decide how many patterns there are in formal language. For this reason, I am giving each group five sentence strips. If you need more, they will be on the front table. If you don't use all of the five I give you, I'll just collect them after the lesson. (I call on a student to place the sentence strips in the middle of each group's table.) Are there any questions? Okay, let's see what you can do. (I visit each group as they work to create the rules for using *am, is,* and *are* in formal language. I assist groups only if they need it.)

Sharing for Understanding

Have the students gather around the partially completed *Am/Is/Are Patterns* chart with their sentence strips.

I saw so many of you thinking as you worked on writing the patterns! Let's see what you decided. Tehjia, how many rules did your team have?

TEHJIA: **Three.**

Would you please share one rule your team wrote?

TEHJIA: ***I* plus *am*.**

How many other teams wrote the same pattern? (The students raise their hands. I tape the rule to the board.) Okay, Samuel, let's hear one of the patterns your group wrote.

SAMUEL: ***We* or *you* or *they* plus *are*.**

Raise your hand if your team also wrote this pattern on one of your sentence strips. (As the students raise their hands, I tape the sentence strip to the board.) Did anyone have any other rules?

I'ANA: ***He, she, it* plus *is*.**

How many of you have this rule written on a sentence strip? (I add the rule to the board.) Did anyone have any other rules? (All of the rules are taped to the board and discussed.) Of course, we want to use the least number of rules possible, and we want to write the rules in a way that is easy to remember, so which of these rules should we use to describe the formal patterns?

ONTIANA: **We have to have three rules because we have *am, is,* and *are*.**

I agree. It would be hard to have fewer than three rules! I saw a number of good ways to express these rules. Which three rules should we use? (The students decide on which version of the rules to use. I have different students add the rules to the chart. We add ***I* + *am*, *he/she/it* + *is***, and **you/we/they + are**.)

Conclude the lesson by prompting students to share what they felt was difficult about the lesson.

Let's take a minute to think about the different things we did during the lesson today. What was the hardest part of today's lesson?

> DESTINY: **When we had to write our own rules.**

Why was that difficult?

> DESTINY: **Because we had to agree on what to write, and I didn't want to write them the same way Quintin did. Quintin wanted to write *we* or *they* plus *are*, but we didn't write it that way on the informal side.**

How many other people found it difficult to work in a group because you had to agree on what to write? (A few hands go up.) How did you work through the problem of agreeing on what to write?

> QUINTIN: **I wrote the one that said *he, she*, or *it* plus *is*, and Destiny wrote that one. (He points to a strip that has *we/they* plus *are* written on it.)**

So you solved the problem yourselves by compromising. Was anything else difficult about this lesson? (I allow several students to share.) Although there were some difficult parts to this lesson, I'm really proud of all of you. You worked so hard today, and it will get easier to use the patterns as you get more practice!

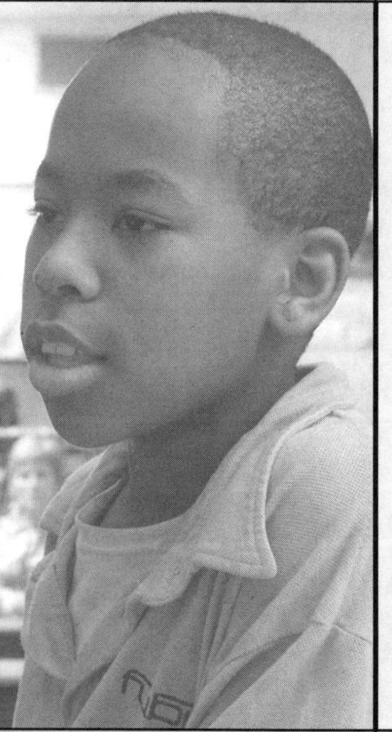

Assessing the Lesson

In assessing this lesson, I review the success of the process students employed in describing the rules for using *am/is/are* inside formal language. As I move from group to group during the Independent Practice portion, I listen to how the students decide to describe the patterns. I want to see that all students are involved in the process and that students are able to defend and discuss the patterns with their peers. Students should be able to describe a pattern and then, through discussions with their classmates, condense the pattern to the simplest terms. Students who are able to successfully describe patterns will be able to use the same process in reviewing data and describing rules for other grammatical patterns.

Classifying *Am/Is/Are* Patterns

Engagement

Have the students gather around the *Am/Is/Are Patterns* chart. Lead the students to review the formal and informal patterns.

Yesterday we worked together – then you worked in groups – to write patterns that showed how different subjects are used with *am, is,* and *are*. Let's start with informal language and review those patterns. What were the *am/is/are* patterns in informal English?

TAJANTA: ***I*** **plus *am* and everything else plus *is*.**

I* plus *am was the first pattern we described. Remember that we decided to describe the subjects that were paired with *is* as **all other subjects plus *is***. We want to make sure we focus on the subjects when we talk about the patterns. What were the formal *am/is/are* patterns?

ANDREW: ***I*** **plus *am*, *he/she/it* plus *is*, and *you/we/they* plus *are*.**

Right, we had three patterns for formal language. (I point to the patterns on the chart.) ***I* plus *am*, *he/she/it* plus *is***, and ***you/we/they* plus *are***.

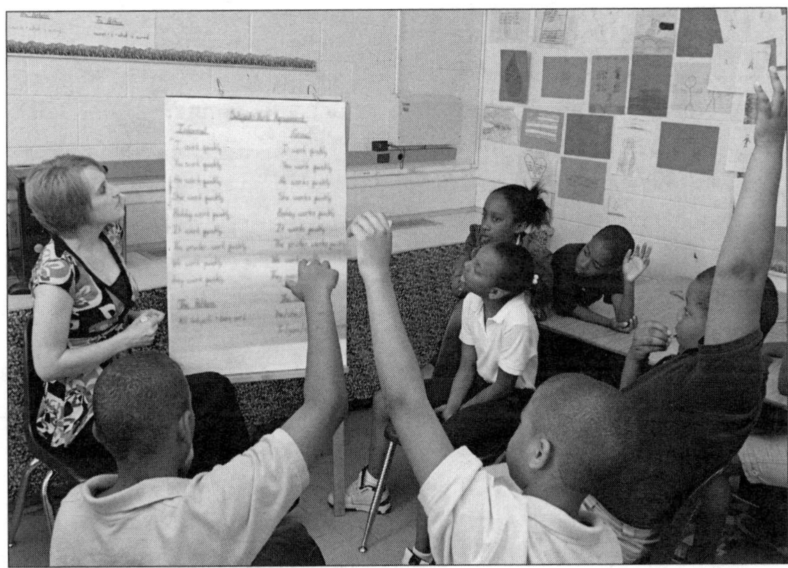

Direct Instruction

Set the purpose of the lesson.

Since most of our writing in school is formal, we are going to focus on the formal patterns today. I have a chart with several different subjects. Our goal for today is to be able to successfully write formal sentences using these subjects and *am, is,* or *are*.

Lesson 2

materials

- *Am/Is/Are Patterns* code-switching chart
- chart paper with a list of subjects plus *am/is/are*
- *Am/Is/Are Sorting* wall chart
- markers, pencils, paper
- sentence strips

goals

STUDENTS WILL:

- Recognize *am/is/are* patterns inside formal and informal language.
- Define *am/is/are* patterns inside formal and informal language.
- Distinguish between formal and informal *am/is/are* patterns.
- Write sentences using formal and informal *is/are* patterns.

Reveal a sheet of chart paper with a list of subjects and the verbs *am/is/are*. Model writing a formal sentence using one of the subjects and the corresponding form of *am/is/are*.

Let's take a look at the chart. (I reveal the chart.)

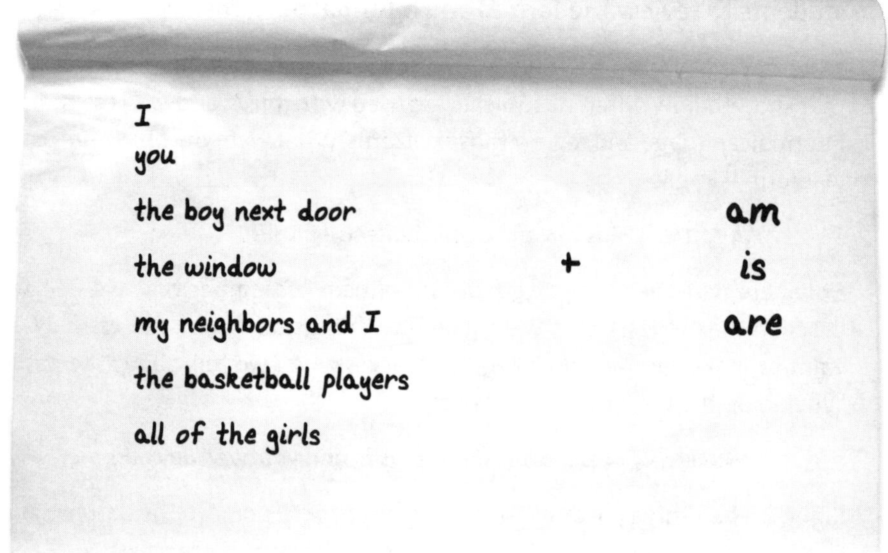

Before you write your own sentences, I'm going to model my thinking as I write a sentence using one of the subjects from the chart. Pay close attention, because this is what you'll be doing on your own in just a few minutes. First, I need to pick a subject. I think I'll use *my neighbors and I.* Since I'm going to start my sentence with *my neighbors and I*, I need to make sure I capitalize *My*. (I write on the chart paper.) Since *My neighbors and I* can be replaced with *we*, I need to use the formal pattern for *we*. The formal pattern is **we plus *are***, so I need to add *are* to my sentence. (I add *are* to *My neighbors and I.*) The people in my neighborhood are having a barbecue, so I'm going to add *having a barbecue* to my sentence. Now I need to add a detail to make my sentence more interesting to read. Since the barbecue is going to be in my neighbor Alfred's backyard, I'm going to add that information to my sentence. (I add *in Alfred's backyard* to the sentence.) I think I'll also add that the barbecue is on Saturday. So now I have *My neighbors and I are having a barbecue in Alfred's backyard on Saturday.* I have *My neighbors and I,* which can be replaced with *we,* plus *are*. That fits the formal pattern. All I need to do is put a period at the end of my sentence!

My neighbors and I are having a barbecue
in Alfred's backyard on Saturday.

Guided Practice

Lead the group in writing another formal sentence using one of the subjects listed on the chart paper.

Now that I've modeled how to write a sentence using the formal *am/is/are* patterns, let's write a sentence together. What do we need to do first?

> HEZEKIAH: **Pick a subject.**

Which subject should we use in our sentence? (Several students raise their hands.) Tajanta?

> TAJANTA: ***All of the girls.***

Tajanta, go ahead and write *All of the girls* on the chart paper while we decide if we need to use *am, is,* or *are* with this subject. (Tajanta writes the subject on the chart paper.) Should we use *am, is,* or *are* with *All of the girls*?

> I'ANA: ***Are.***

How do you know?

> I'ana: ***They* plus *are*. (She points to the *Am/Is/Are Patterns* chart on the wall.) That's the pattern.**

Since we can replace *All of the girls* with *they*, the pattern we need to use is *they* plus *are*. I'ana, you can add *are* to the sentence. (I'ana writes *are*.) What should we say about *All of the girls*?

> DAR'ASIA: **They are good singers.**

Okay, would you please add good singers to our sentence? (Dar'Asia writes *good singers* on the chart paper.) Let's see if we can add a detail to make the sentence more interesting. What could we add to the sentence *All of the girls are good singers*?

> BOBBY: **Because they practice a lot.**

"Because they practice a lot." Let's go ahead and add that to our sentence. (Bobby completes the sentence on the chart paper.) Quatasia, would you please read our sentence aloud?

> QUATASIA: **All of the girls are good singers because they practice a lot.**

Excellent sentence! We followed the formal *am/is/are* pattern of *they* plus *are*, and we wrote a sentence with a detail. Nice work!

All of the girls **are** good singers
because they practice a lot.

what if...

the students have a difficult time adding details?

I simply offer more assistance in writing the sentence. For example, in the sentence that begins *All of the girls are good singers,* I might prompt the students by saying, "All of the girls are good singers because..." This type of prompting allows me to lead the students without providing the answers for them.

Independent Practice

Have the students write three more formal sentences using the subjects listed on the chart paper. Make sure they write one sentence using each form of the verb *am/is/are*.

Now that we've taken the time to write a sentence together, it is your turn to showcase what you can do on your own. You will be writing three sentences using the formal *am/is/are* patterns. Here's the tricky part, though. You must write one sentence that uses the word *am*, one in which you use the word *is*, and one in which you use the word *are*. So choose your subjects carefully! Make sure you are using the formal *am/is/are* patterns, and make sure you include details in your sentences. If you finish early, challenge yourself to write a sentence using any subject you choose. Are there any questions? (I answer any questions the students ask. As the students write their sentences, I circulate around the room to answer questions and provide assistance. I also put a sentence strip on the corner of each student's desk.)

Have students write their favorite sentence on a sentence strip to share with the class.

As you wrote your sentences, some of you may have noticed that I put a sentence strip on the corner of your desk. Before we meet as a group, I would like you to choose one sentence that you really like and copy that sentence onto the sentence strip. Once you have done that, tape your sentence on the board in the *am* column, the *is* column, or the *are* column. (The students copy their favorite sentences and tape them under the appropriate heading on the wall.)

Sharing for Understanding

Allow the students to review the sentences and check for formality and placement in the correct column.

Let's take a few minutes to review your sentences. Once you have read through all of the sentences, come back to the carpet so I will know you are ready to begin discussing the sentences. Are there any questions? (I answer any questions the students ask before giving them about five minutes to look at the sentences.)

Let's start with this one. (I point to a random sentence under the *am* column). *I am in the fifth grade.* Which formal pattern is our sentence following?

BOBBY: ***I* plus *am*.**

(I point to another random sentence under the *am* column and lead students to discuss it in the same way. I then move to two or three sentences under the *is* and *are* columns.)

Have students evaluate the success of meeting the goal of the lesson.

I want you to think about what we did today. I modeled writing a formal *am/is/are* sentence for you, we wrote a sentence together, and you wrote some sentences on your own. Remember that our goal today was to be able to write formal *am/is/are* sentences. Thumbs-up if you think we met the goal, thumbs-down if you do not think we met the goal, and thumbs to the side if you think we sort of met the goal. Does anyone want to share their opinion?

DAJON: **I put thumbs to the side.**

Why?

DAJON: **I wrote formal sentences, but it was hard.**

So you think a little more practice might help?

DAJON: **Yeah.**

Anyone else want to share their opinions? (I take two or three more student responses.)

Assessing the Lesson

In assessing this lesson, I am focused primarily on the students' abilities to use *am, is,* and *are* to write sentences inside formal English. I note how quickly students complete the Independent Practice and how confident they are with their sentences. I also watch the students' reactions to their classmates' sentences during the Sharing for Understanding. I make a mental note of those students who are unable to verbalize how the sentences follow the formal rules. I also listen to the students' opinion about whether the goals of the lesson were met. I will work individually or in small groups during the next lesson with students who showed thumbs to the side or thumbs-down. I do not expect students to complete this lesson effortlessly, as we have not been working with this pattern for very long. However, given the similarities between this lesson and previous lessons, I expect students to be comfortable enough with the process to accurately use the patterns we have described.

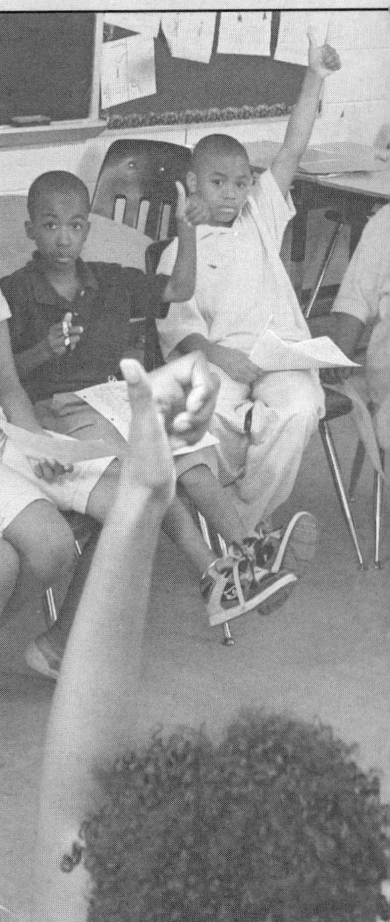

Lesson 3

Practicing Formal *Am/Is/Are* Patterns

Engagement

Have the students gather around the *Am/Is/Are Patterns* code-switching chart. Review writing sentences using the formal *am/is/are* patterns.

Yesterday we used our knowledge of *am/is/are* patterns to write our own formal sentences. Let's come up with a few sentences for these two subjects. (I write the subjects on the board.)

Who has a formal sentence using the first subject, *my aunt*?

> my aunt
>
> the children

DESTINY: **My aunt is going to Chicago next week.**

Destiny gave us an excellent sentence with details. Which formal pattern did she follow?

ANDREW: ***She* plus *is*.**

She plus *is*. That's a pretty easy pattern to remember because it is the same as the informal pattern, isn't it? Let's take one more sentence. Doris?

DORIS: **My aunt is taking me shopping after school.**

Another juicy sentence! Let's look at the next subject, *the children*. Who thinks they can give us a formal sentence using *the children*? (I allow two students to share.)

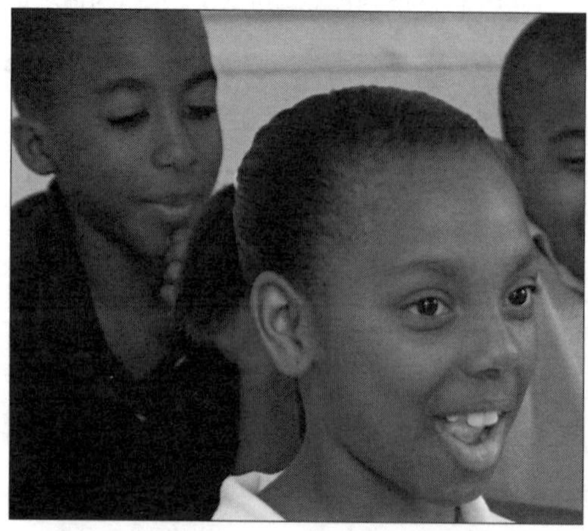

materials

- *Am/Is/Are Patterns* code-switching chart
- chart paper with the practice paragraph "Spring Break"
- chart paper with a writing sample for subject–verb agreement editing (one for each small group)
- markers, pencils, paper
- sentence strips

goals

STUDENTS WILL:

- Recognize *am/is/are* patterns inside formal and informal language.
- Define *am/is/are* patterns inside formal and informal language.
- Distinguish between formal and informal *am/is/are* patterns.
- Edit pieces of writing for the formal *am/is/are* patterns.

Direct Instruction

Introduce the focus of the lesson.

Now that we have worked on writing formal sentences, we are going to take it one step further and practice editing papers to make sure the formal *am/is/are* patterns are being used. You will be editing papers written by students in this class, and you will be working in groups of four. Of course we will practice editing together before you start editing on your own.

Show students the chart paper with the paragraph "Spring Break." Model the process of editing for formal use of *was/were*.

Let's take a look at the paragraph. (I reveal the paragraph written on chart paper and read it aloud.)

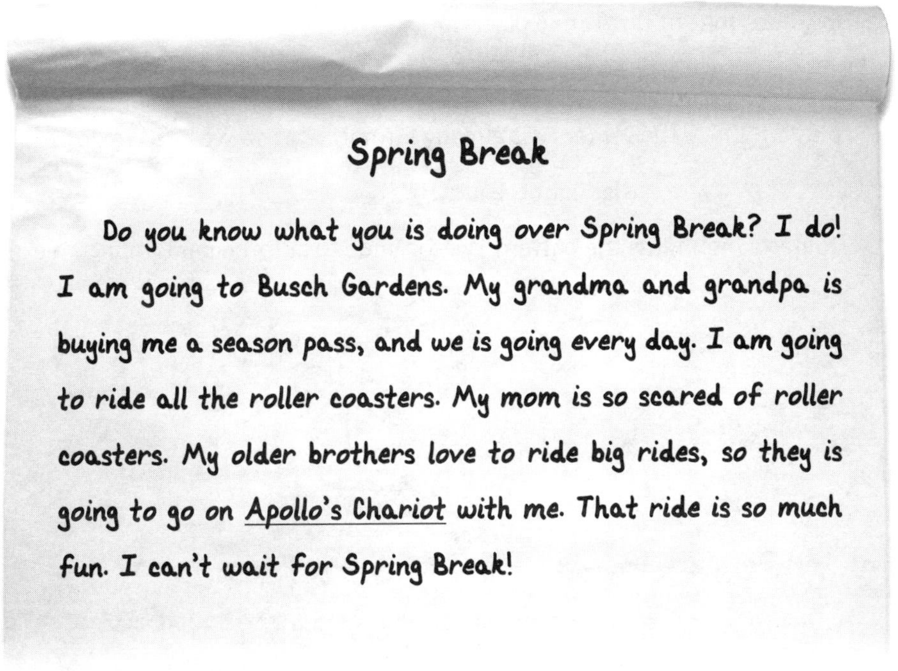

Spring Break

Do you know what you is doing over Spring Break? I do! I am going to Busch Gardens. My grandma and grandpa is buying me a season pass, and we is going every day. I am going to ride all the roller coasters. My mom is so scared of roller coasters. My older brothers love to ride big rides, so they is going to go on Apollo's Chariot with me. That ride is so much fun. I can't wait for Spring Break!

note

A customizable version of the paragraph "Spring Break" is available on the CD-ROM.

Since we are only working on editing for the formal *am/is/are* patterns today, I am now going to go through the paragraph and look at each sentence, one at a time. *Do you know what you is doing over Spring Break?* As I reread that sentence, I immediately notice the word *is,* so I know one of our patterns is in this sentence. *You is* – the subject is *you.* Now I need to remember what the formal pattern is when *you* is the subject. Let me refer to our *Am/Is/Are Patterns* chart to check the formal pattern for *you*. Okay, the pattern is ***you + are***. Now I know that the pattern in our sentence is informal, so I'm going to put a line through *is* and write *are* above it. (I put a line through *is* and write *are* above it on the chart paper.) *Do you know what you are doing over Spring Break?* Now I have the formal pattern, so I am going to highlight *you are*. I modeled the first sentence for you; now we're going to finish editing the paragraph together.

Guided Practice

Lead the students to edit the remainder of the paragraph.

Quintin, would you please read the next sentence?

QUINTIN: **"I do!"**

Do we have an *am/is/are* pattern in that sentence?

STUDENTS: **No!**

I'ana, please read the next sentence.

I'ANA: **"I am going to Busch Gardens."**

Do we have an *am/is/are* pattern in this sentence?

BOBBY: **"I am."**

How does that fit the formal pattern?

BOBBY: ***I* plus *am*.**

I plus *am*. Since the sentence is already formal, what do we need to do next?

QUATASIA: **Highlight the pattern.**

(Quatasia highlights the pattern. We continue to edit the paragraph as a class.)

Spring Break

Do you know what you ~~is~~ are doing over Spring Break? I do! I am going to Busch Gardens. My grandma and grandpa ~~is~~ are buying me a season pass, and we ~~is~~ are going every day. I am going to ride all the roller coasters. My mom is so scared of roller coasters. My older brothers love to ride big rides, so they ~~is~~ are going to go on Apollo's Chariot with me. That ride is so much fun. I can't wait for Spring Break!

Independent Practice

Have the students work in groups to edit authentic paragraphs written by members of the class.

Today you are going to work with your group to edit pieces written by some of your own classmates. I have rewritten the paragraphs on chart paper to make them easier to see. I want you to work together while you're editing. I'll start by giving each group one of the paragraphs.

If I hand you the paragraph, your job is to be the reader. You will read the paragraph aloud for your group and then read each sentence as you edit. I am going to give one person the black marker. If you have the black marker, your job is to mark out informal patterns and write the formal patterns. One person will be in charge of highlighting. If you have the highlighter, your job is to highlight the formal *am/is/are* patterns. The last person will be the pattern checker. The pattern checker is responsible for looking at the chart and explaining how each pattern is formal. The pattern checker will also be choosing one of the patterns from the paragraph and explaining how the pattern is formal. Does everyone understand what to do? (I begin handing out the chart paper, black markers, and highlighters.) You may begin. (I give the students about ten minutes to complete the assignment. As the students work together, I go to each group to monitor the students' progress and to answer any questions.)

Sharing for Understanding

Allow the students to share their reflections on what they liked and disliked about the assignment.

Let's take a few minutes to think about what we did today and how we did it. I want you to think about how we edited the paragraph as a class and how you worked in groups to edit a paragraph one of your classmates wrote. What did you like about this lesson?

GARRETT: **I liked that I got to be in a group with Dar'Asia and Dajon.**

Why did you like working with Dar'Asia and Dajon?

GARRETT: **They listen to me and I listen to them.**

So you worked well with your group. Did anyone have anything else they liked about the lesson? (I allow two or three more students to share.) Now I want you to think about what you disliked, or did not like, about the lesson.

TYREEK: **I didn't like when we had to decide to use *is* or *are*.**

You had a hard time knowing when to use *is* and *are*?

TYREEK: **Yeah because *is* sounds right, but sometimes it's supposed to be *are* when it's formal.**

The formal pattern can be tricky. That's why we're practicing it together. Does anyone else want to share something they disliked about the assignment? (I allow one or two students to share.) Let's do a thumbs-up, thumbs-down. Thumbs-up if you think you need a little more practice with the formal *am/is/are* patterns; thumbs-down if you do not think you need any more practice with the formal *am/is/are* patterns.

Assessing the Lesson

While I make mental notes about different students' understanding of editing for formal *am/is/are* patterns during Guided Practice, I focus on the Independent Practice portion of the lesson. As I listen to the students discuss the sentences during the editing process, I am able to recognize which students truly understand the formal patterns and which students are relying on their peers. When I find students who have little to add to the discussion, I ask questions of those students to include them in the dialogue. For example, I might ask, "What do you think we need to do to this sentence to make it formal?" or "What pattern is this sentence following?" In subsequent lessons and editing sessions, I will focus on those students who continue to have difficulty with editing even after my questioning. I do not take a formal assessment at this point because students are in the beginning stages of editing for this particular pattern.

Editing for Formal *Am/Is/Are* Patterns

Engagement

Have the students gather around an easel with two or three sentences using the formal and informal *am/is/are* patterns written on chart paper.

We have been working with *am/is/are* patterns for several days now. We have discovered and described the formal and informal patterns for *am/is/are*. We have practiced writing sentences using the formal *am/is/are* patterns. And yesterday we edited paragraphs that contained formal and informal *am/is/are* patterns. Let's review the process we use for editing patterns. On the chart, I have written some sentences I found in some of your work. (I reveal the sentences.)

My mom is my best friend.

Shanae and Brittany is coming to my birthday party.

We is going to stay up all night.

Let's look at the first sentence, *My mom is my best friend.* Who or what is the subject in that sentence?

DAWNNELLA: ***My mom.***

My mom is the subject. We have *My mom* plus *is*. Is that formal or informal?

STUDENTS: **Formal!**

Since the sentence is already formal, what do we do next?

CHA'ZON: **Highlight *My mom is.***

We highlight the pattern. (I hand Cha'zon the highlighter, and he highlights *My mom is*. We edit the remaining two sentences in this way.)

My mom is my best friend.

Shanae and Brittany ~~is~~ are coming to my birthday party.

We ~~is~~ are going to stay up all night.

Lesson 4

materials

- chart paper with sample sentences using informal and formal *am/is/are* patterns
- *Am/Is/Are Patterns* code-switching chart
- chart paper with "Why I Am Sad" writing sample
- student journals with current writing assignments
- paper, markers, pencils, highlighters

goals

STUDENTS WILL:

- Recognize *am/is/are* patterns inside formal and informal language.
- Define *am/is/are* patterns inside formal and informal language.
- Edit their work for formal *am/ is/are* patterns.

Direct Instruction

Set the purpose for the lesson. Show students the chart paper with the "Why I Am Sad" writing sample.

Yesterday we practiced editing paragraphs in a group. Today you are going to edit your own work. You will be editing the piece of writing we started last week. Before you get started, I will model the editing process, and then you will help me edit. Let's take a look at the paragraph.

note

A customizable version of the paragraph "Why I Am Sad" is available on the CD-ROM.

Why I Am Sad

My best friend Kiera and I is both nine years old. We is in the same class this year. I am really sad because I just found out that next year we is going to be in different classes. I am going to be in Mrs. White's class. Kiera is going to be in Mrs. Hall's class. A lot of my friends is going to be in my class, but I am still sad that Kiera is not. Even if we is not in the same class, Kiera and I is still going to be best friends.

Model editing the first sentence for *am/is/are* patterns.

The first thing I am going to do is read the entire paragraph. (I read the paragraph aloud.) Now I'm going to go back and edit for the formal *am/is/are* patterns by starting back at the beginning of the paragraph and editing one sentence at a time. If I find an informal pattern, it will be my job as the editor to change the pattern to make it formal. As I read, I'm going to highlight all of the formal patterns. Even if I had to change a pattern from informal to formal, I'm going to highlight it once I make it formal.

Let's get started. The first sentence says *My best friend Kiera and I is both nine years old.* As soon as I read the word *is,* I know there is a pattern in that sentence. Now I have to decide if the pattern is formal or informal. The subject is *My best friend Kiera and I.* Since that can be replaced with *we,* I know that this sentence is following the informal pattern: all subjects plus *is.* The formal pattern for *we* is ***we + are***, so I need to cross out *is* and write *are* above it to make it formal. Now I have *My best friend Kiera and I are both nine years old.* Since I have the formal pattern, I can highlight *My best friend Kiera and I are.* (I highlight the pattern.) Does everyone understand what I did? (The students nod.)

Guided Practice

Have the students take the teacher role as they finish editing the piece of writing.

Now it's your turn to practice editing. Let's look at the second sentence. Who would like to take the teacher role and lead us through editing the next sentence? Dajon?

DAJON: ***We is in the same class this year.*** **What is the pattern?**

ANDREW: ***We is.***

DAJON: **Is that formal or informal?**

SEVERAL STUDENTS: **Informal.**

DAJON: **What is the formal pattern? Doris?**

DORIS: ***We* plus *are.***

DAJON: **Okay.**

(Dajon changes the *is* to *are* and highlights *We are.*) Nice job, Dajon! Who would like to take the teacher role for the next sentence? (We finish editing the paragraph in this fashion.)

Independent Practice

Have the students individually edit their own formal writing.

Now you've had a chance to practice exactly what you will be doing with your own writing. You are going to take out the writing you started last week and read through the entire piece. What will you do next?

ONTIANA: **Edit one sentence at a time.**

You will go back and edit one sentence at a time. What will you do if you find a formal pattern?

QUINTIN: **Highlight it.**

What will you do if you find an informal pattern?

TAJANTA: **Make it formal and highlight it.**

Exactly. Are there any questions? (I give the students five to ten minutes to complete the assignment. As the students edit their paragraphs, I work individually with students who are struggling with the assignment.)

what if...

students are unable to take on the teacher role independently or it takes too much time?

If students are unable to take on the teacher role on their own, offer support by whispering prompts. For example, if, after Dajon read the sentence, he didn't know what to do, I might whisper "ask if the pattern is formal or informal." Eventually students will become more comfortable in the leadership role. If time is the issue, edit a few of the sentences and save the rest for a later time.

Sharing for Understanding

Allow the students to share their work with the class.

As you come back to the carpet, I would like you to choose one sentence to share with the class. Since we just finished editing, all of the sentences we share will be formal or informal?

STUDENTS: **Formal!**

Okay, who would like to get us started? Tehjia?

TEHJIA: **My grandma is moving to North Carolina.**

My grandma is. How does that follow the formal *am/is/are* pattern?

GARRETT: ***She* plus *is*.**

Excellent. Quintin, what is your sentence? (We continue to share in this manner. I stop periodically to ask students to articulate what formal pattern is being followed.)

Close the lesson by asking the students to assess how useful they felt the lesson was.

I want you to think about how helpful today's lesson was. Do you think today's lesson helped you to edit *am/is/are* patterns? If you think the lesson was helpful, show a thumbs-up. If you do not think the lesson was helpful, show a thumbs-down. If you think the lesson was a little useful, show a thumbs to the side. (The students signal their opinions.) Would anyone like to share their opinion?

ANDREW: **I don't think it was helpful because I already use the formal pattern.**

Okay. Did anyone have a different opinion?

DAR'ASIA: **It helped me because I had a lot of informal patterns, and now I already did the editing for them.**

Good. Anyone else want to share? (I allow a few students to share their opinions.)

Assessing the Lesson

In this lesson, I expect students to be able to accurately edit their own work for the formal *am/is/are* patterns with relatively few mistakes. I assess the students' ability to edit their work independently. Although I offer support and guidance to those students who need it, the goal is for students to be able to edit for the patterns on their own. I pair students who struggle with editing for the *am/is/are* patterns with students who more readily grasp the concept when editing subsequent assignments. Students who are having difficulties often do better with these assigned peer editors.

9 Using *Be*

Lessons

THIS UNIT INCLUDES THE FOLLOWING LESSONS:

1. Defining Informal and Formal Patterns for Using *Be*
2. Practicing Code-Switching with *Be* Patterns from Literature

Here we continue working on the contrasts between verbs in vernacular and Standard English. The subject of this unit is "using *be*." (*She walking the dog* vs. *She's walking the dog.*)

In our other units on verbs, we looked at subject–verb agreement for regular verbs (*Mama walk to the store* vs. *Mama walks to the store*) and for *Be* in present and past tense (*They is working* vs. *They are working*; *We was talking* vs. *We were talking*). We also looked at showing past time by context (*a story about what happen to me last week*) or primarily by verb endings as in Standard English (*a story about what happened to me last week*).

Be adds a new dimension: In certain instances in vernacular English, the verb *be* itself is not necessary. So in these lessons students look for the presence or absence of the verb *be* and they actively use comparison and contrast as they identify the *be* pattern in informal English.

UNIT 9

Using *Be*

The Pattern

In this unit, we explore another verb pattern. Indeed, we'll look at another form of the verb *be*. In Units 7 and 8, we saw how African American English and Standard English contrasted in subject–verb agreement patterns for *was/were and am/is/are* (*we was* vs. *we were*; *we is* vs. *we are*). Here, we explore another contrast in the use of the verb *be* between this vernacular and Standard English. The contrast lies in whether we use or do not use the word *be*.

Vernacular pattern:
I* + *am
Otherwise, subject + rest of sentence

Standard English pattern:
Subject + a form of *be*

The Code-Switching Chart

Identifying vernacular *be* patterns in kids' work

Identifying vernacular instances of *be* understood in students' work is easy. You'll immediately notice that the verb *be* appears to be "missing." That's the clue that a pattern in a different language variety is afoot.

This student has used the informal pattern for *be* understood: **any (other) subject (besides *I*) plus rest of sentence**.

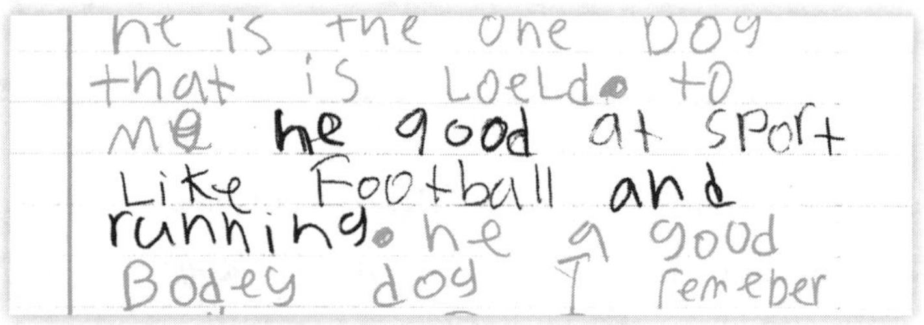
he is the one Dog
that is Loeld to
me he good at Sport
Like Football and
running. he a good
Bodey dog I remeber

He good at sports like football and running.

Choosing/creating the examples

In choosing examples for your chart, look for a blend of where *be* would occur in Standard English as a full verb and where it would occur as an auxiliary. As always when working with verbs, you'll look for examples of all the persons and numbers (*I, you, he/she/it, we, you, they*). This will show the full range of places where the vernacular patterns contrast with the patterns in Standard English.

Don't worry if you don't find examples of all the persons and numbers of subjects. If you find a selection using *he/she/it,* and maybe *you* and *they*, you can construct the rest of the chart yourself. As time goes on, you'll collect authentic examples to flesh out your Using *Be* code-switching chart.

Creating the code-switching chart

We title our chart Using *Be*. As always, we list informal sentences from student writing on the left, writing their formal translations next to them on the right. And as always, we correct any spelling or punctuation and change any other vernacular patterns to their Standard English equivalents. Finally, we write *The Pattern* under each column of the chart, leaving space to write the pattern during the lesson.

Notice that the pattern for first-person sentences will be the same across both vernacular and Standard English: *I am watching the movie.* For first-person singular, vernacular English requires a form of *be* (*am*) to be present, just as in Standard English.

The details for predicting when vernacular English can omit *be* are fairly complex (Pullum, 1999). Fortunately, we don't have to predict; we just have to springboard from when students actually use the vernacular *be* pattern. Students will discover that vernacular English keeps *be* for sentences with first-person singular subjects (*I*) and may delete it when Standard English could contract *be*. (*She's fine!*)

USING *BE*

INFORMAL	**FORMAL**
I am watching the movie.	I'm watching the movie.
I'll play when you ___ finished.	I'll play when you're finished.
She ___ my best friend.	She's my best friend.
David ___ playing basketball.	David's playing basketball.
It ___ my turn.	It's my turn.
We ___ walking to school.	We're walking to school.
They ___ happy.	They're happy.
THE PATTERN	**THE PATTERN**
I + am **otherwise, subject + rest of sentence**	**subject + a form of *be***

Now we're ready for the lesson!

Lesson 1

Defining Informal and Formal Patterns for Using *Be*

Engagement

▶ **Have the students gather around the easel. Review contractions as a group.**

We're going to start today by reviewing something you learned a long time ago. Think back to when you learned about contractions. What is a contraction?

> TEHJIA: **When you put two words together and leave some of the letters out, like *don't*.**

Exactly! Let's look at some contractions and see if you can tell me which two words are used to make the contraction in each of these sentences. (I show the students a piece of chart paper with several sentences containing contractions.)

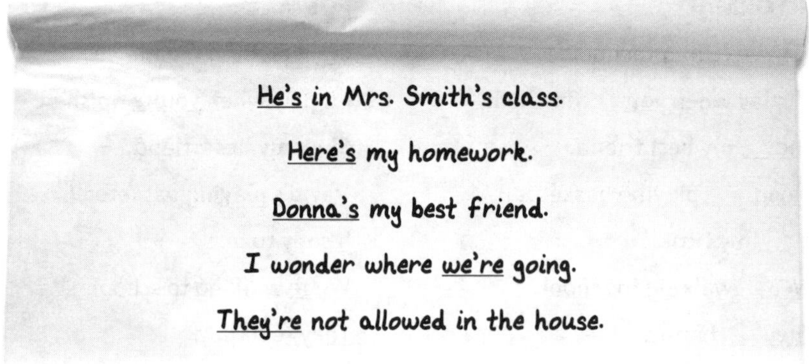

He's in Mrs. Smith's class.
Here's my homework.
Donna's my best friend.
I wonder where we're going.
They're not allowed in the house.

Which two words make up the word *He's* in the first sentence?

> DAJON: ***He is.***

Yes, because *He is in Mrs. Smith's class* makes sense. What about *Here's*?

> ONTIANA: ***Here is.***

Here is my homework. That has the same meaning! Here's a tricky one. Which two words are contracted to make up *Donna's* in the third sentence?

> TAJANTA: ***Donna is.***

Donna is my best friend. Wow! You're good! Let's try *we're* in the fourth sentence.

> QUINTIN: ***We are.***

I wonder where we are going. Good. (We finish the last sentence in the same manner.)

materials

- chart paper with sample sentences for reviewing contractions
- chart paper with sample sentences for combining subject + *be*
- *Using Be* code-switching chart
- chart paper, markers, pencils, paper

goals

STUDENTS WILL:

- recognize *be* patterns inside formal and informal language.
- define *be* patterns inside formal and informal language.
- distinguish between formal and informal *be* patterns.

Direct Instruction

Introduce the topic for today's lesson. Have students combine subjects and *be* verbs to form contractions.

We have discussed and described a lot of different formal and informal patterns this year. The pattern we're going to talk about today is a little more complicated, but I know you can do it. Today we are going to be using our understanding of contractions that use different forms of the verb *be*. That means we are going to look at patterns in which *am, are,* and *is* are a part of a contraction. Let's start by looking at some sentences that contain *am, are,* and *is*. (I reveal the sentences.)

I am watching the movie.

I'll play when you are finished.

She is my best friend.

David is playing basketball.

It is my turn.

We are walking to school.

They are brothers.

The first thing we are going to do is look at the underlined subject and *be* verb and combine them to make a contraction. Let's look at the first sentence. *I am watching the movie.* What is the contraction for *I am*?

DORIS: *I'm.*

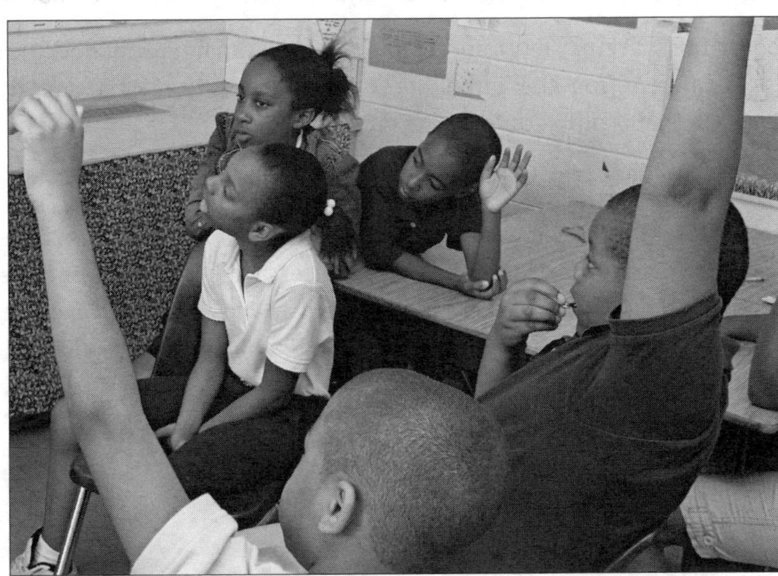

note

Since contractions will play such a large part in our rules for Using *Be*, we spend some time reviewing this form.

Exactly. I cross out *I am* in the sentence and write *I'm*. (We go through each sentence in the same manner.) Now that you have changed all of the subject–*be* verb combinations to contractions, you have just created the formal side of our code-switching chart! (I show the students the chart.)

USING *BE*

INFORMAL	*FORMAL*
I am watching the movie.	I'm watching the movie.
I'll play when you finished.	I'll play when you're finished.
She my best friend.	She's my best friend.
David playing basketball.	David's playing basketball.
It my turn.	It's my turn.
We walking to school.	We're walking to school.
They brothers.	They're brothers.
THE PATTERN	THE PATTERN

note

The Using *Be* pattern is an advanced one appropriate to the higher grades (fifth or sixth and beyond).

Focus students' attention on how the informal and formal sides differ.

Look at the chart for a few minutes and see if you can figure out how the informal side is different from the formal side. What do you notice? What does the formal side have that is different from the informal side?

DAR'ASIA: **The formal side has contractions.**

On the formal side, each subject is contracted with *am, are*, or *is*. It seems that inside formal language, *are* and *is* are necessary, but that is not the case in informal English. And actually, formal English adds a form of *be* where other languages, like Russian, do not, so informal English is a lot like Russian in this pattern!

Identify and summarize the formal pattern.

Let's see if we can describe the formal pattern.

> ONTIANA: **Subject plus apostrophe *-m*, or apostrophe *-s*, or apostrophe *-re*.**

That seems to describe the pattern. Since *am, are,* and *is* are all forms of the verb *be,* we could say the pattern is **subject plus a form of *be***. Let's make sure that it works in each sentence before we write it down. *I'm watching the movie.* Do we have a subject plus a form of *be*, an apostrophe *-m*, *-s,* or *-re*?

> STUDENTS: **Yes!**

What is the pattern?

> DORIS: ***I'm.***

Yes, so the first sentence follows our pattern of subject plus *be*. (We go through each formal sentence in the same way. I write **subject + a form of *be*** under the formal column.)

Identify and summarize the informal pattern.

Now let's look at the informal pattern. Where does it change?

> ONTIANA: **It doesn't have a *be* verb. Well, except for the first sentence.**

Let's hold off on the first sentence. The rest of the sentences don't have a *be* verb. What do they have?

> ONTIANA: **A subject.**

Exactly. Our pattern is **subject plus the rest of the sentence**, and we could even say *be* is understood. We *understand* that the *be* is not necessary in informal language. Let's check to make sure each of our informal sentences follows the pattern of **subject plus rest of sentence**. (We check each sentence to make sure the pattern is correct. I write **subject + rest of sentence** under the informal heading.) Now let's go back to the first sentence. What is the pattern?

> HEZEKIAH: ***I* plus *am*.**

Exactly. So we have ***I* plus *am*** and **otherwise, subject plus rest of the sentence**. (I write the patterns on the informal side.)

THE PATTERN	THE PATTERN
I + am	*subject + a form of be*
otherwise, subject + rest of sentence	

Guided Practice

Aid the students in writing sentences that contain the Using *Be* pattern.

Now that we have described the patterns, let's take a moment to write a sentence using one of the patterns. We are going to pretend we are talking to our friends using *it* or *we* for the subject. Do you think we should use formal or informal language?

SEVERAL STUDENTS: **Formal!**

SEVERAL STUDENTS: **Informal!**

Actually, you're all right. Since you are talking to your friends, you can choose to use formal or informal language. What would you like to use for the sentence we are going to write together? Formal or informal?

TAJANTA: **Formal.**

OK, do we want to use *it* or *we* as our subject?

I'ANA: ***It.***

Now what is going to come after the word *it*? We have a couple of choices for formal language. What are our choices?

NIJE: **We can use *is*.**

We could use *is*, or we can use the contraction for *it is*, which is ...

SEVERAL STUDENTS: ***It's*!**

Which should we use?

GARRETT: ***It's*, because it's shorter to write!**

Okay, Garrett, go ahead and write *It's* on the board. (Garrett writes *It's*.) That's the beginning of our sentence. What do we want the rest of our sentence to say?

BOBBY: **It's raining outside.**

Let's write that on the board. (Bobby adds *raining outside* to *It's*.) How does this sentence fit our formal pattern?

I'ANA: **Subject plus *be*.**

Right, subject plus a form of *be*. What is the subject?

I'ANA: ***It.***

And what is the *be* verb?

QUATASIA: ***Is.***

So our sentence fits the pattern because we have the subject *it* plus *is*, which is a form of the *be* verb. Nice job!

It's raining outside.

Independent Practice

Have the students write a sentence showing the formal or informal *be* patterns.

We've written a sentence together, and I want you to try just one sentence on your own. Pretend you're talking to your friend just like we did when we wrote our sentence together, so you can write an informal sentence or a formal sentence. You may use either *it* or *we* as the subject of your sentence. When we come back together as a group, you will have the chance to read your sentence to the class. Are there any questions? (I answer any questions the students ask before giving them five minutes to write their sentences. I help students on an individual basis.)

Sharing for Understanding

Have the students share their sentences with the class.

Here is your chance to shine! We're just going to go around the circle. When it's your turn, read your sentence aloud for everyone to hear. The rest of us will be listening, and we will give the sign language sign for *I* if the *be* pattern is informal and we'll give the sign language sign for *F* if it is formal. (I show the students the signs.) Who would like to go first?

GARRETT: ***My dad painting my room today.***

Show your sign language letters. (The students show their signs.) Good. Garrett's sentence is informal. How does he follow the informal pattern? What is the subject, and how does Garrett make it informal?

ANDREW: **The subject is *dad* and then the rest of the sentence.**

How do you know this is using the *be* pattern?

ANDREW: **For formal language it would be *my dad IS painting my room today*.**

Yes, you're exactly right. Formal English would say *My dad is painting my room today* or *My dad's painting my room today*. So we know Garrett is following the informal *be* pattern. Tehjia? (Each student has the opportunity to share. I stop periodically to ask how a particular pattern is being followed.)

Conclude the lesson by allowing the students to evaluate how easy or difficult the lesson was for them.

We're going to stop here for today. But before you go back to your seats, let's reflect, or think about, what we did today. We defined the formal and informal Using *Be* patterns. We wrote sentences using either the formal or informal *be* patterns. Finally, we listened to our classmates' sentences and classified them as either formal or informal. Thumbs-up if you felt that today's lesson was easy for you to understand, thumbs-down if you think today's lesson was difficult to understand, and thumbs to the side if some of it was easy and some of it was difficult. (The students show their thumbs.) I know this is a difficult type of pattern, but we'll continue to work on it when we edit our work.

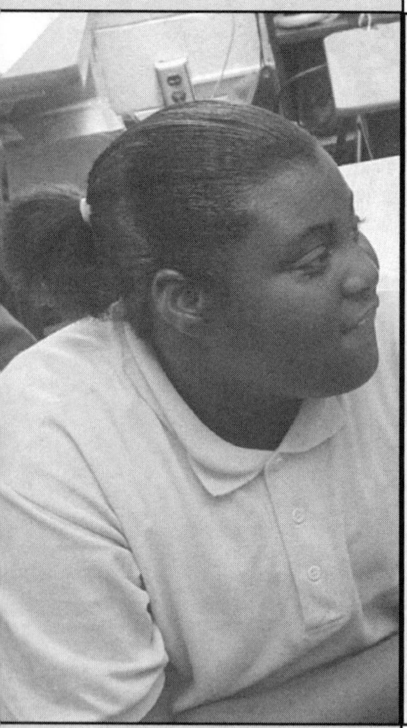

Assessing the Lesson

This is a difficult concept, and I expect the students to struggle with it a little bit. To assess the success of this lesson, I closely monitor students during their Independent Practice. I make a mental note of which students struggle the most. I will work with these students individually or in a small group in subsequent lessons. I also note which students do not recognize whether the patterns are formal or informal during sharing time. Often I will see students waiting until they see what their classmates are doing. I will focus on these students during the Guided Practice in my next lesson to check that they understand the patterns. Students who cannot classify the patterns will certainly not be able to edit for the formal *be* pattern.

Practicing Code-Switching with *Be* Patterns from Literature

Engagement

Have the students gather around the Using *Be* chart they helped to complete yesterday. Review the formal and informal patterns.

Yesterday we learned about a new type of language pattern. Who remembers the name of the pattern?

SEVERAL STUDENTS: **Using *Be*.**

Let's review the informal and formal patterns by looking at a few sentences and describing how these sentences use the *be* patterns. (I show the students the first sentence, which I have written on a sentence strip.)

My brother's a teacher in New York.

Is this sentence informal or formal?

SEVERAL STUDENTS: **Formal!**

How does it follow the formal *be* pattern?

NIJE: **It has a subject plus *is*.**

What is the subject?

NIJE: ***My brother.***

We have the subject *My brother* plus *be* contracted, which in this case is *'s*.

Let's look at the next sentence. (I show the students another sentence written on a sentence strip.)

My mom at home today.

Does this sentence follow the informal or formal *be* pattern?

SEVERAL STUDENTS: **Informal!**

How does it fit the informal pattern?

DAJON: **The subject is *mom*; then it's just the rest of the sentence.**

Exactly!

Lesson 2

materials

- sentence strips with sentences showing the formal and informal Using *Be* pattern
- various books that contain sentences with the informal *be* pattern (see list on page 215)
- two or three overheads of pages from the literature that use the informal *be* pattern
- chart paper, markers, pencils, paper

goals

STUDENTS WILL:

- recognize Using *Be* patterns in formal and informal language.
- define Using *Be* patterns in formal and informal language.
- locate informal *be* patterns in literature.
- translate informal *be* patterns into formal patterns.

ways of talking

Since our treatment of formal and informal language has been to help students recognize the power of choice when it comes to language, students should not feel that they are editing or looking for errors within the literature. Rather, we want students to understand the process involved in creating a chart. Additionally, it is important to let students know that future lessons will address when and how authors use informal language in their work.

Direct Instruction

Set the purpose of the lesson. Explain how you'll be using examples of the informal *be* pattern in literature to build a code-switching chart. Remind students that authors can choose to use informal English when having their characters speak.

Now that we've taken a few minutes to review the *be* patterns, we're going to use that knowledge to create our own code-switching charts in groups.

Remember when we were reading *Flossie and the Fox,* we compared how the characters spoke? Who can tell me what we learned?

GARRETT: **Flossie spoke informal and the fox spoke formal!**

That's right, the author of *Flossie and the Fox* chose to use different language styles for her characters. She had Flossie speak informally and the fox speak formally. We'll see that authors often use informal language to create a character. Today, you're going to use different literature to create a code-switching chart. Normally, when I create a chart, I use examples of informal patterns from your writing. Then I translate the sentence to formal English so we can compare and contrast the different patterns. That's what we are going to do today, but we're going to find examples for our chart in literature.

I'm going to give each team a piece of chart paper with a blank Using *Be* chart (I hold up a piece of the paper) and several books. You're going to look through different books to find examples of the informal *be* pattern. Once you find an informal *be* pattern, you're going to write the sentence with the pattern on your chart paper. Then you're going to translate that sentence into formal English.

Demonstrate finding an example of the informal *be* pattern in literature and adding it to the code-switching chart.

Let me show you what this will look like. This is a transparency of a page from *Nettie Jo's Friends.* (I put a transparency of page one on the overhead for the students to see.) I'm going to read through the page. As I'm reading, I'm looking for informal *be* understood patterns. (I begin reading through the page.) Oh, here's an example of the informal *be* understood! *Annie Mae, we goin' to a wedding.* I know this is an example of informal *be* because after the subject, which is *we,* I could add *are* for formal English. So in this sentence, the *be* is not written because it is understood. That is the informal pattern. I'm going to write this sentence on the informal side of my chart. When I write my sentence, I'm going to leave a blank after *we* to show that the *be* is understood. (I write "Annie Mae, we ____ goin' to a wedding.") Now I have to code-switch to formal English. To make this sentence formal, I will need to add *are* or *'re* after *we.* (I write "Annie Mae, we are goin' to a wedding." on the formal side of the chart.) Does everyone understand what I did?

Guided Practice

Guide the students in locating and code-switching informal examples of using *be*.

Let's try one together. Here is a page from *William and the Good Old Days*. (I put a transparency of page eight on the overhead.) Go ahead and read it to yourselves. When you think you see the informal *be* pattern, hold up one finger. (The students read silently, several fingers going up as they read.) Wow! I see a lot of people who think they've found the pattern! Let's see if you're right. Garrett, would you read the sentence with the informal *be* pattern?

GARRETT: ***I know you not talking to Mama like that.***

Thumbs-up if you agree with Garrett, and thumbs to the side if you disagree. It looks like we're in agreement. Where is the *be* pattern in this sentence? How will we write it on our chart?

ONTIANA: ***You* and then a line.**

You and then a blank. Quatasia, would you please write our sentence in the informal column? Don't forget the line to show where the *be* understood is. (Quatasia writes "I know you ___ not talking to Mama like that.") Now for our chart we need to code-switch to formal English. How will we change this sentence to make it formal?

DORIS: **Write "you're."**

Give us the whole sentence.

DORIS: ***I know you're not talking to Mama like that.***

And we have the subject *you* plus an apostrophe *-re*, which is a contracted form of *you are*. So this sentence follows our pattern. Bobby, please write our translated sentence under the formal column. (Bobby writes the sentence.) What should Bobby underline in the sentence?

DESTINY: ***You're.***

Bobby, would you please underline the formal pattern in the sentence. (Bobby underlines *you're*.) Let's try one more together, since this pattern is a little more difficult than some of the others we have done. This is a page from *The Patchwork Quilt*. (I put the transparency on the overhead machine for the students to view.) Read the page quietly to yourselves, and put one finger up when you think you've found the informal *be* understood pattern. (I give the students a few minutes to read. Several students give the sign that they have found the pattern.) Which sentence contains the pattern?

HEZEKIAH: ***Makin' this quilt gonna be a joy.***

How does this sentence show the informal *be* pattern? (We think through the pattern in this sentence in the same manner as the first sentence. A student writes the informal pattern on the chart. Then the students code-switch the sentence, making it formal. Another student writes the formal sentence on the chart.)

what if...

the students are unable to locate the informal *be* patterns in the example pages?

If this happens, I give students a smaller selection of sentences to choose from by highlighting a paragraph or a few sentences on the page. If the students are really struggling, I recommend creating an entire chart as a class, then having the students find one or two examples of the pattern on their own. I might also take two days to teach this particular lesson. I would stop after the Guided Practice on the first day and begin with a brief review before having students complete the independent work the next day. This is a difficult pattern, and the students may need more support to master it.

Independent Practice

Have the students work in groups to create their own code-switching chart for the *be* patterns.

You did an excellent job finding the informal *be* understood patterns and helping to create a class chart. Now you're going to create your own charts in your groups. I have already drawn and labeled your charts. You will be responsible for using the books I have on each table to find examples of the informal *be* pattern. This is what we just did as a group. To help you find the example sentences, I have put a sticky note on the pages that contain the informal pattern in each book, so you do not need to read through the entire book; just read the pages with the sticky notes on them.

Once you find an informal example, you're going to write it under the informal column on your chart. Then you are going to translate, or code-switch, the informal pattern to formal language. Make sure you underline the patterns in your sentences, just like we did together.

note

It is important for students to understand when and why authors use informal language when they write. However, this is not the focus of this unit. We will explore the use of character and voice in literature in Unit 11.

Remember that the authors chose informal language for specific reasons. We will discuss when and why authors use informal language in their writing in a couple of weeks. For today, we are using the literature to find examples of the informal *be* pattern. Are there any questions? (I answer questions.) I will leave the chart we started together out so you can use that to help you. (As I walk around the room, I help individuals and groups who are having difficulties. I also take this opportunity to ask questions about the process the groups are using to create their charts.)

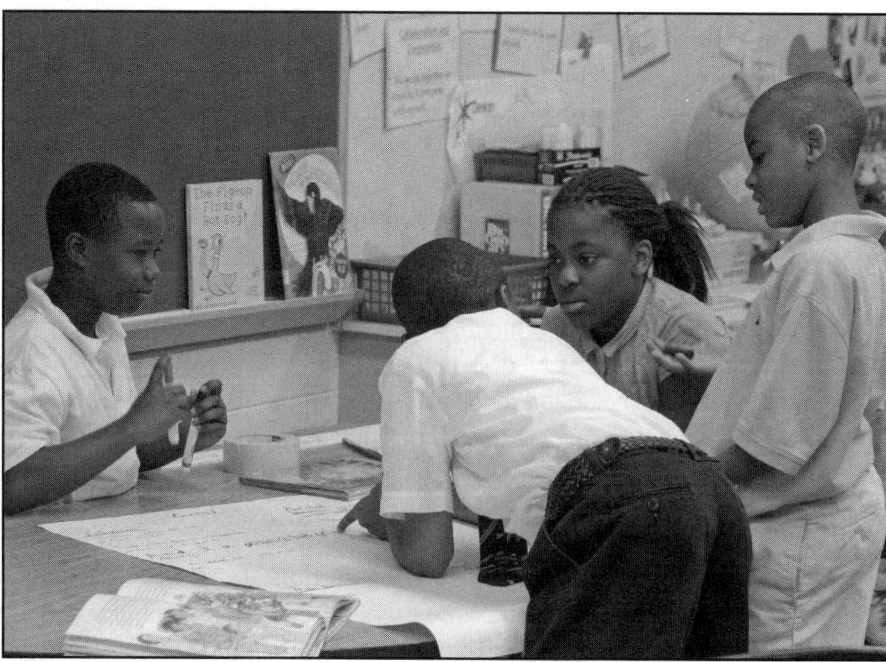

Sharing for Understanding

As the students complete their charts, post them in a central location. Allow each group to share one of the examples from their chart.

Wow! You all did a fantastic job of finding sentences with the informal *be* pattern. This was a difficult pattern, but you worked through it! I am going to have each group share one of the sentences they found in the literature. Once you read your informal sentence, I want you to read your formal sentence. Those of us who are listening are going to give a thumbs-up if we agree with how you've translated to formal English and a thumbs to the side if we disagree with you. Let's start with Dar'Asia's group. Dar'Asia?

DAR'ASIA: **In *Flossie and the Fox*, we found *I don't believe you a fox.***

And how did you change that to formal English?

DAR'ASIA: ***I don't believe you're a fox.***

Thumbs-up or thumbs to the side? I agree. This group did a great job with this sentence. I saw a lot of examples of sentences from *Flossie and the Fox*! Let's hear from Dawnnella's group. (Each group shares one example from their chart.)

Conclude the lesson by allowing several students to share what was difficult about the lesson.

I know this type of pattern was a little more challenging than some of the other patterns we have studied. I want you to think about today's lesson and the *be* patterns. What was difficult about this lesson or the patterns?

TEHJIA: **It was hard to find the patterns in the books.**

What was hard about it?

TEHJIA: **There wasn't any words to look for. Like when we did *is*, we just looked for that word.**

This was a more difficult type of pattern because there wasn't a specific word to look for. How many of you thought that was something difficult about the lesson? (Several students raise their hands and nod their heads in agreement.) What else was difficult about the lesson? (I allow several students to share.) As we continue to work with these patterns, you will find it much easier to code-switch between informal and formal English.

Remember that the authors chose informal language for specific reasons. We will discuss when and why authors use informal language in their writing in a couple of weeks. For today, we are using the literature to find examples of the informal *be* pattern.

suggested literature

Flossie and the Fox, by Patricia McKissack, illustrated by Rachel Isadora. New York: Scholastic (1986).

Mirandy and Brother Wind, by Patricia McKissack, illustrated by Jerry Pinkney. New York: Knopf (1988).

Nappy Hair, by Carolivia Herron, illustrated by Joe Cepeda New York: Dragonfly Books (1998).

Nettie Jo's Friends by Patricia McKissack, illustrated by Jerry Pinkney. New York: Knopf (1989).

The Patchwork Quilt, by Valerie Flournoy, illustrated by Jerry Pinkney. New York: Dial (1985).

Pink and Say, by Patricia Polacco. New York: Philomel (1994).

William and the Good Old Days, by Eloise Greenfield, illustrated by Jan Spivey Gilchrist. New York: HarperCollins (1993).

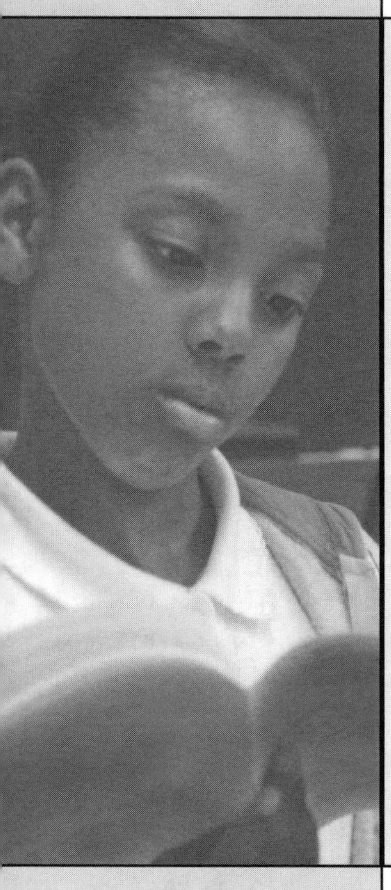

Assessing the Lesson

This is a very difficult lesson for elementary students. To assess this lesson, I focus on the students' understanding of the process used in creating a chart in addition to their understanding of the Using *Be* pattern. As I informally assess these two things, I make adjustments to the lesson based on the students' abilities. While students are using the same process they have used before, they're extending their abilities as they explore this more difficult type of pattern.

The most challenging part of this lesson is locating the informal *be* pattern in various texts, because the students have to remember to look for where formal English would use *be*, either in its full or its contracted form. This is why I mark the pages where the patterns can be found. If students still can't find the informal patterns in the books, I will often pull them back together as a whole group, and we will complete the chart together.

Extending the Lesson

Students do not have to master these patterns for the lesson to be successful. Nevertheless, you may find that your students need more practice with the Using *Be* pattern before they are ready to begin editing writing on their own. Here are a couple ideas for additional lessons that focus on editing student work.

1. Mimic previous units by rewriting selected student paragraphs on chart paper. The selected paragraphs should contain either the informal *be* pattern or a combination of the formal and informal *be* patterns. Have your students work with a partner or in small groups to edit the paragraphs for the Using *Be* pattern. Make sure you follow the established routine of highlighting formal examples of the pattern and changing informal patterns to formal and then highlighting the now-formal pattern.
2. Have your students use a recent formal writing or allow them to look through their writing folders so that they can edit their own writing for the formal *be* pattern. As your students edit their work, meet with individuals to clear up any misconceptions, offer help in locating patterns, and provide positive feedback.

10 Multiple Patterns

Lessons

THIS UNIT INCLUDES THE FOLLOWING LESSONS:

1. Editing Multiple Patterns Within a Single Sentence
2. Peer-Editing with Multiple Patterns
3. Editing for Multiple Patterns

So far, in each lesson, we've presented students with only one vernacular pattern per sentence in order to help focus their learning. But of course, writing is not so tidy or simple. Often, we find more than one vernacular pattern in a sentence. So students need to be able to handle multiple vernacular patterns in one sentence. That's what this unit accomplishes – it helps students integrate their learning to handle more complex writing environments, and become ever more independent in their abilities to choose the language to fit the context.

We do this unit after we have finished teaching the code-switching units (diversity, possessive, plural, past time, etc.). By then, we know our students are ready to begin addressing more of the grammar complexities of real writing, combining and reinforcing their learning from all our earlier code-switching units.

UNIT 10

Multiple Patterns

The Patterns

These are the range of grammar patterns students have explored so far:

SHOWING POSSESSION

INFORMAL	FORMAL
Christopher family moved to Spain.	Christopher's family moved to Spain.
THE PATTERN	**THE PATTERN**
owner + what is owned	**owner + *'s* + what is owned**

PLURAL PATTERNS

INFORMAL	FORMAL
I have two brother. I fit all the book in my bag. I love cat.	I have two brothers. I fit all the books in my bag. I love cats.
THE PATTERN	**THE PATTERN**
number words **other signal words** **common knowledge**	**noun + *s***

PAST TIME PATTERNS

INFORMAL	FORMAL
Yesterday I trade my MP3 player. Martin Luther King, Jr., talk to the people.	Yesterday I traded my MP3 player. Martin Luther King, Jr., talked to the people.
THE PATTERN	**THE PATTERN**
time words and phrases **common knowledge**	**verb + *ed***

SUBJECT-VERB AGREEMENT

INFORMAL	**FORMAL**
He walk to school every day. You walk to school every day.	He walks to school every day. You walk to school every day.
THE PATTERN subject + bare verb	**THE PATTERN** *he/she/it* subject + verb + *s* any other subject + bare verb

WAS/WERE PATTERNS

INFORMAL	**FORMAL**
I was working. You was working. They was working.	I was working. You were working. They were working.
THE PATTERN any subject + *was*	**THE PATTERN** I, *he/she/it* subject + *was* any other subject + *were*

AM/IS/ARE PATTERNS

INFORMAL	**FORMAL**
I am working. The car is working. We is working.	I am working. The car is working. We are working.
THE PATTERN *I* + *am* any other subject + *is*	**THE PATTERN** *I* + *am* *he/she/it* subject + *is* any other subject + *are*

USING *BE*

INFORMAL	**FORMAL**
I am watching the movie. She my best friend. They happy.	I'm watching the movie. She's my best friend. They're happy.
THE PATTERN *I* + *am* otherwise, subject + rest of sentence	**THE PATTERN** subject + a form of *be*

No code-switching chart for this unit!

Unlike most other units, we will not be using a code-switching chart in this unit. Instead, we will make sure all our other code-switching charts are posted around the room or available for students in notebook-sized form so they'll have the resources they need.

Choosing or creating examples for practice with multiple patterns

In this unit, we present students with sentences that contain two, three, and even four vernacular grammar patterns. The task will be for them to identify the grammar patterns and translate them to Standard English. Of course, we work with sentences exemplifying the grammar patterns we've studied so far.

While we sometimes find examples of naturally occurring sentences with multiple vernacular patterns in them, sometimes we find we need to create sentences for student practice. Whether we use naturally occurring sentences or ones we create, here are a set of tips that help us support student learning. We make sure that ...

Possessive sentences have	• two full nouns sitting side by side to show owner + owned (*The book is on Jason desk.*)
Plural sentences show plurality through	• number words (*four, both...*) or • other signal words (*all, lots of, several...*) or • common knowledge (*Send this to the fifth grade teacher in the school* – we know that there are three fifth grade teachers)
Past time sentences have	• a single regular main verb (take an *-ed* ending inside Standard English) • no helping verbs • a time word or show past time through common knowledge
Subject–verb agreement sentences have	• a single regular, main verb (take an *-s* ending inside Standard English) • no helping verbs
Was/were sentences have	• a *you* style subject or • a *we* or *they* style subject (these are the places of contrast with Standard English)
Am/is/are sentences have	• a *you* style subject or • a *we* or *they* style subject (these are the places of contrast with Standard English)
Using be sentences have	• a *you* style subject or • a *he/she/it* style subject or • a *we* or *they* style subject (these are the places of contrast with Standard English)

Editing Multiple Patterns Within a Single Sentence

Engagement

Have the students gather around the chart paper. Ask them to recall previously taught patterns.

We have been spending a considerable amount of time working with formal and informal language. I want you to think about the different patterns we have learned about. Which patterns have we discussed?

ONTIANA: **Plurals.**

Plurals. (I start a list by writing *Plurals* on chart paper). What other patterns have we discussed?

BOBBY: **We did past time.**

Past time. (I add this to the list.)

GARRETT: ***Was* and *were*.**

I'ANA: ***Is* and *are*.**

Good. (I add these to the list. I continue to allow students to share until all of the previously taught patterns have been named. The list includes possessives, plurals, past time, subject–verb agreement, *was/were*, *is/are*, and using *be*.)

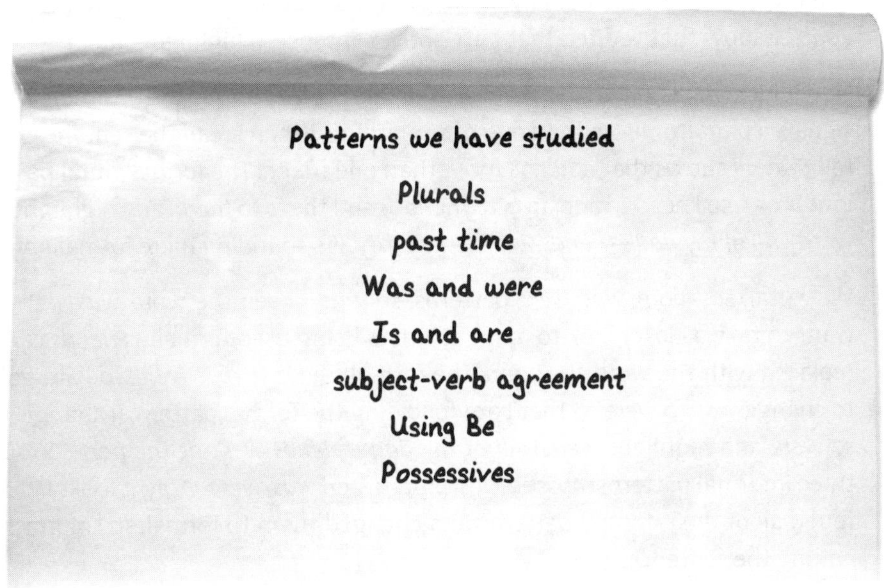

Patterns we have studied
Plurals
past time
Was and were
Is and are
subject-verb agreement
Using Be
Possessives

Lesson 1

materials

- chart paper with sample sentences containing multiple informal patterns
- two sentence strips for each pair of students (each with a different sentence that contains multiple informal patterns)
- sticky notes
- flip-chart paper
- markers, pencils, paper

goals

STUDENTS WILL:

- recognize various informal patterns that have been taught in previous lessons.
- identify informal language patterns in writing.
- edit multiple informal patterns within a single sentence to formal patterns.

Direct Instruction

Introduce the topic for today's lesson.

We have learned about a lot of different patterns, haven't we? We have spent time defining, or describing, the patterns, and we've spent time editing for these patterns. I want you to remember that for most school assignments, you should be using formal language. So when you edit, you want to make sure you used formal language in your work. Today we're going to put all of the knowledge we have about formal and informal patterns together and edit sentences that contain more than one informal pattern. This may be a bit of a challenge, but I know you'll be able to do it! I'll model a sentence for you, then we'll try one together.

Model the process of editing a sentence with multiple patterns.

Let's look at this sentence. (I reveal the sentence on a piece of chart paper).

> All of my dad friend was at the party.

When I see this sentence, the first thing I notice is that there is an informal possessive pattern, *dad friend*. The *friend* belongs to *dad*. Since this is a school writing, and we need to be formal for most school writings, I am going to have to change this informal possessive pattern to the formal possessive pattern. The formal possessive pattern is **owner + apostrophe *-s* + what is owned**, so I need to add an apostrophe *-s* to *dad*. (I add the *'s* to *dad*). Just look on our wall charts if you need to remind yourself of any of our grammar patterns. I'm going to highlight *dad's* to show that I edited that part of the sentence. (I highlight *dad's*.)

Now I have *All of my dad's friend was at the party*. I notice the word *all* which signals a plural, or more than one of something. When I read the sentence, I can tell that *all* shows that dad has more than one friend. The formal plural pattern is **noun + *s***, so I need to add an *-s* to *friend*. (I add the *-s* to *friend* and highlight the word). *All of my dad's friends was at the party*. It's sounding more formal now!

We've talked about *was/were* patterns, so when I see the word *was,* I always want to take a closer look to make sure it is being used formally. *Friends* can be replaced with the word *they*, and the formal rule is **they + *were***, so I am going to change *was* to *were* so that I am following the formal pattern. (I change *was* to *were* and highlight *were*.) *All of my dad's friends were at the party*. I found three informal patterns: possessives, plurals, and *was/were*. Okay, it looks like I've found all of the informal patterns and changed them to formal, so I'm finished editing the sentence.

> All of my dad's friends ~~was~~ were at the party.

Guided Practice

Guide the students through the process of editing a sentence with multiple informal patterns.

Now that you've had the opportunity to watch me edit a sentence with more than one informal pattern, we're going to practice one together. Let's take at the sentence you are going to edit. (I show students the sentence).

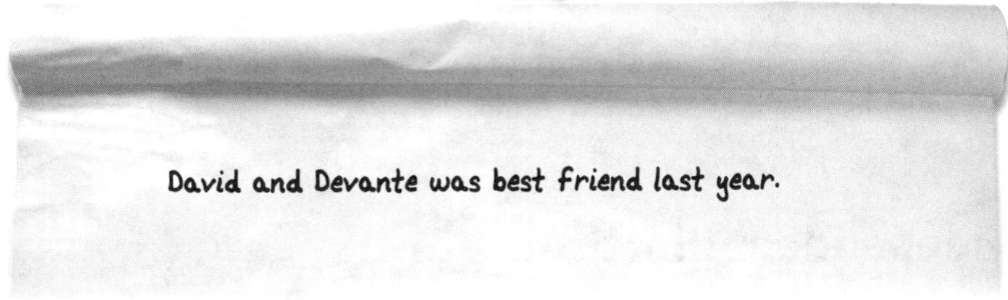
David and Devante was best friend last year.

Dajon, would you please read the sentence aloud for us.

DAJON: ***David and Devante was best friend last year.***

Thank you, Dajon. Does anyone notice any informal patterns in this sentence?

I'ANA: ***Friend*** **is informal.**

Why?

I'ANA: **Because there are two people.**

There is more than one person. What is the name of the pattern that shows more than one?

SEVERAL STUDENTS: **Plurals!**

What do we need to do to make *friend* plural?

ONTIANA: **Add an** ***–s*** **to the end of** ***friend.***

Thumbs up if you agree with Ontiana, thumbs to the side if you disagree. Okay Ontiana, it looks like your classmates agree with you. Go ahead and add the *–s* to *friend* and highlight it so we can remember what you have already edited. Any other informal patterns in this sentence?

GARRETT: ***Was*** **needs to be changed to** ***were.***

Since we want the sentence to be formal, we have to look closely at the *was/were* pattern. How would *were* follow the formal pattern?

GARRETT: ***David and Devante*** **is like** ***they. They*** **goes with** ***were.***

ways of talking

When Garrett says a word "needs to be changed" he continues to embody a deficit view of community language. We reframe in terms of choosing language to fit our purpose and audience by saying something like "Since we want the sentences to be formal in this writing, let's check to see if we've followed the formal pattern."

Thumbs up if you agree, thumbs to the side if you disagree. You're right, the formal pattern is **they + were**. Go ahead and change *was* to *were* and highlight the pattern for us. (Garrett makes the change and highlights *David and Devante were*). Now we have *David and Devante were best friends last year.* Are there any more informal patterns in our sentence? (The students shake their heads).

were
David and Devante was best friends last year.

Independent Practice

Have the students work in pairs to edit sentences with multiple informal patterns.

Now that we've edited a sentence together, you are going to work with a partner to edit two sentences that contain multiple informal patterns. I took some of the sentences from writings you completed and some of them from literature. Each team has different sentences. When you're finished editing your sentences, we will put them up on the board and you will get a chance to check your classmates' work! So double, triple, quadruple check your work before you put it on the board. I will hand out the sentence strips with the sentences you will be editing written on them. Make sure you highlight the patterns you edit. Are there any questions? (I answer any questions). You may begin.

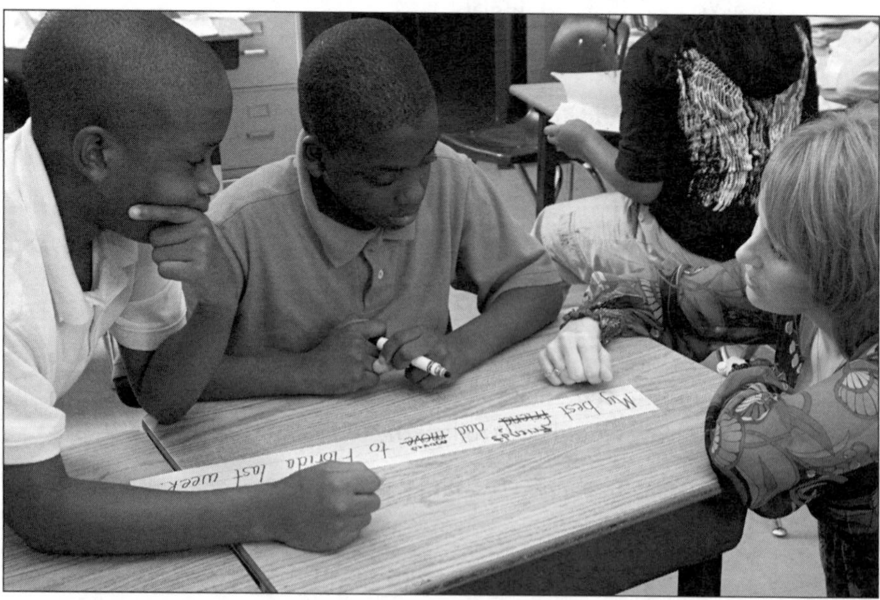

Sharing for Understanding

Display the sentences on the board for students to review. Have the students share the strategies they used to edit the sentences.

I have put all of the sentences you edited on the board. Take a few minutes to look over the sentences your classmates have edited. If you see a sentence that still contains an informal pattern, put a sticky note on it, and we'll discuss it as a class. You don't have to write anything on your sticky note. Remember, you're only putting a sticky note on sentences that still contain an informal pattern. (I give the students a few minutes to review the sentences. If there are any sticky notes, we discuss those sentences as a class. Since the students know ahead of time that their peers will be evaluating their edited sentences, they are usually pretty thorough and rarely leave an informal pattern unedited.)

I want you to think about the strategies you used during the editing process. What did you do to make sure you found all the informal patterns?

BOBBY: **I looked for the easy ones first. Then I did the hard ones.**

What do you mean?

BOBBY: **I looked for *was/were* and *is/are* first because they are the easiest. Then I looked for ownership and more than one because they are sort of easy. Then I looked for subject-verb and past time because those are the hardest.**

That's a great strategy. You edited what you found easiest first. Then edited the more difficult patterns. Did anyone have a different strategy?

DAR'ASIA: **I just read the sentence and if it sounded informal, I changed it.**

Good. Any other strategies? (I allow students who have additional strategies to share them with the class.)

Conclude the lesson by allowing several students to share what they felt was difficult about the lesson.

This lesson was a little more challenging than some of our other lessons. What did you find to be most difficult about it? Let's take five responses. If you agree with someone's answer, show a thumbs-up. Who would like to share?

ONTIANA: **It was hard to find all the patterns because I didn't know exactly which patterns to look for.**

You had a hard time figuring out which patterns needed editing?

ONTIANA: **Yeah. (Several students give a thumbs-up to show they also had difficulty with this.)**

What other difficulties did you find with this lesson? (I allow four more students to share.)

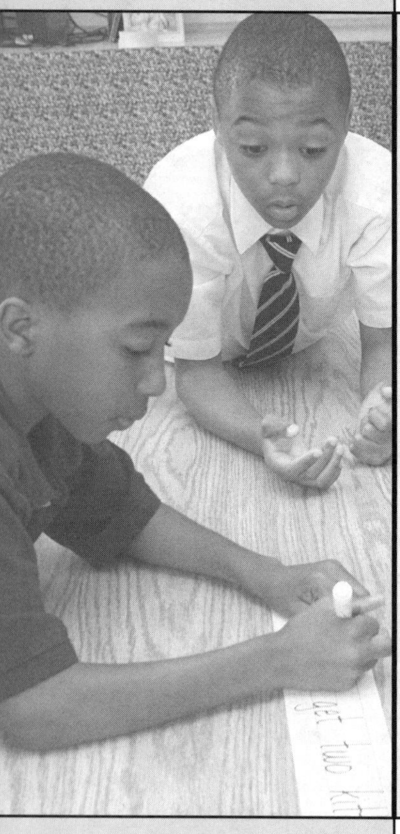

Assessing the Lesson

When I assess this lesson, I take a close look at the process each team uses to edit their sentences. I do not expect students to have too many difficulties editing sentences with multiple informal patterns. I'm not really teaching anything new in this lesson. Rather, I'm requiring students to combine what they already know. As I visit with each team, I am assessing how quickly the students are able to recognize informal patterns within the sentence and how readily they recall the comparable patterns. I help students who are constantly referring to the charts by pulling them into small groups and working with them on editing for two or three patterns at a time. I continue to add patterns until they are editing for all of the informal patterns in a single editing session. The goal is, of course, for students to become proficient in both using and editing for formal language.

Peer-Editing with Multiple Patterns

Engagement

Have the students gather around the easel with a sample sentence written on chart paper. Review the process of editing a sentence with multiple patterns.

Yesterday we edited sentences, and each of the sentences contained more than one of these patterns. Let's see if you remember how to do this. I have a sentence that contains multiple informal patterns. (I show the students the sentence).

All of my friend is going to be at my brother birthday party.

This is a tough one! *All of my friend is going to be at my brother birthday party.* Which informal patterns do you see in this sentence?

DAR'ASIA: ***All of my friend.***

Let's make that formal. What do we need to do?

DAR'ASIA: **Change it to *All of my friends.***

Okay. (I change *friend* to *friends* and highlight it). I have to highlight it so I know I already edited it. What other patterns do you see?

DAJON: **There's a possessive pattern because it says *my brother birthday party.***

Good! What do we need to do to *my brother birthday party* to make it formal?

TEHJIA: **Put an apostrophe *-s* on the end of *brother.***

Exactly. (I add the apostrophe *-s* and highlight *my brother's birthday party.*) To make a possessive pattern formal, I have to put an apostrophe *-s* on the owner. Are there any other patterns? (We finish editing the sentence together). So in this sentence, we found three informal patterns. We found the plural pattern, *am/is/are,* and the possessive pattern. (I point to each pattern in the sentence as I name it.) We often use more than one pattern when we write.

All of my friend^s ~~is~~ are going to be at my brother's birthday party.

Lesson 2

materials

- chart paper with a sample paragraph for editing written on it
- a copy of the Code-Switching Shopping List for each pair of students
- a copy of a student writing sample to edit for each pair of students
- sentence strips
- markers, pencils, paper

goals

STUDENTS WILL:

- recognize various informal patterns that have been taught in previous lessons.
- identify informal language patterns in writing.
- edit multiple informal patterns within a single paragraph to formal patterns.

Direct Instruction

Explain the purpose of today's lesson.

So yesterday we edited sentences that contained more than one informal pattern. We just finished editing a sentence that contained three informal patterns. Today we're going to take it one step further and edit a whole paragraph that contains more than one pattern. Some of the sentences in the paragraph may contain more than one pattern, some might have one informal pattern, and some sentences might not have any informal patterns. So you will have to read very carefully.

Introduce the sample writing paragraph and the code-switching editing sheet.

Let's take a look at a paragraph written by a student a few years ago. (I reveal the paragraph, which I have written on chart paper.)

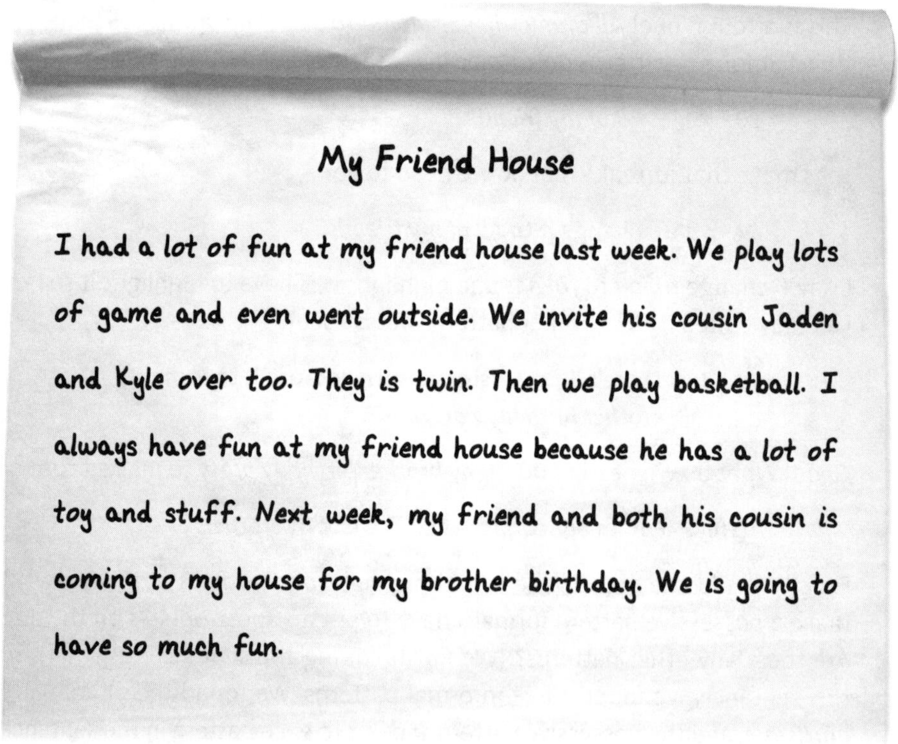

My Friend House

I had a lot of fun at my friend house last week. We play lots of game and even went outside. We invite his cousin Jaden and Kyle over too. They is twin. Then we play basketball. I always have fun at my friend house because he has a lot of toy and stuff. Next week, my friend and both his cousin is coming to my house for my brother birthday. We is going to have so much fun.

Let's take a minute to read the paragraph together. (The students read the paragraph aloud.)

Before we start editing, I want to show you the editing sheet that we're going to be using. (I hold up the editing sheet.) This is our Code-Switching Shopping List (see page 233). Remember how when you go to the store, you write down what you need to look for on a list, so you won't forget? It works the same way with our grammar patterns. As you can see, I have listed all of the patterns we have studied this year so we can remember what to look for. That's why we call it a Code-Switching Shopping List. Every time we find an informal pattern in the paragraph, we're going to put a tally mark next to that pattern on our editing sheet. When we've finished editing, we will know which patterns the author had the most difficulty using. Why would that be important?

ANDREW: We can be more careful when we write.

The sheet will let the author know that in future papers he or she will need to pay close attention to those patterns.

Model the process of editing each sentence for informal patterns using the editing sheet.

Let's go ahead and look at the paragraph. We've already read it, so we can get started with editing. When I start editing, I always begin with the title. When I read the title, *My Friend House*, I immediately see a possessive. The *house* belongs to *my friend*. I know that the formal possessive pattern is **owner + 's + what is owned**, so I need to add an apostrophe *-s* to *friend* to make the title formal. (I add the apostrophe *-s*). Now I'm going to highlight the pattern to show that I have already edited it. Let me put a tally mark next to *possessive* on my editing sheet before I go on to the first sentence. (I mark the editing sheet.) The first sentence says *I had a lot of fun at my friend house last week*. Oh, here's that possessive pattern from the title, *my friend house*! Well that's an easy one, since I just edited the exact same pattern. (I add the *'s* and highlight *my friend's house*. I also add a tally mark next to the *possessive* on the editing sheet.) *I had a lot of fun at my friend's house last week*. I notice the words *last week* in this sentence, so I know that the author is going to talk about events that have already happened. I'll keep that in mind as I edit the rest of the paragraph.

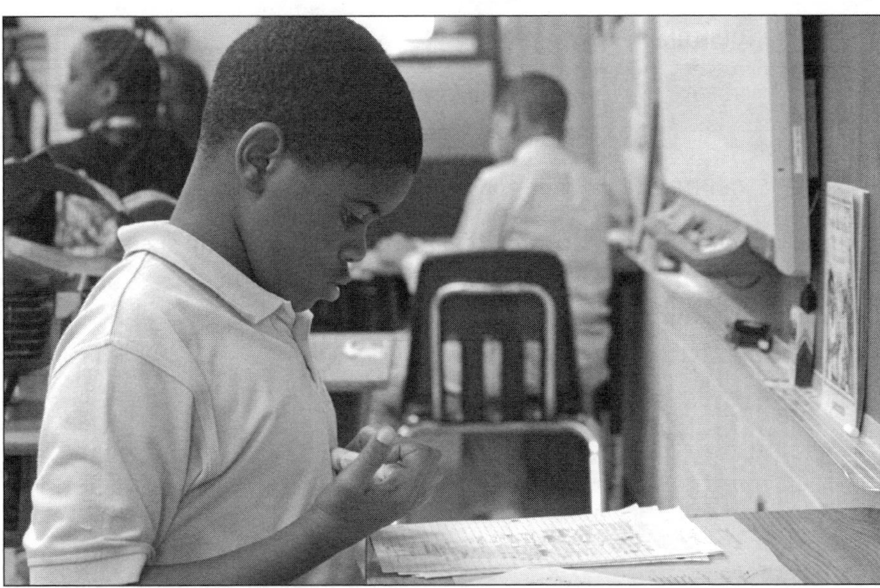

Guided Practice

Allow different students to take the teacher role in editing the remainder of the paragraph.

Let's finish editing the paragraph together. Let's have someone else take over the teacher role for the next sentence. Quintin, would you be our teacher for the next sentence? Start with reading the sentence aloud.

QUINTIN: **Okay. *We play lots of game and even went outside.* I see one!**

Go ahead and talk us through one pattern.

QUINTIN: **I have to change *game* to *games* because there is more than one.**

How do you know?

QUINTIN: **It says *lots.***

Tell us what you're doing as you edit the pattern.

QUINTIN: **I'm adding an *-s* to *game*, and then I'm highlighting *lots of games.***

Don't forget about the editing sheet.

QUINTIN: **Oh, I have to put a mark next to *plural.***

Go ahead and ask your classmates if they see any other patterns in this sentence.

QUINTIN: **Are there any other patterns?**

BOBBY: **You need to change *play* to *played* because it shows past time.**

QUINTIN: **How do you know?**

BOBBY: **Mrs. Swords read *last week* in the first sentence, so it happened last week.**

QUINTIN: **Okay. And I have to put a mark next to *past time.***

(Quintin puts a tally mark next to *past time* on the editing sheet. Then he edits the pattern and highlights it. I choose another student to take on the teacher role, and we finish editing the paragraph as a class.)

Independent Practice

Have the students work in pairs to edit authentic pieces of student writing.

Now that we've edited a paragraph together, it's your turn to edit some of your classmates' writings. You will work with a partner to do exactly what we just did together with *My Friend's House*. Read through the entire piece of writing aloud before you start editing. Make sure you remember to highlight any editing you do. This will let the author know what you changed. Use the editing sheet to help you remember all the patterns. Are there any questions? (I answer any questions the students ask.) You may begin! (The students work in pairs to edit authentic pieces of writing. As they work, I visit each pair to check for understanding.)

Sharing for Understanding

Allow the students to share what they felt was most useful about the assignment.

I saw a lot of great editing today! I saw partners working together and talking about the editing choices they were making. I want you to think about the process you used to edit your paragraphs. In what ways was this activity useful? How was it helpful?

DAWNNELLA: **We got to work with a partner.**

How was that helpful?

DAWNNELLA: **Dar'Asia found some patterns that I didn't even see.**

So working with a partner was helpful because there were two of you looking for the patterns. Well, two brains are better than one! What else was helpful about this lesson? (I allow a couple more students to share).

Conclude the lesson by allowing the students to evaluate their own success in meeting the goal.

The goal of today's lesson was to work with a partner to edit a paragraph that contained many different informal patterns. I want you to think about how successful you were with editing your paragraph. Were you able to find the patterns? Was it difficult or easy to edit? If you understood the lesson and were able to find all the patterns, you're going to give a thumbs-up. If you found some of the patterns or had a few problems with the lesson, you're going to give a thumbs to the side. If you weren't able to find any patterns or had a really hard time with this lesson, you're going to give a thumbs-down. Go ahead and show your thumbs. Good. It looks like most of you are confident with your ability to find informal patterns. For those of you who had some difficulty, we're going to continue to work on this, so don't worry if it was a little rough today. It will get easier!

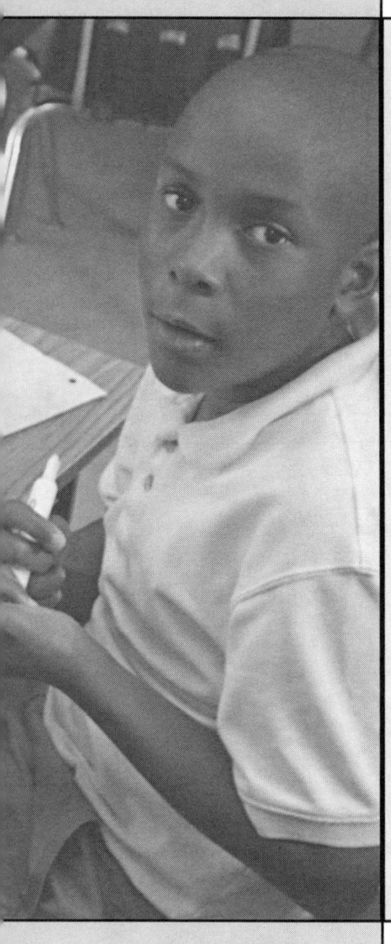

Assessing the Lesson

Although the students are not learning anything new, it can be overwhelming for some children to look for so many patterns at once. As I interact with the students during their independent practice, I assess their ability to locate various informal patterns. I take written notes of what I notice. For example, I might note that a particular student failed to locate any subject–verb agreement patterns. I also note which students rely too much on their partners. When I see this happening, I tell the pair to take turns finding patterns. I watch for a few minutes to make sure that both students are taking equal responsibility in editing. I expect students to become more proficient in locating and editing informal patterns as they practice with authentic pieces of writing during self and peer editing. I work with students who continue to have difficulty in small groups or individually as they get to the editing stage of their writing. I also assign stronger students to peer-edit with those students who are weaker in locating and editing informal patterns.

The Code-Switching Shopping List

Informal vs. Formal English Patterns		✓
Possessive		
Informal	**Formal**	
The dog tail	The dog's tail	
Plural		
Informal	**Formal**	
Three cat	Three cats	
Showing past time		
Informal	**Formal**	
I finish	I finished	
Subject–Verb agreement		
Informal	**Formal**	
She walk	She walks	
Was/were		
Informal	**Formal**	
You was sleeping	You were sleeping	
Am/is/are		
Informal	**Formal**	
They is tall	They are tall	
Gonna/going to, wanna/want to		
Informal	**Formal**	
He's gonna go home I wanna leave soon	He's going to go home I want to leave soon	
Be		
Informal	**Formal**	
He cool with me	He's cool with me	

The Code-Switching Shopping List. Modified from Wheeler & Swords (2006). *Code-Switching: Teaching Standard English in Urban Classrooms*, Urbana, IL: NCTE.

Lesson 3

materials

- one sentence strip for each student containing a sentence with a previously studied informal pattern
- magnets or tape for attaching the sentence strips to the board
- chart paper with sample paragraph for editing
- current or previous formal writing assignments
- markers, pencils, paper

goals

STUDENTS WILL:

- recognize various informal patterns that have been taught in previous lessons.
- identify informal language patterns.
- edit multiple informal patterns within a single piece of writing.

Editing for Multiple Patterns

Engagement

Give each student a sentence strip with a sentence that contains one informal pattern that they have already studied. Have them hang their sentence under the corresponding pattern heading you have written on the board.

I have written each of the patterns we have studied on the board. In my hand I have sentence strips. Each strip has a sentence that contains one of the informal patterns we have studied. I am going to give each of you a sentence strip. I want you to read your sentence to yourself and then attach it to the board under the heading that tells which informal pattern your sentence contains. So you'll read your sentence, find the informal pattern, and hang the strip under that pattern's name. (The students receive and hang their sentences.)

Let's see how we did. We have two sentences under the *Possessive* heading. When I point to your sentence, you will read it aloud to the class. Those of you who are listening will give thumbs-up if you agree the example shows an informal possessive pattern, thumbs to the side if you disagree. (I point to the first sentence.)

TAJANTA: ***I broke my grandma lamp.***

Thumbs-up or to the side? Good. *Grandma lamp* is an informal possessive. (I point to the next sentence.)

DAJON: ***Mrs. Smith class went on a field trip.***

Thumbs up or to the side? (I go through each heading and each sentence in this way.)

Direct Instruction

Introduce the topic for today's lesson.

Now that I know you can find informal patterns, we're going to put that knowledge to work. We have been working on formal and informal patterns for some time now. Today is the day you get to put all of that information together and edit your own work. Your goal today is to edit the piece of writing we finished last week by changing all of the informal patterns into formal patterns. This is just what we did yesterday except today you will be editing your own work. This is important because most of our school writing needs to be formal. When we finish today's lesson, you will have finished a large part of your editing. Before you edit your own work, let's practice a paragraph together. (I show students the paragraph I have recorded on chart paper.)

My Worst Day

One day last year my dad car stop at a red light and die. He try and try to get it started but it did not go. Then these two big guy walk over and help us. They was strong so they push the car to the gas station. My dad call his friend to help him. They work and work but still they did not get the car fixed. Then my dad friend call a tow truck. We wait for two hour until the tow truck help us. We was so happy when that day was over!

Let's take a minute to read through the paragraph before we start editing. (I read the entire paragraph aloud.) I always start with the title because sometimes the title is informal. *My Worst Day.* Nope, I don't see any informal patterns in this title. Now we're going to look through the paragraph and edit any informal patterns we see. All of the patterns we have studied are listed on the board, so look carefully to make sure we find all of the informal language.

Guided Practice

Lead the students in editing multiple informal patterns within a single paragraph.

Okay, let's take a look at the first sentence. *One day last year my dad car stop at a red light and die.* Which informal patterns do we have here?

I'ANA: Past time.

Where do you see a past time pattern?

I'ANA: *Stop* and *die*.

How do you know these actions happened in the past?

I'ANA: It says *last year*.

Good. How can we make this formal?

I'ANA: Make it *stopped* and *died*.

note

A customizable version of the paragraph "My Worst Day" is available on the CD-ROM.

what if...

the student writing you want to use has informal patterns you haven't covered?

Sometimes when we use student writings, we need to edit them slightly to help focus on the matters at hand. Originally, the student had written *He try and try to get it* ***start****...* and later in the paragraph, *but still they did not get the car* ***fix***. We edited the student's vernacular *get start* and *get fix* to match the standard form *get started, get fixed*. While it's true these examples take an *-ed* inside Standard English, they're not examples of the vernacular past time pattern.

Thumbs-up if you agree, thumbs to the side if you disagree. Wow, you all are on fire today! Okay, I'ana make the editing changes and highlight them so we can show what we have changed. (I'ana makes the changes and highlights them.) Are there any other informal patterns in the first sentence?

BOBBY: Oh! *My dad car*!

Which pattern is that?

BOBBY: Possessive.

How can we make it formal?

BOBBY: Add an apostrophe *-s* to *dad*.

Thumbs-up or thumbs to the side? We're in agreement. Bobby make the changes and highlight them. (We finish editing the paragraph as a group.)

Independent Practice

Have the students edit their own writing by changing informal patterns to formal.

Think about the process we used to edit *My Worst Day*. Remember that we read the entire piece of writing and then focused on one sentence at a time. We edited informal patterns only. As you edit your own writing today, you are just looking for informal patterns. You should have finished editing for punctuation and capitalization last week. Today we are just practicing editing informal language. Are there any questions about what you will be doing once you go back to your seat? (I answer any questions the students have about the assignment.) You may get started! (I work individually with students who are having difficulties.)

Sharing for Understanding

Have several students share a sentence they edited from their own work.

I saw a lot of great work as I walked around the room! I saw so many of you carefully reading through your papers and finding those patterns to edit! Now's your chance to share some of the sentences you edited. If you would like to share, pick one juicy sentence. After you share your sentence, tell us which informal patterns you edited in the sentence. You highlighted everything you edited, so it should be pretty easy to find those patterns! Who would like to go first?

QUATASIA: *I played lots of games with my sister.*

Which patterns did you edit?

QUATASIA: Past time and plural.

Good. Who else would like to share? (I allow several students to share.)

Conclude the lesson by allowing all of the students to share how they felt while editing their work.

I want you to think about how you felt as you were editing your papers. I want you to use this sentence. (I write *I felt* _______ *because* _______ on the board.) If you would rather not share, just say *pass* and we'll keep going. Who would like to start?

> NIJE: **I felt frustrated because there was too much patterns.**

Okay, we'll work on that. Maybe tomorrow you can find an editing partner to help you. Destiny?

> DESTINY: **I felt happy because I found a lot of patterns.**

Good job! Garrett? (I allow each child to share.)

Assessing the Lesson

I assess this lesson by reading each of the students' edited pieces of writing and noting whether or not they were able to locate and edit all of the informal patterns in their writing. I'm looking to see that most or all of the informal structures were changed to formal. If I notice a student seems to miss a particular pattern, I will talk with the student before he/she completes the final draft. I might say, "When I read through your paper last night, I noticed you had several informal subject–verb agreement patterns that you hadn't edited. Let's take a few minutes to review that pattern." Once we review the pattern, I have the student edit for that specific pattern. If I had a student who missed several patterns, I would start by pairing the student with a peer editor. This is often the only help students need. However, if the student continued to struggle with editing informal patterns, I would work with that student one-on-one. In order to meet state and national standards for English, students must be able to edit their work for grammar usage, so it is extremely important for students to master this skill.

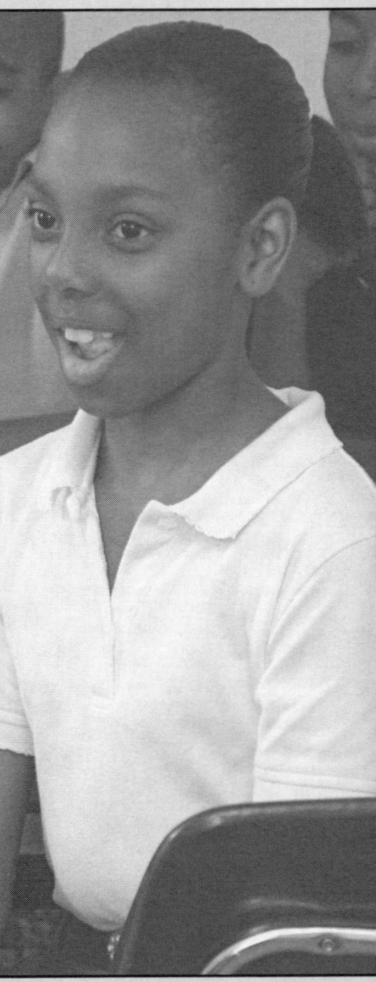

Character and Voice in Literature

11

Lessons

THIS UNIT INCLUDES THE FOLLOWING LESSONS:

1. Identifying Author's Purpose for Language Selection
2. Creating Dialogues Using Informal and Formal Language

This unit brings our work in code-switching full circle. In Unit 1, *Diversity in Life and Language,* we explored how we all vary our style and language to fit the setting, the time, and the place. We vary our clothing, and even our posture and behavior to suit the setting. In Units 2–10, we focused on strategies for helping students build on their existing knowledge – the informal language of their community – to add new knowledge, the more formal, academic English expected in school. In this final unit, we lead students to appreciate the richness of language and voice in the larger context of literature – the literature they read and the stories they themselves craft – and to continue choosing language to suit the situation.

UNIT 11

Character and Voice in Literature

The Code-Switching Model

Unlike almost all other units, we'll not be using a code-switching chart in this unit. Instead, a piece of literature becomes the model for language diversity and the springboard for appreciating and creating characters whose language is central to who they are. Of course we will make sure all our other code-switching charts are posted around the room or available for students in notebook form so they'll have the resources they need as they analyze literature and create their own stories.

Choosing a Literary Model

The goal of this unit is for students to determine when and why authors choose informal language when they write. Students will read literature that includes informal language and discuss why they think the author chose to use informal language.

As we prepare for teaching this unit, we begin by selecting a range of literature that will aid us in teaching our objectives. Of course our literary choices must be dialectically diverse, but that is only one criterion we use when selecting literature. We also want to make sure the authors' purpose is varied so that the students recognize different reasons for employing informal language. For example, in *Nappy Hair,* the author uses informal language to mimic the call and response method of story telling used by slaves. *Working Cotton* also uses informal voice to tell a story of slavery. But our literary choices should expand beyond one point in history, as we don't want students to equate informal language with slavery. For this reason, stories such as *Ashpet: An Appalachian Tale* and *Cindy Ellen: A Wild Western Cinderella* are good choices for this unit of study. These books employ different styles of informal language for students to analyze. Additionally, we look for text that varies in difficulty so that we can meet the needs of all our students.

Teaching the lessons

We begin with a poem "Tough Kids," from *Hey You! C'mere!* by Elizabeth Swados, and continue with a range of dialectally diverse children's literature.

In Lesson 1, students discover that authors use language to let us *see, hear,* and *feel* their characters. Through language, we can see and experience a character even if the story doesn't have pictures. Students discover that authors think very carefully about their language choices: they use informal language to make the text entertaining and to make their characters seem more realistic. So authors consider the setting of the story, the purpose for writing, and the type of character they want to create as they use lively language to create dialogue. Above all, we want students to recognize that language choice is a purposeful and powerful decision the author makes. This is important because we want students to take ownership of their own language choices in their writing.

In Lesson 2, students extend their understanding of voice in literature to their own writing. They explore thinking about their purpose – why they are writing a story, and their audience – who will be reading their work. Students write a dialogue, a conversation between two characters. Students name their characters and then decide if they will have two formal speakers, two informal speakers, or one formal speaker and one informal speaker.

In this unit, students learn that as they create stories and narratives, they have the power to choose the language that will tell their story best – just as they do in life.

SUGGESTED BOOK TITLES

Ashpet: An Appalachian Tale, by Joanne Compton, illustrated by Kenn Compton. New York: Holiday House (1994).

Cindy Ellen: A Wild Western Cinderella, by Susan Lowell, illustrated by Jane Manning. New York: HarperCollins (2001).

Flossie and the Fox, by Patricia McKissack, illustrated by Rachel Isadora. New York: Scholastic (1986).

Hey You! C'mere! A Poetry Slam, by Elizabeth Swados, illustrated by Joe Cepeda. New York: Arthur A. Levine (2002).

Mirandy and Brother Wind, by Patricia McKissack, illustrated by Jerry Pinkney. New York: Knopf (1988).

Nappy Hair, by Carolivia Herron, illustrated by Joe Cepeda. New York: Dragonfly Books (1998).

Nettie Jo's Friends by Patricia McKissack, illustrated by Jerry Pinkney. New York: Knopf (1989).

The Patchwork Quilt, by Valerie Flournoy, illustrated by Jerry Pinkney. New York: Dial (1985).

Pink and Say, by Patricia Polacco. New York: Philomel (1994).

William and the Good Old Days, by Eloise Greenfield, illustrated by Jan Spivey Gilchrist. New York: HarperCollins (1993).

Working Cotton, by Sherley Anne Williams, illustrated by Carole Byard. San Diego: Harcourt (1992).

Lesson 1

Identifying Author's Purpose for Language Selection

Engagement

Gather the group in the reading area. Review appropriate situations for using informal language.

We have spent many weeks learning about formal and informal language. I want you to think about some situations in which informal language would be an appropriate choice. Where might you be when informal language could be used? What might you be doing?

SAMUEL: **When you're on the basketball court with your boys.**

On the basketball court is a good one. How about some more examples? (I allow three or four students to share.)

Direct Instruction

Explain the goal of today's lesson. Direct students to focus on informal language in literature.

We have spent a lot of time looking at, discussing, and using the patterns found inside formal language. Today we are going to focus on informal language. Specifically, we are going to look at informal language in literature. We have read several books in which the authors used informal language. Our goal today is to determine when and why authors choose informal language when they write. Your job will be to read some examples of literature that includes informal language and discuss, with your group, why you think the author chose to use informal language.

Read the poem "Tough Kids"

Let's take a look at what this will look like using a poem. I have here a poem called "Tough Kids" by Elizabeth Swados. Listen to the language she uses. What do you notice about the language choice? When does she use informal language? Why do you think Elizabeth Swados decided to use informal language? (I read the poem.)

materials

- the poem "Tough Kids," from *Hey You! C'mere! A Poetry Slam* by Elizabeth Swados
- a selection of books (multiple copies if possible) that contain informal language (see *Suggested Book Titles*)
- chart paper, markers

goals

STUDENTS WILL:

- recognize the author's purposeful use of informal language.
- determine author's purposes for selecting informal language.

Guided Practice

Have the students discuss informal language in the poem "Tough Kids."

In small groups take a few minutes to discuss when and why Elizabeth Swados uses informal language in this poem. (I give the students three or four minutes to discuss their responses.) Okay, let's share your thinking. When did Swados use informal language?

HEZEKIAH: **When the bully was talking.**

Hmm, why do you think she did that?

HEZEKIAH: **To make him look tough.**

What do you mean *to make him look tough*? There aren't any pictures.

HEZEKIAH: **Yeah, but when I think about him, he looks tough to me.**

Oh, so Elizabeth Swados used informal language to help you visualize, or see, the character. Very interesting. We'll have to keep that in mind as we read more literature.

Independent Practice

Have the students work in pairs to read and discuss literature that includes informal language.

Now you are going to read a book and see if you can decide when and why the author chose to use informal language. You're going to work in pairs to complete this assignment. Once you read the book, talk with your partner about when the author uses informal language and why you think the author chose informal language. Write these on a piece of paper. (I give the students ten to fifteen minutes to complete the task.)

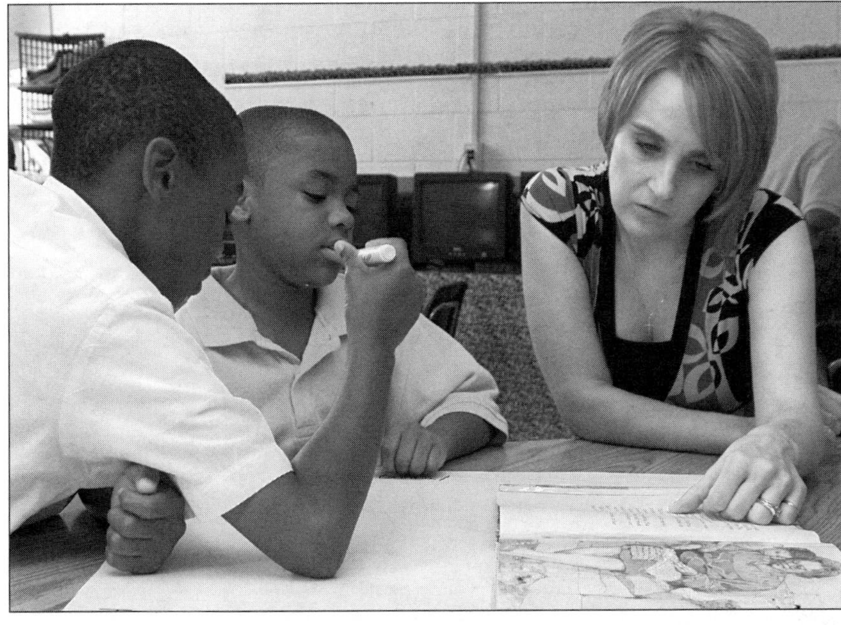

Sharing for Understanding

Have the students share their understanding of when and why authors use informal language in literature.

Let's take a few minutes to share what you discussed with your partners. Your goal was to determine when and why authors use informal language in literature. Who would like to get us started? Tell us which book you looked at first.

> BOBBY: **We read *Working Cotton*, and they was slaves.**

She used it to show how slaves might have spoken?

> BOBBY: **Yeah. Because they didn't go to school so they didn't talk formal.**

So the author created realistic characters using informal language.

> GARRETT: **Me and Quatasia read *Flossie and the Fox*, and the author used informal language even when she was talking ABOUT Flossie.**

Why do you think she did that?

> GARRETT: **Same thing as Bobby's story – to make Flossie's character. And so it would be fun to read.**

Sure, for entertainment. Did anyone have a different reason an author might have for using informal language? (I allow additional students to share.)

Reiterate the purpose for using informal language in literature.

So to summarize, it seems like the authors thought very carefully about their language choices. They used informal language to make the text entertaining and to make their characters seem more realistic. So the author must have considered the setting of the story, the purpose for writing, and the type of character he or she was creating in deciding to use informal language. Tomorrow you will have the opportunity to experiment with informal language in your own writing.

Assessing the Lesson

The goal of this lesson is to expose students to a range of literature in which the author has elected to utilize informal language. Additionally, I want students to recognize and understand when and why an author might choose to use informal language. There are no wrong answers. For this reason, the success of this lesson is based on teacher observation of the independent practice and sharing portion of this lesson. Above all, I want students to recognize that language choice is a purposeful decision that the author makes. This is important because I want students to take ownership of their own language choices in their writing.

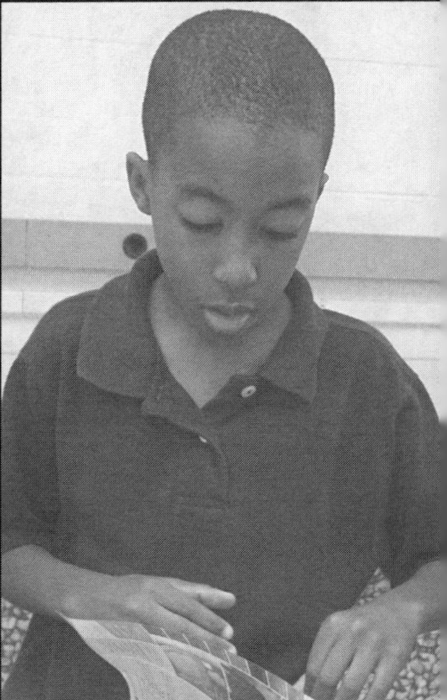

Lesson 2

materials

- chart paper, markers, paper, pencils

goals

STUDENTS WILL:

- create characters with specific language patterns.
- write a dialogue while maintaining distinct voices.

Creating Dialogues

Engagement

Review the reasons authors use informal language.

Let's review some of the reasons authors use informal language when they write. What are some of the reasons we found yesterday?

ANDREW: **To make the story more interesting.**

What other reasons did we find? (I allow three or four more students to share.)

Direct Instruction

Explain that there must always be a purpose for the style of language a writer chooses.

Up to this point, we have focused on using formal language in our own writing. But, as we found in the last lesson, there are several reasons that authors use informal language. There are times when you, as an author, may choose to use informal language in your writing. It's important to make sure that you have a purpose for whatever style of language you use. You have to think about the purpose of your writing. Why are you writing? And you have to consider your audience. Who is going to read your work?

Describe how students will complete today's assignment.

Today you are going to write a dialogue, a conversation between two characters. You will need to decide if you want both characters to speak formally, both characters to speak informally, or one character to speak informally and one to speak formally. For today's assignment, your characters will be two friends. To help you get started, you will choose one of the scenarios I have on the board.

TWO FRIENDS

- discuss what they are going to do after school
- argue over who is the better soccer player
- talk about their summer vacation

We're going to start by practicing this together before you begin writing on your own.

Guided Practice

Complete a shared writing dialogue with the class.

Let's start by naming our characters. Which names should we use?

> ONTIANA: **Joe.**
>
> BOBBY: **Maggie.**

Okay, which of the are we going to use? Raise your hand if you want to use the conversation about what to do after school. Who wants to write an argument about the better soccer player? Anybody want to have the characters discuss their summer vacation? Okay, it looks like Joe and Maggie will be arguing over who is the better soccer player. Do we want Joe to speak formally or informally?

> STUDENTS: **Formally!**

What about Maggie?

> STUDENTS: **Informally!**

I'll start the dialogue. Then we'll do some shared writing. I'm going to start with Joe. I have to make sure my sentence is formal because Joe is our formal speaker. I'm going to write, *"I am the best soccer player on our team!" said Joe.* (I write the sentence.) Now Maggie needs to respond. I'll need to use informal language for her. *"How you gonna say you better than me?" Maggie responded.* (I write the sentence as I say it aloud.) Now, what should Joe say to Maggie?

> I'ANA: ***I scored more points yesterday.***

Did she keep Joe formal?

> STUDENTS: **Yes!**

Okay, add it to our dialogue. (I'ana writes on the chart paper.)

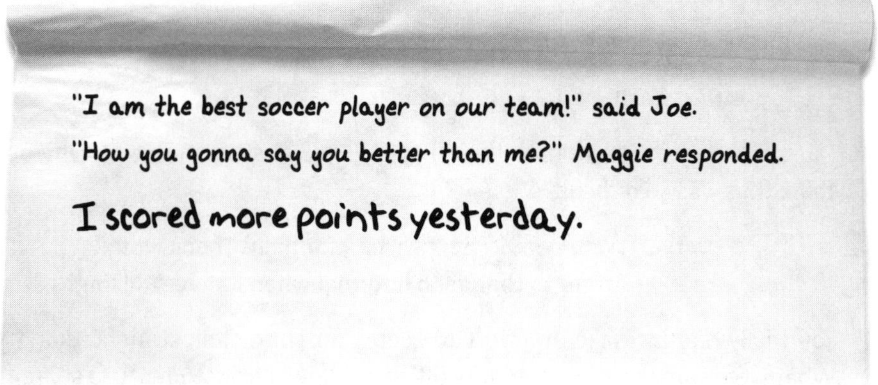

"I am the best soccer player on our team!" said Joe.
"How you gonna say you better than me?" Maggie responded.
I scored more points yesterday.

What should happen next? (We complete several lines of the shared writing.)

Independent Practice

▶ **Have the students choose whether their characters will speak formally, informally, or a mix. Then have students write their own dialogues.**

Now you are going to write your own dialogue. First decide which conversation your characters will have. Name your characters. Then decide if you are going to have two formal speakers, two informal speakers, or one formal speaker and one informal speaker. Are there any questions? Who plans on having two formal speakers? (Several students raise their hands.) Those of you who raised your hands may return to your seats and get started. Who is planning to use two informal speakers? (The students raise their hands.) You may go ahead and get started. Are the rest of you using one formal and one informal speaker? (The students nod.) You may get started. (I walk around the room, assisting students on an individual basis.)

Sharing for Understanding

▶ **Have the students share their dialogues and the strategies they used to edit the sentences.**

Let's have a few of you share your dialogues with the class. If you are part of the audience, I want you to see if you can figure out whether the characters are speaking formally or informally. Do we have any volunteers? (I allow two or three students to share. If additional students want to share, I allow them to share during class meeting or at the onset of writing over the next several days.)

▶ **Allow the students to debrief the most difficult aspect of the assignment.**

What did you find to be the most difficult part of this assignment?

> I'ANA: **It was hard to switch back and forth.**

You mean between formal and informal language?

> I'ANA: **Yeah.**

Did anyone else find that to be difficult? (Several students nod.) Why do you think that was so difficult?

> ONTIANA: **Well, I would start writing formally. Then I would forget to change to informal when Kat was talking.**

You really had to make an effort to keep your characters straight, didn't you? What were some of the other difficulties? (I allow a few students to share).

I know this was a difficult assignment, but I saw some really amazing writing from so many of you. As you continue to create stories and narratives, remember that you have the power to choose the language that will best tell your story. I'm proud of you for rising to the challenge today!

Assessing the Lesson

In evaluating this lesson, I am not expecting students to demonstrate expert command over the language. Therefore, I do not assess the dialogues by grading them. I want the students to take risks with language. If they fear poor grades, they will not be risk-takers in their writings. I do expect the language choices to be clear because the assignment was for them to make a conscious decision about their language choices. They should be able to maintain a single voice for each character throughout the dialogue. In future writings, I encourage students to purposefully select and thoughtfully utilize the language that is most appropriate for a particular piece of writing.

Efficacy Research

The problem: Current practices are not sufficiently successful in teaching Standard English in urban classrooms

When African American students write *I have two sister and two brother, My Dad jeep is out of gas,* or *My mom deserve a good job,* teachers traditionally diagnose "error" and "poor English." Teachers find that the students are "having problems," or making "mistakes" with plurality, possession, or verb agreement, etc.

In response, the teacher "corrects" the child's writing, showing them the "right" way to convey these grammatical points. However, research and longstanding student performance have demonstrated that the traditional correction methods fail to teach vernacular speaking students the requisite Standard English writing skills.

> "Current literacy practices do not close the Black/White gap as students advance up in grades."

Literacy achievement gap remains

NAEP reports in Black White Achievement Gaps (July 14, 2009) that a significant achievement gap remains across our nation.

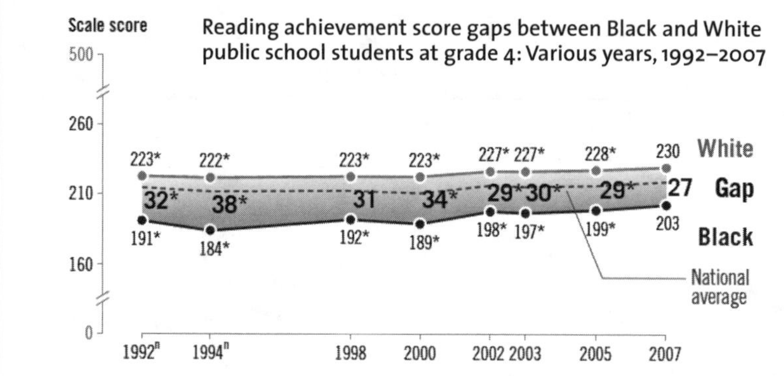

ⁿ Accommodations were not permitted for this assessment.
* Significantly different (p<.05) from 2007.
SOURCE: U.S. Department of Education, Institute of Education Sciences, National Center for Education Statistics, National Assessment of Educational Progress (NAEP), various years, 1992–2007 Reading Assessments.

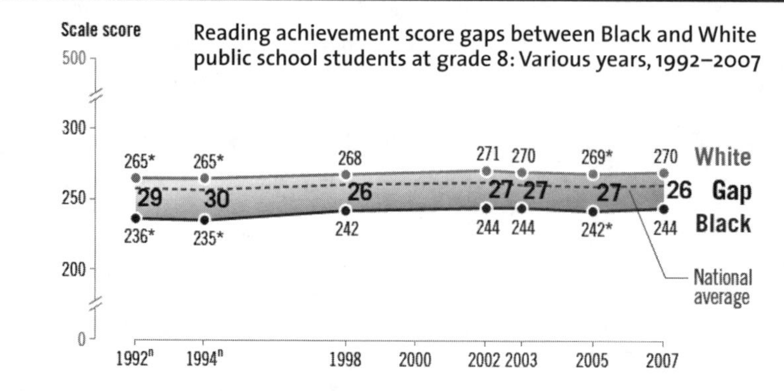

ⁿ Accommodations were not permitted for this assessment.
* Significantly different (p<.05) from 2007.
NOTE: Data were not collected at grade 8 in 2000.
SOURCE: U.S. Department of Education, Institute of Education Sciences, National Center for Education Statistics, National Assessment of Educational Progress (NAEP), various years, 1992–2007 Reading Assessments.

http://nces.ed.gov/nationsreportcard/pdf/studies/2009455.pdf (p. 29)

Current literacy approaches misdiagnose student performance. *Code-switching Lessons* correctly assesses student performance

When traditional approaches assess student language as "error-filled," they misdiagnose student writing performance.

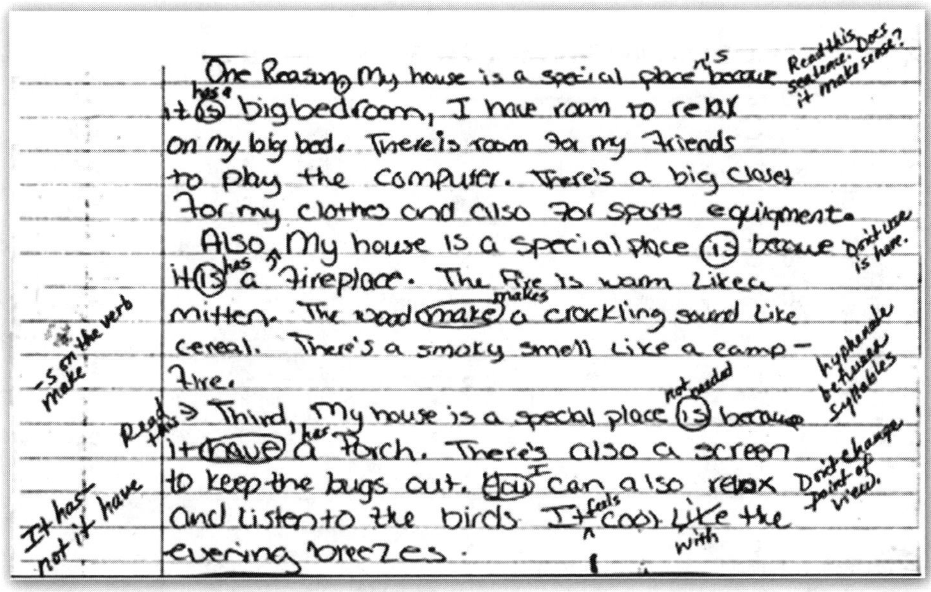
One Reasing My house is a spacial place becaue
it is big bedroom, I have room to relax
on my big bed. There is room for my friends
to play the computer. There's a big closet
for my clothes and also for sports equipment.
Also, My house is a special place is becaue
it is a fireplace. The fire is warm Like a
mitten. The wood make a crackling sound Like
cereal. There's a smoky smell Like a camp-
fire.
Third, My house is a special place is becaue
it have a porch. There's also a screen
to keep the bugs out. You can also relax
and listen to the birds It cool Like the
evening breezes.

Teachers correct vernacular grammar in student writing.

Linguistics correctly diagnoses the language facts: Students using vernacular language (*My goldfish name is Scaley*, etc.) are not making errors in Standard English. Instead, they are writing correctly in the language patterns of the home dialect.

> "Students using vernacular language are not making errors in Standard English. Instead, they are writing correctly in the language patterns of the home dialect."

Code-switching Lessons offers a targeted, successful response to teach Standard literacy

Code-Switching Lessons offers a research-based solution:
Contrastive analysis and **code-switching**.

Contrastive Analysis: Applies Marzano's #1 strategy to grammar

In contrastive analysis, the teacher draws upon the linguistic insights that all language is patterned and that dialects systematically contrast with each other. Accordingly, she leads students to contrast the grammatical patterns of home speech to the grammatical patterns of school speech thus applying Marzano et al.'s #1 strategy – compare and contrast – to grammar discovery (Marzano et al., 2004).

Code-Switching Lessons applies strategies of critical thinking (analysis and synthesis) to grammar discovery. Indeed teachers use the scientific method (observe data, seek grammar pattern, describe pattern, test, refine pattern) to lead grammar discovery.

Code-switching: Students choose their language to fit the setting

As the child then learns to code-switch between the language of the home and the language of the school, teachers add another linguistic code, Standard English, to the child's linguistic toolbox.

Under experimental conditions, 3rd graders taught with the traditional approach showed only a slight improvement or actually lost ground in their Standard English performance. Students taught with contrastive analysis showed a marked increase in their command of Standard English grammar.

A 2007-2008 study funded by the State Council of Higher Education of Virginia (SCHEV), demonstrated that students in code-switching classrooms increased their Standard English usage in high fidelity by 32.19% from fall to spring, in contrast with students from low fidelity classrooms who increased their Standard English performance by only 9.9%.

Efficacy results

Classroom experience and research results affirm the efficacy of Contrastive Analysis and Code-switching to teach Standard English among African American students.

Elementary

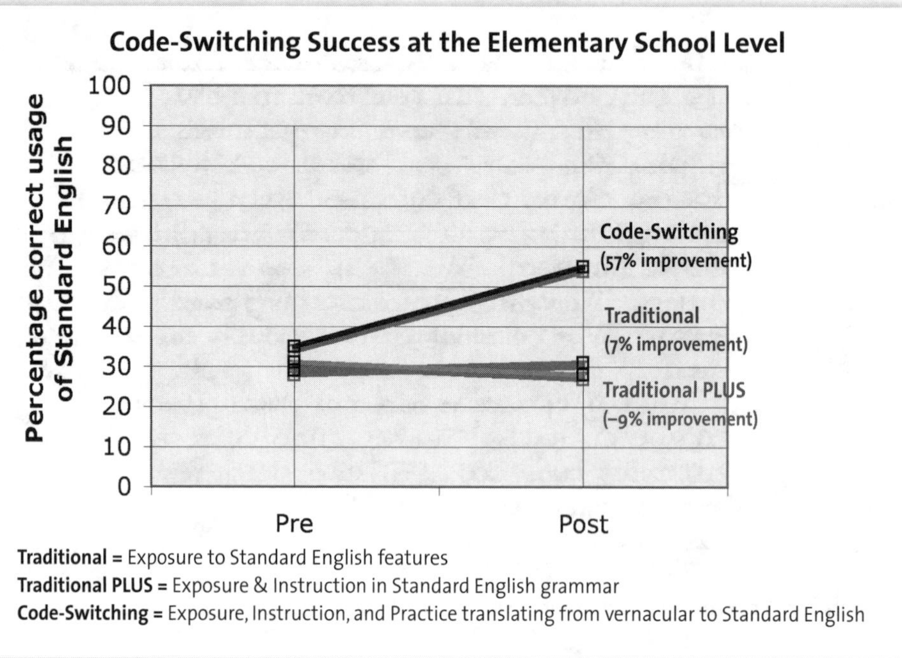

Traditional = Exposure to Standard English features
Traditional PLUS = Exposure & Instruction in Standard English grammar
Code-Switching = Exposure, Instruction, and Practice translating from vernacular to Standard English

Fogel, H. & Ehri, L. (2000) "Teaching Elementary Students Who Speak Black English Vernacular to Write in Standard English: Effects of Dialect Transformation Practice." *Contemporary Educational Psychology* 25: 212-235.

Middle School

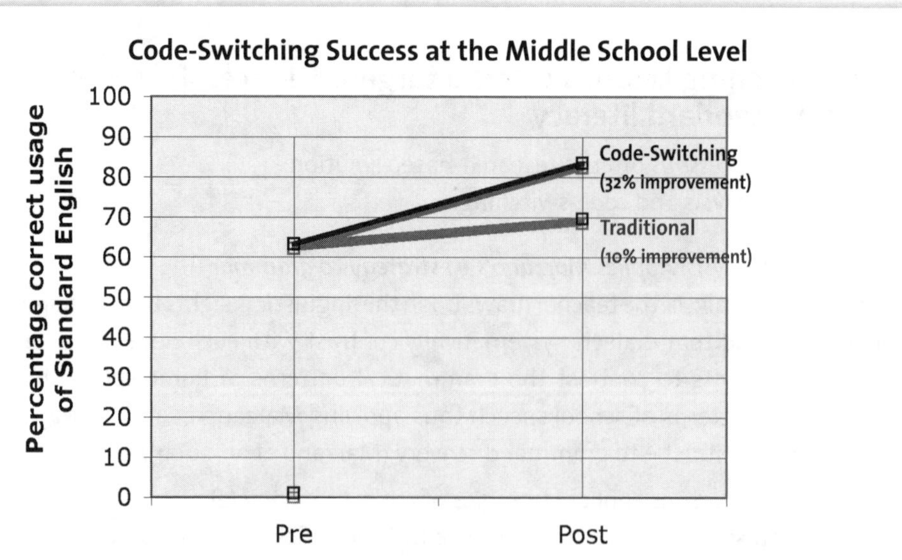

Scores are for tests taken by sixth graders at the beginning of the school year and again at the end of the school year. Groups were divided into classrooms that implemented code-switching with high fidelity *vs.* classrooms that followed more traditional approaches to teaching Standard English.

2007-2008: Wheeler, Principal Investigator: SCHEV (State Council on Higher Education of Virginia), TELES: Technology Enhanced Learning of English and Science in Middle School. With Co-PI, Dr. Raj Chaudhury, CNU Department of Physics and Co-PI Diane Gladstone, Director of Curriculum and Instruction, Northampton Middle School. Amount funded: $93,564 under the Title II, Part A – Improving Teacher Quality State Grants of the No Child Left Behind Program.

College level

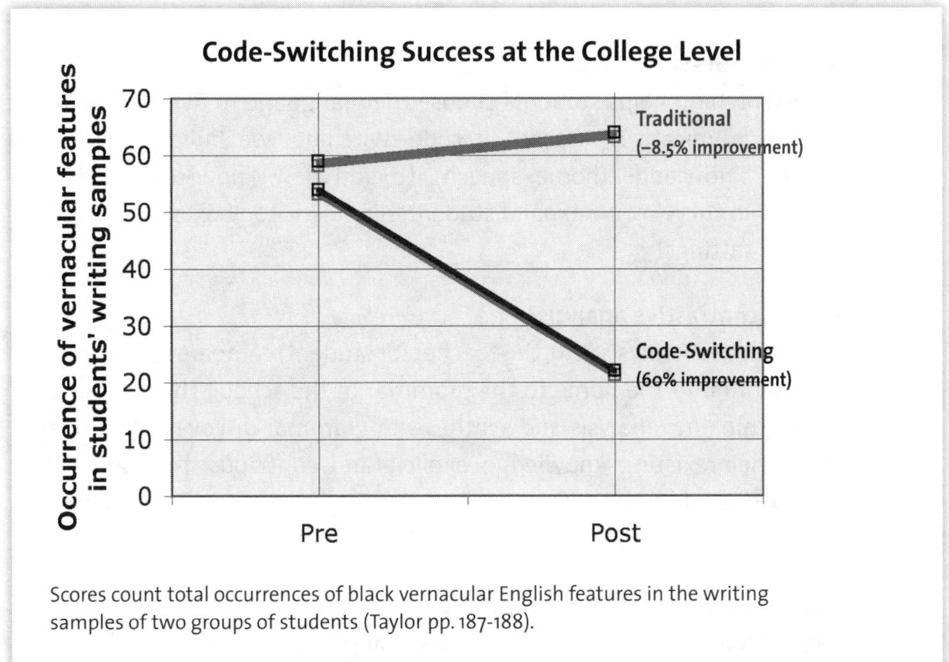

Scores count total occurrences of black vernacular English features in the writing samples of two groups of students (Taylor pp. 187-188).

Taylor, H. (1991). *Standard English, Black English, and Bidialectalism: A Controversy.* New York: Peter Lang.

Students taught with traditional methods actually used 8.5% more vernacular features in their formal writing. Students using contrastive analysis showed remarkable success. These students used 59.3% fewer African American vernacular features in their formal writing. Contrastive Analysis brings substantial improvement in vernacular speaking students' command of Standard literacy skills (Taylor, 1991).

Individual elementary classroom results

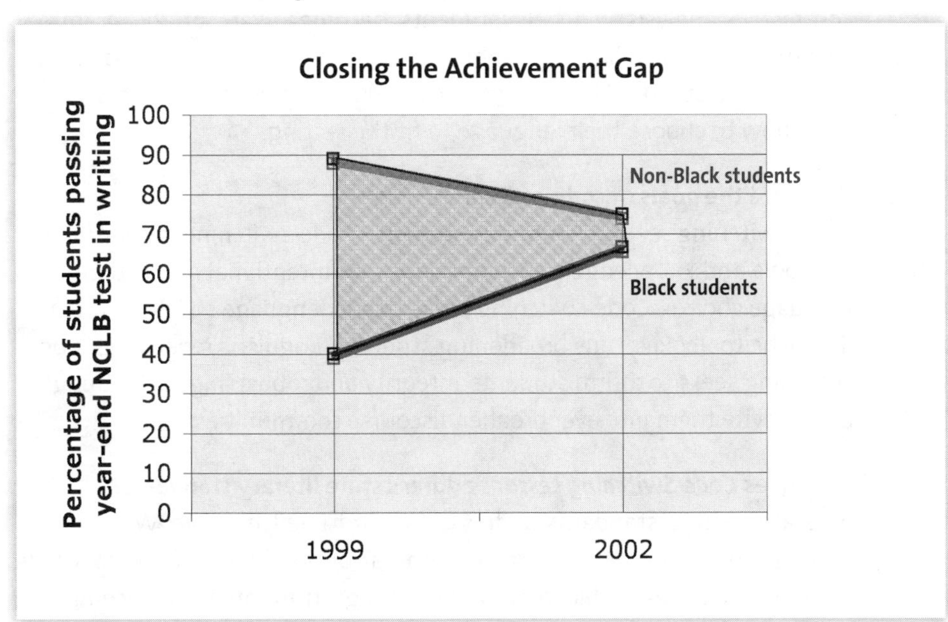

Individual results, Year-end testing, Virginia Standards of Learning under NCLB, 1999 and 2002

Before Rachel Swords began working with code-switching in her urban elementary school, her Black and White students showed a 30 point gap in scores and a greater than 50-point achievement gap in passing the NCLB test. The very year she implemented code-switching (2002), she closed the achievement gap in her classroom, and in 2006, her last testing year, 100% of African American students passed 100% of the NCLB tests.

Collectively, these results point to the powerful promise of code-switching and contrastive analysis to foster Standard English mastery among our linguistically diverse writers.

Frequently Asked Questions

Q: What is Code-Switching?

A: Code-switching helps students choose their language to fit the time, place and communicative purpose. In code-switching, we build on students' existing knowledge (home speech), to add new knowledge (Standard English). In this way, we expand students' linguistic toolboxes. More tools to fit more settings!

Q: What is contrastive analysis?

A: In Contrastive Analysis (CA), the teacher (or student) compares and contrasts the grammar of the home to the grammar of the school. They use skills of critical thinking, analysis and synthesis in grammar discovery. As students make their existing knowledge explicit and conscious, they are better equipped to add new knowledge, Standard English. Contrastive Analysis can foster students' keen attention to the structures and rhythms of language.

Q: Is code-switching relevant for my students?

A: Code-switching is a powerful tool for any linguistically or dialectally diverse classroom. Your students may speak a vernacular variety of English or a regional variety of English. They may speak English as a Second (third or fourth) language, or an international form of English. Or, your US students may slip text-speak into their formal school papers. In all these cases, contrastive analysis will help students become aware of the grammar patterns they are following. From that point, *Code-Switching Lessons* will help you add Standard English to your students' linguistic repertoires. They'll learn how to choose their language to fit the setting.

Q: What are the goals of code-switching?

A: Code-Switching seeks to empower students. Code-switching gives students the tools and knowledge to be conscious and intentional about their own language choices. Code-switching seeks to add language styles to students' linguistic toolboxes, thus broadening students' linguistic repertoires. Code-switching seeks to affirm students' integrity and robust linguistic strengths as we invite them into ever broader discourse communities.

Q: How does *Code-Switching Lessons* address state literacy standards?

A: All state writing standards address Standard English usage. Whether it's called proper grammar, or correct grammar or good English, all standards require students to be able to use Standard English grammar. By teaching kids how to compare and contrast the grammar of the home and the grammar of the school, *Code-Switching Lessons* gives students a leg up on mastering Standard English. Most standards also address issues of character, voice, and dialect diversity in literature. Code-switching Lessons supports students as they come to understand how linguistic diversity enriches our cultural and literary landscape.

Q: What results might I expect?

A: You can expect your students to light up as they identify with exploring formal & informal English. You can expect them to become much more conscious of and intentional about their language choices. You should expect them to rejoin the enterprise of learning. And you should expect test scores across all subjects to improve.

Q: Should I correct a child's grammar when they read out loud or speak?

A: No, do not correct a student's grammar when they are reading or speaking. Correction simply doesn't work to teach Standard English equivalents. It derails the educational moment and may humiliate the child. After being told repeatedly that they're wrong, wrong, wrong, children may turn away... disengaging from education and learning.

Besides, as you'll see in *Code-Switching Lessons*, the child is often not making mistakes inside Standard English; they're correctly following the patterns of their community language variety. So, from that perspective, there's nothing to correct! Instead, we'll compare and contrast the grammar of home and school, to better add Standard English. Students will learn standardized English much more efficiently this way.

Q: If I don't correct students' home speech grammar, what do I do?

A: Make note of the grammar patterns the student is following. Then, after school, build code-switching lessons in response. This book offers you many code-switching lesson units; it provides a bank of code-switching charts for vernacular patterns beyond those in our lesson units; and we show you how to extend *Code-Switching Lessons* to address any language difference in your classroom.

Q: What if I'm not comfortable with grammar, can I still use code-switching?

A: You do not need a degree in linguistics to do code-switching. All you need is a sense of "error." From that point, we show you how to collect examples of a similar grammar issue, and reframe your perception so you can find the pattern inside vernacular, regional, or International English, etc. From that basis, you can lead your students in contrastive analysis and code-switching as they expand their linguistic repertoires. We provide lots and lots of resources to support you.

Q: How do I talk to parents about code-switching?

A: Explain to parents that you are using research-proven strategies for teaching Standard English. Explain that you are building on students' existing knowledge (community grammar) to add new knowledge (Standard English).

What if . . . ?

Q: What if my principal sees me not correcting a student's grammar?

A: If your principal (or another teacher) asks why you didn't correct a student's grammar, tell them that research has shown correction doesn't work to teach Standard English. Instead, you are addressing grammar needs systematically in your writing workshop. Tell the principal that you are using Code-Switching, a linguistically-informed, research-based approach to addressing language diversity in the classroom. In this approach, you use a teacher's log to keep track of students' grammar issues. Then, based upon students' needs, you use code-switcing lessons during writing workshop. In this way, you're using effective methods for teaching Standard English. Soon, you will have test score results to support these best practices (Wheeler, 2006).

Q: What if my class is half African American and half White OR What if half my class speaks vernacular English and half speaks Standard English?

A: Even though her classes are now virtually 100% African American, for the first several years Rachel's classroom was half Black and half white, half vernacular speakers and half Standard speakers. In this context, she taught the full range of code-switching units.

Code-switching helps *all* students understand how dialect contributes to character, voice and setting in literature. *Code-Switching Lessons* directly affirms national standards that require students to appreciate diverse cultures and dialects. Further, the technique of contrastive analysis embodies critical thinking — skills of observation, description, hypothesis formation, and hypothesis testing — skills of analysis and synthesis that enhance the abilities of all students.

Q: What if the majority of my students all speak Standard English?

A: *Code-switching Lessons* is still relevant even when a large majority of your class are speakers of Standard English (even over 80%). You'll still want to assure all students develop an "understanding of and respect for diversity in language use, patterns, and dialects across cultures, ethnic groups, geographic regions, and social roles" (NCTE/IRA Standard 9). And an understanding of diverse grammar patterns from various language varieties directly serves students' understanding and ability to critique literature. Indeed, one middle school teacher I've worked with used code-switching lessons to enable her honors students to better understand the dialogue in Mark Twain and Zora Neale Hurston, among others.

To support students' exploration of diversity in language in literature, begin with our unit on formal & informal places and clothing, and then continue with the first lesson of each of each Code-Switching unit. This will enable students to recognize that language structure varies by time, place, and setting. You might also use the basic code-switching chart in extended uses — explore the contrast between Appalachian English and Standard English as seen in literature your class is reading, between British English and American English;

use the code-switching chart to explore the difference between sentence fragments and full sentences, between text messaging and full sentences, and so on. In all these cases, comparison and contrast develops students' critical thinking skills and enhances their awareness of how language functions in different times, places, cultures, regions and so on.

Q: What if I have many different language groups in my class?

A: Perhaps you have students from Thailand, Russia, China, Pennsylvania, or Alabama. You'll probably have a sense that students from these different countries or regions show characteristic "errors." What you're likely seeing are instances where patterns from the students' first language or dialect transfer into school expression. Time for code-switching charts!

I could imagine you collecting examples from Thai students to build a chart for showing past time, and another chart drawing on examples from Russian students to show patterns for using (and not using) *be*. You might teach code-switching first with our Diversity unit and then our unit on possessives. From that foundation, you could differentiate learning, grouping students by nationality or region, and helping them build their own code-switching chart addressing grammar patterns characteristic of their language group or region. Then students could share their discoveries with the rest of the class. In this way, students continue learning that language differs by time, place and purpose. Students continue developing skills of analysis, synthesis and critical thinking, and you've addressed grammar issues in a classroom with numerous and diverse language groups.

Responses to Frequent Assertions

Assertion: "We should get rid of that bad grammar in the home."

Response: In the schools, we can offer students choices; we can teach the types of English grammar expected by our schools, colleges and the world of enterprise. What choices mama and papa and grandma and grandpa make, those are surely the private matters of the family.

Assertion: "This language is just flat out wrong, incorrect, and we ought to just say so! Enough of this political correctness. I don't have time for it."

Response: Actually, "correct" and "incorrect" are blunt, dull instruments. A 3rd grader once told us "you couldn't use that formal English on my street corner and get away with it." We all need to choose language to fit the setting. Sometimes that's vernacular, sometimes it's standard, sometimes it's written or casual, or text-speak, or regional. It's about fitting one's style to the context. Further, if we want to succeed in teaching Standard English, we'd best look beyond simple correction. Decades of experience shows that correction doesn't work to teach Standard English. Students are still making the same "mistakes." It's time for an approach that works!

Bibliography

Bibliography

Adger, C. T., Wolfram, W., & Christian, D. (2007). *Dialects in schools and communities* (2nd ed.). Mahwah, NJ: Lawrence Erlbaum Associates.

Baratz, J. C., Shuy, R., (Eds.) (1969). *Teaching Black Children to Read.* Washington, DC: Center for Applied Linguistics.

Brown, D. W. (2009). *In Other Words: Lessons on Grammar, Code-Switching and Acadmemic Writing.* Portsmouth, NH: Heinemann.

Charity, A., Scarborough, H., & Griffin, D. (2004). Familiarity with School English in African American Children and its Relation to Early Reading Achievement. *Child Development,* 75(5), 1340-1356.

Craig, H. K., & Washington, J. A. (2006). *Malik Goes to School: Examining the Language Skills of African American Students from Preschool – 5th grade.* Mahwah, NJ: Lawrence Erlbaum.

Fogel, H. & Ehri, L. (2000) "Teaching Elementary Students Who Speak Black English Vernacular to Write in Standard English: Effects of Dialect Transformation Practice." *Contemporary Educational Psychology* 25: 212-235.

Godley, A., Sweetland, J., Wheeler R. S., Minnicci, A., & Carpenter, B. (November 2006). "Preparing teachers for the dialectally diverse classroom." *Educational Researcher.* Vol. 35, No 8., pp. 30 – 37.

Green, L. J. (2002). *African American English: A linguistic introduction.* Cambridge, UK: Cambridge University Press.

Labov, W. (1972). *Language in the Inner City: Studies in the Black English Vernacular.* Philadelphia: University of Pennsylvania Press.

Labov, W. & Baker, B. (n.d.) *The Penn Reading Initiative on the Reading Road.* Retrieved October 20, 2009 from http://www.ling.upenn.edu/~wlabov/PRI/index.html.

Meier, T. (2008). *Black Communications and Learning to Read: Building on Children's Linguistic and Cultural Strengths.* New York, NY: Lawrence Earlbaum.

Montgomery, M. B. (2004). "Appalachian English: Morphology and Syntax." *A Handbook of Varieties of English: Morphology and Syntax.* New York: Mouton de Gruyter. 244-280.

Piestrup, A. M. (1973). *Black Dialect Interference and Accommodation of Reading Instruction in First Grade.* Berkeley, CA: Language and Behavior Research Laboratory.

Pullum, G. (1999). African American Vernacular English is Not Standard English with Mistakes. In Rebecca S. Wheeler (Ed.), *The Workings of Language: From Prescriptions to Perspectives,* 39 – 58. Westport, CT: Praeger.

Redd, T. M., & Schuster, K. (2005) *A Teacher's Introduction to African American English: What a Writing Teacher Should Know. NCTE.*

Rickford, J.R. (1998, March 25). Using the vernacular to teach the standard. Paper presented at 1998 California State University Long Beach [CSULB] Conference on Ebonics. Retrieved October 25, 2007, from http://www.standford.edu/~richford/papers/VernacularToTeachStandard.html

Rickford, J. R. (1999). *African American Vernacular English: Features, Evolution, Educational Implications.* New York, NY: Wiley-Blackwell.

Rickford, J. R. and Rickford R. J. (2000). *Spoken Soul: The Story of Black English.* New York, NY: Wiley.

Scarborough, H. S., Hannah, D., Charity, A. H., & Shore, J. (2004). Distinguishing dialect differences from reading errors in oral text reading by speakers of African-American Vernacular English (AAVE). In A. Pincus (ed.), *Tips from the experts: A compendium of advice on literacy instruction from educators and researchers* (pp. 113-117). [International Dyslexia Association, NJ Branch.]

Shaughnessy, M. (1977). *Errors and Expectations: A Guide for the Teacher of Basic Writing.* NY, NY: Oxford University Press.

Smitherman, G. (2000). *Talkin that talk: Language Culture and Education in African America.* New York, NY: Routledge.

Smitherman, G. (1994). *Black talk: Words and phrases from the hood to the amen corner.* Boston, MA: Houghton Mifflin.

Sweetland, J. (2006). *Teaching writing in the African American classroom: A sociolinguistic approach.* Unpublished doctoral dissertation, Stanford University.

Taylor, H. (1991). *Standard English, Black English, and Bidialectalism: A Controversy.* New York: Peter Lang.

Turner, K. (2009). "Flipping the Switch: Code-Switching from Text Speak to Standard English" *English Journal* May 2009. 98.5,:60-65.

Wheeler, R. (2008). Becoming Adept at Code-Switching, *Educational Leadership.* Themed-issue on Poverty and Learning, April 2008. Association of Supervision and Curriculum Development (ASCD). 65(7), 54–58.

Wheeler, R. (2005). Code-switch to teach Standard English. *English Journal, 94*(5), 108–112.

Wheeler, R. (Ed.). (1999). *The Workings of Language: From Prescriptions to Perspectives.* Westport, CT: Praeger.

Wheeler, R. & Swords, R. (2010) *Code-switching Lessons: Grammar Strategies for Linguistically Diverse Writers.* Portsmouth, NH: Heinemann.

Wheeler, R. & Swords, R. (2006) *Code-switching: Teaching Standard English in Urban Classrooms.* Urbana, IL: National Council of Teachers of English.

Wheeler, R., & Swords, R. (2004) "Code-switching: Tools of language and culture transform the dialectally diverse classroom." Language Arts, NCTE. Vol. 81, No. 6. July 2004, 470 – 480.

Wheeler, R., Cartwright, K. B., Swords, R., & Savage, D. (forthcoming, Spring 2010). "Factoring Dialect into Reading Assessment and Intervention." *Reading in Virginia.*

Wolfram, W. (1969). *A sociolinguistic description of Detroit Negro Speech.* Washington, DC: Center for Applied Linguistics.

Wolfram, W., Adger, C.T., & Christian, D. (1999). *Dialects in schools and communities (*2nd ed.). Mahwah, NJ: Lawrence Erlbaum Associates.

Wolfram, W. & Schilling-Estes, N. (2006). *American English.* 2nd edition. Malden, MA: Blackwell.

Childrens' Literature

Compton, J., & Compton, K. (1994). *Ashpet: An Appalachian Tale.* New York: Holiday House.

Flournoy, V., & Pinkney, J. (1985). *The Patchwork Quilt.* New York: Dial.

Greenfield, E., & Gilchrist, J. S. (1993). *William and the Good Old Days.* New York: HarperCollins.

Herron, C., & Cepeda, J. (1998). *Nappy Hair.* New York: Dragonfly Books.

Lowell, S., & Manning, J. (2001). *Cindy Ellen: A Wild Western Cinderella.* New York: HarperCollins.

McKissack, P., & Isadora, R. (1986). *Flossie and the Fox.* New York: Scholastic).

McKissack, P., & Pinkney, J. (1988). *Mirandy and Brother Wind.* New York: Knopf.

McKissack, P., & Pinkney, J. (1989). *Nettie Jo's Friends.* New York: Knopf.

Polacco, P. (1994). *Pink and Say.* New York: Philomel.

Swados, E., & Cepeda, J. (2002). *Hey You! C'mere! A Poetry Slam.* New York: Arthur A. Levine.

Williams, S. A., & Byard, C. (1992). *Working Cotton.* San Diego: Harcourt.